Measuring Second Language Vocabulary Acquisition

Mixed Sources
Product group from well-managed
forests, controlled sources and
recycled wood or fibre
www.fsc.org Cert no. SA-COC-002112
© 1996 Forest Stewardship Council
FSC

SECOND LANGUAGE ACQUISITION
Series Editor: Professor David Singleton, *Trinity College, Dublin, Ireland*

This series brings together titles dealing with a variety of aspects of language acquisition and processing in situations where a language or languages other than the native language is involved. Second language is thus interpreted in its broadest possible sense. The volumes included in the series all offer in their different ways, on the one hand, exposition and discussion of empirical findings and, on the other, some degree of theoretical reflection. In this latter connection, no particular theoretical stance is privileged in the series; nor is any relevant perspective – sociolinguistic, psycholinguistic, neurolinguistic, etc. – deemed out of place. The intended readership of the series includes final-year undergraduates working on second language acquisition projects, postgraduate students involved in second language acquisition research, and researchers and teachers in general whose interests include a second language acquisition component.

Full details of all the books in this series and of all our other publications can be found on http://www.multilingual-matters.com, or by writing to Multilingual Matters, St Nicholas House, 31-34 High Street, Bristol BS1 2AW, UK.

SECOND LANGUAGE ACQUISITION
Series Editor: David Singleton, *Trinity College, Dublin, Ireland*

Measuring Second Language Vocabulary Acquisition

James Milton

MULTILINGUAL MATTERS
Bristol • Buffalo • Toronto

Library of Congress Cataloging in Publication Data
A catalog record for this book is available from the Library of Congress.
Milton, James, 1955–
Measuring Second Language Vocabulary Acquisition/James Milton
Second Language Acquisition: 45
Includes bibliographical references and index.
1. Language and languages–Study and teaching. 2. Vocabulary–Study and teaching.
3. Second language acquisition. I. Title.
P53.9.M55 2009
418.0071–dc22 2009026147

British Library Cataloguing in Publication Data
A catalogue entry for this book is available from the British Library.

ISBN-13: 978-1-84769-208-5 (hbk)
ISBN-13: 978-1-84769-207-8 (pbk)

Multilingual Matters
UK: St Nicholas House, 31-34 High Street, Bristol BS1 2AW, UK.
USA: UTP, 2250 Military Road, Tonawanda, NY 14150, USA.
Canada: UTP, 5201 Dufferin Street, North York, Ontario M3H 5T8, Canada.

The policy of Multilingual Matters/Channel View Publications is to use papers that are natural, renewable and recyclable products, made from wood grown in sustainable forests. In the manufacturing process of our books, and to further support our policy, preference is given to printers that have FSC and PEFC Chain of Custody certification. The FSC and/or PEFC logos will appear on those books where full certification has been granted to the printer concerned.

Typeset by Datapage International Ltd.
Printed and bound in Great Britain by Short Run Press Ltd.

Contents

Introduction

Much of the literature on second language acquisition as a general process (e.g. Mitchell & Myles, 2004; Lightbown & Spada, 1999) pays little attention to vocabulary learning. This is not just a recent phenomenon. O'Dell (1997: 258) comments that vocabulary and lexis are absent from major books on the syllabus and theory of language teaching throughout the 1970s and 1980s. Its omission may have an even longer history. Wilkins (1972: 109), writing at the beginning of the 1970s, suggests it dates from the development of structural linguistics. For much of the last half century or so, therefore, the consideration of vocabulary in the process of language learning, testing and teaching appears to have been sidelined and, as Meara (1980) describes it, turned into a Cinderella subject.

I think there are three reasons for this. One is a product of the structural and other approaches to language teaching that have become highly pervasive in language teaching. Outside the arena of specialist vocabulary studies there seems to be a long-standing idea that words are just words, and that learning words is unsystematic. Vocabulary is unchallenging as a pedagogical or an academic issue, as a consequence. In structural approaches to learning, the part of language learning which is really important is how language rules and systems are acquired, and with this approach we need not be too concerned about the words to which these rules and systems apply. It is assumed that these rules would develop regardless of which words, or how many words, were being used to form them. Commonly, a structural linguistic approach to teaching deliberately reduces the volume of vocabulary input at the earliest stages of learning to only what is necessary for the presentation of language structures, or what is essential to motivate learners. So powerful has this approach been, that it has pervaded later approaches where a greater emphasis on vocabulary ought to be apparent. Notional-functional and, in the UK, communicative approaches have likewise seen vocabulary learning sidelined.

The second reason is the persistent belief among teachers, learners and educational administrators, that it is possible to become highly proficient in a foreign language, and even a sophisticated user, with only very limited vocabulary resources. I am constantly surprised, for example, by the number of teachers who quote Ogden's (1930) *Simple English* at me, apparently in all seriousness, and are under the impression that they can teach a complete western European language with only 850 words. Ogden's *Simple English* even continues to crop up in the most recent academic literature, for example in Häcker's (2008) examination of the vocabulary loading of German course books. While Häcker recognises that Ogden's 850 words cannot form a fully communicative lexicon for a modern European language, the idea that it can do so is widespread and even occurs in otherwise reputable media. A recent BBC news article by Alex Kirby (2004), for example, suggested that since only 'about 100 words are needed for half of all reading in English' it would follow that a parrot with 950 words should cope 'with a wide range of [English] material'. Ogden's work, and structural linguistics, pre-date modern corpus analysis that gives a much better idea of the kind of vocabulary resources that learners need. These can tell us about the occurrence and frequency of words in language, and this provides reliable information on which words, and how many, are really used by normal speakers. It turns out that thousands of words are needed even for basic communication, let alone for fluency. But the idea that teaching modern foreign languages requires only a handful of words persists, probably because it is also a product of wishful thinking. Learning a language is an enormous task. To perform like a native speaker you need to learn thousands of words. You need to discover which words can be combined and which cannot, and master many rules of language. It can take years of effort to achieve even basic levels of command and understanding. Teachers have to try to fit all of this into a restricted timetable and maintain the motivation of learners at all times. Everyone would like to believe that you can reduce the burden of learning to something much smaller, say, a few hundred words instead of many thousands, and still achieve worthwhile results.

The third reason is the widely held belief that time spent in explicit vocabulary teaching is wasted because 'few words are retained from those which are "learned" or "taught" by direct instruction' (Harris & Snow, 2004: 55), and 'most L2 vocabulary is learned incidentally, much of it from oral input' (Ellis, R., 1994: 24). The best way to deal with vocabulary, therefore, is not to teach it at all because learners will soak it up as though by osmosis from the language which surrounds them inside or outside class. This is also wishful thinking. The evidence suggests that the vocabulary uptake from truly incidental language exposure is usually negligible and that successful learners acquire large volumes of vocabulary from the words explicitly taught in the classroom and supplement their learning by targeting vocabulary in activities, like learning the words of songs, outside of class.

Too often, it seems, wishful thinking and time restrictions seem to outweigh hard evidence in the construction of teaching syllabuses and in teaching practice.

While the study of vocabulary has recently become much more fashionable at an academic level, this interest has yet to transfer itself to the foreign language teaching mainstream. The most recent manifestation of the Common European Framework of Reference for Languages (The Council of Europe, 2001), for example, has omitted its early work on vocabulary lists, and concentrates on descriptions of skills and knowledge, almost entirely free of vocabulary. Suites of exams, such as UCLES's First Certificate in English and Proficiency in English, retain specific papers on Use of English, which concentrate on knowledge of language structures, but have no equivalent papers on vocabulary knowledge. This knowledge must be assessed coincidentally through skills assessment in reading, speaking and writing. In the UK, our national Centre for Information on Learning and Teaching recently hosted a seminar 'steering teachers away from the dangers of purely vocabulary based teaching and towards a methodology that focuses on the development of skills and transferable language'. The implication is that an emphasis on vocabulary is still thought to be damaging to learners and it could and should be avoided, even where communication is the principal goal of language learning. The effect in UK schools seems to be a reduction both in the volumes of vocabulary presented to learners (Häcker, 2008) and in the volumes of vocabulary learned (Milton, 2008).

Of course, vocabulary is not an optional or unimportant part of a foreign language. Still less is it an aspect of knowledge that can be disposed of without much effect on the language being learned. Words are the building blocks of language and without them there is no language. As Wilkins succinctly notes (1972: 111), 'without grammar very little can be conveyed, without vocabulary *nothing* can be conveyed'. Recent language learning theory suggests that reducing the volumes of vocabulary acquired by learners may actually harm the development of other aspects of language; for example, word learning may actually drive the development of structural knowledge. It is possible, then, to challenge at a theoretical level the approaches to learning that sideline vocabulary or reduce it to minuscule levels. It is possible too, to use recent work on comprehension and coverage, to provide a very practical justification for teaching vocabulary in greater volumes. The measurements we have of learners' vocabulary resources challenge the myth that it is possible to be an accurate and highly communicative language user with a very small vocabulary. The measurement of second language vocabulary knowledge is not a recondite area of study, therefore, interesting only to a handful of scholars. It should be of interest to everyone involved in the business of language education. It can help teachers and administrators set appropriate targets for learning so that learners can have the language skills that are expected. It can help teachers and learners monitor progress so they can tell whether they have achieved the kind of knowledge needed for an examination or a trip to a foreign country. It can even help academics to understand the nature of language knowledge and the learning process.

For almost 20 years, Swansea University has had a research group investigating the vocabulary of second language learners. We have devised tests to measure vocabulary knowledge, we have models of how vocabulary is learned and how it is forgotten, and we have data from many researchers in many different countries around the world. I have drawn on this huge resource in writing this book and I have tried to bring together the many disparate strands which our research students and colleagues have been working on to make a cogent whole.

The purpose of writing this book is threefold.

In the first section, it is intended to lay before the interested reader how useful measurements of vocabulary knowledge can be made. Useful measuring systems should be systematic so that results from different learners or schools or language levels can be compared. Too often in the past, researchers have used *ad hoc* tests where the results gained from one set of learners provide little insight for learners and teachers in other language teaching environments. This section will consider how to make the tests we use systematic by addressing issues such as the unit of measurement, and what knowing a word means. Vocabulary knowledge is multi-faceted and, in the current state of knowledge, no single measurement can satisfactorily encapsulate a learner's knowledge. This section will also explain, and will seek to justify, why many recently constructed tests use frequency information and concentrate their analysis on the most frequent words in language. It will examine the relationship between frequency of occurrence and learning. It will also consider the relationship between coverage, the proportion of words in a text that a learner knows, and comprehension.

The second section will explain the tests used to make measurements of vocabulary knowledge and will present some of the measurements that have been made of learners' knowledge. The intention is to provide teachers and learners with normative data against which they can begin to compare themselves or their classes, and the learning they undertake. Because vocabulary knowledge is multi-faceted, this section is broken down into some of the aspects of vocabulary knowledge that we commonly consider. These include passive vocabulary size or breadth, or the number of foreign language words a learner knows. It will include productive vocabulary knowledge, or the number and nature of words that a learner can use to express their ideas and communicate. It will tackle areas of knowledge that are less well researched and understood, such as vocabulary depth. It will also address the levels of vocabulary knowledge that learners need to reach in order to tackle formal examinations and where this vocabulary comes from; I will argue that vocabulary levels can be built into the Common European Framework of Reference for Languages.

Finally, this book will consider how the measurements can confirm or challenge the models of language learning we use, and so allow us to refine and improve the methods and techniques we use in foreign language teaching.

Chapter 1

Explanations and Definitions

The intention in this chapter is to give working explanations of vocabulary and the various ways it can be measured. The chapter will not discuss every option and detail about why these measures have evolved exactly as they have, but should provide readers with an understanding of the terms used in this book. It will cover:

- *What is vocabulary and what is meant by a word?*
- *What is word knowledge?*
- *How can vocabulary knowledge be measured?*

We live in a society where we measure things all the time: our height, our weight, our shoe size, our car speed. We do it automatically and rarely think about the units we use for measurement until, that is, the units change for some reason. For example, exactly how fast is the maximum speed limit of 120 kph on roads in continental Europe when your car (my car, at least, it's an old one) only gives miles per hour (mph) on the speedometer? In order to measure anything, therefore, we need to understand the units of measurement and use them appropriately. Measuring language, and vocabulary knowledge in particular, is no exception. Misunderstand the units, or use the wrong units, and we are likely to learn very little about the language we are trying to understand. The purpose of this opening chapter is to explain what these units of measurement are in describing vocabulary acquisition and how we set about measuring vocabulary knowledge.

Measuring language is not as easy as measuring distance or weight. Language knowledge is not a directly accessible quality and we rely on learners to display their knowledge in some way so it can be measured. If learners are tired or uninterested, or misunderstand what they are expected to do, or if we construct a test badly, then they may produce language that does not represent their knowledge. A further problem arises with the qualities of language we are interested in monitoring. Grammar, for example, does not come in conveniently sized packages that can be counted. The techniques we frequently use to elicit language from learners, such as writing an essay, provide data that are not easy to assess objectively. We tend to *grade* performance rather than *measure* it and this can lead to misinterpretation. For example, if two essays are given a mark out of 10, and one is given 8 and the other 4, this does not mean that the first learner has twice the knowledge or ability as the second, even though the mark is twice as large. The use of numbers for grading suggests this ought to be the case, but it is not so. In these circumstances, it is hard to characterise second language knowledge and progress accurately or with any precision; it is hard to *measure* language.

One of the advantages of examining vocabulary learning in a second language is that, superficially at least, it is a quality that appears to be countable or measurable in some meaningful sense. You can count the words in a passage or estimate the number of words a learner knows, and the numbers that emerge have rather more meaning than a mark out of 10 for an essay. A passage of 400 words is twice as long as a passage of 200 words. A learner who knows 2000 words in a foreign language can be said to have twice the knowledge of a learner who knows only 1000 words. While the principle of this looks very hopeful, in reality, assessing vocabulary knowledge is not quite so easy. It is not always clear, for example, exactly what is a word, and what appears to be a simple task of counting the number of words in a text can result in several possible answers. Again, in estimating the number of words a learner knows, it is possible to come up with several definitions of knowledge, some more demanding than others, which might produce very differently sized estimates. The following sections will explain the terms that are used in measuring vocabulary knowledge and learning, and will set some ground rules for the terms used in this book.

What is Vocabulary and What is Meant by a Word?

One thing the reader will find in accessing the literature on vocabulary knowledge, is that we tend to use the word 'word', presumably for ease and convenience, when we are really referring to some very specialist definitions of the term, such as *types, tokens, lemmas, word families* and even the attractively named *hapax legomena*. This can be very confusing, even depressing. My undergraduate students, for example, having read that native speakers of English know something like 200,000 words (Seashore & Eckerson, 1940), are mortified to find that their vocabularies appear less than one tenth of this size when they try out Goulden *et al.*'s (1990) or Diack's (1975) vocabulary size tests. The reason is that early estimates of the vocabulary knowledge of native speakers, such as Seashore and Eckerson's, used a dictionary count where every different form of a word included in the dictionary, was counted as a different word. Words such as *know, knows* and *knowing* were all treated as different words and counted separately. Later attempts to systematise such counts and use frequency information for greater accuracy, such as that of Goulden *et al.*, include a treatment of all the common inflections and derived forms of words as a single word family. By this method, *know, knows* and *knowing* and many other similar forms are all treated as a single unit. Not surprisingly, this method of counting comes up with a smaller count than Seashore and Eckerson's – but often the result is still called a word count.

So, what is a word and how do we count it? In one sense, it can be very simple. Faced with a sentence like,

> *The boy stood on the burning deck,*

we can count up the number of separate words in the sentence. In this case, there are seven separate words. This type of definition is useful if we want to know how many words there are in a passage, for example, or how long a student's essay is. It is also the type of definition used by dictionary compilers and publishers to explain how big the corpus is, which they use to find real examples of word use. When counting words this way, words are often called *tokens* to make it quite clear what is being talked about. So, we would say that the example sentence above contains seven tokens.

Sometimes you will see the expression *running words* used with much the same meaning. Where dictionaries give information about how frequent a word or expression is, you may be told that a word occurs once every so many thousand or million words or running words. The most common words in languages are much more frequent than this. In English, the three most frequent words (usually *the, and* and *a/an*) might make up 20% of a corpus. In a fairly normal text, therefore, you might expect to encounter one of these words once in every five running words rather than every thousand or million. In French, the two most frequent words make up 25% of Baudot's (1992) corpus, and in Greek the definite article alone comprises nearly 14% of the Hellenic National Corpus (Hatzigeorgiu *et al.*, 2001). At the other end of the continuum, the uncommon words are much less frequent and even in the largest corpora a huge number of words occur once only. In Baudot's corpus of approximately 1.1 million words, for example, just under one third of all the entries fall into this category. There is a term for words that occur only once in any corpus or text: *hapax legomena*, often shortened to *hapax*.

In addition to knowing about the size of a piece of writing or speech, the number of words produced, we may also be interested in the number of different words that are used. The terms *types* and *tokens* are used to distinguish between the two types of count. *Tokens* refers to the number of words in a text or corpus, while *types* refers to the number of different words. Look again at the example,

> *The boy stood on the burning deck.*

There are seven tokens, but only six types because *the* occurs twice. It will be appreciated that *types* are much more interesting to us in measuring the vocabulary knowledge of learners, as we usually want to know how many different words they have at their disposal, rather than how much they can produce regardless of repetition.

When dealing with word counts in writing, this catch-all type of definition appears quite straightforward. But, in dealing with spoken text in particular, knowing exactly what to count as a word can be difficult. How do you count the *ums* and *ers* that we sprinkle throughout our speech while we struggle to remember a word or think of what to say next? And how should we count the expressions we contract in speech, such as *don't* and *won't*; should these be counted as one word or two; *do not* and *will not*? How do you count numbers such as 777? In writing, it looks like it could be treated as a single expression, but the same expression in speech requires five words, *seven hundred and seventy seven*. There are few hard and fast answers to these questions, but there are conventions that most writers adhere to most of the time. In producing frequency lists for estimating vocabulary size, in general, numbers, proper nouns and names, and false starts and mistakes are now excluded from word counts. By contrast, the corpora used by dictionary compilers and other researchers may well include many of these things and even *ums* and *ers* can be recorded and categorised.

A *type* count uses the kind of definition of a word which Seashore and Eckerson (1940) applied in making calculations of the vocabulary knowledge in the 1920s and 1930s. It gives a very workable figure that is easily understood. Adult, educated native speakers may know several tens or even hundreds of thousands of words. So why do more modern researchers choose to use a different definition that counts different forms of a word as a single unit? The answer lies in the regularity of the rules by which words are inflected and derived in any language. A good example of this is the way plurals are formed in English. Words like *dog* and *cat* are made plural simply by adding *–s* to make *dogs* and *cats*. Once this rule is mastered, and it is generally learned very early, it can be applied to a huge number of other nouns. Learners do not have to learn these plural forms as separate items from the singular form. If you know one form, you can just apply the rule and you automatically have other words of this kind. Unfortunately, not all plurals are this regular and the over-application of these rules can lead to errors. Young children may use the word *foots* instead of *feet*, for example, until time and experience teach them the plural for this particular word is irregular. Irregular plural forms, such as *child* and *children*, and *sheep* and *sheep*, will need to be learned individually. Nonetheless, it makes sense, to assume, for most learners that if one form of a word is known, then other, very common derivations and inflections will also be known.

This has important implications for testing and for our understanding of how learners build very large vocabularies. In testing, it simplifies the process of choosing the words to include in a test. Instead of having to choose from hundreds of thousands or even millions of words in a dictionary, we can choose from a few thousand word families. This should give better coverage. We can test a bigger proportion of the words in a language, and make a more reliable test. It also helps explain how learners can master the several hundred thousand words which Seashore and Eckerson referred to and which appears an insuperable barrier to foreign language learners. With only a few hundred hours of classroom time available for learning, how do you learn the hundreds of thousands of words you see in a dictionary and which appear necessary for fluency? The answer is that you do not learn these words as separate items. Once you encounter and learn one form of a word, you can apply the rules for making plurals, or past tenses of verbs, or comparative and superlative adjectives, and you have a whole family of words at your disposal. This does not mean that learning vocabulary is a small or simple task. A learner still needs to learn thousands of new words in a foreign language to become competent, but it does make the task approachable in scale. Further, using the word family as the unit of measurement, it is possible to construct tests which can tell us a number of things: how vocabulary is learned, which words are being learned and when these words are being learned. Learning vocabulary in a second language becomes much more understandable when words are considered as a basic form with rule-based variations, than if every different form of the word is measured separately. It can make good sense, therefore, to count word families in some form rather than every different inflected form or spelling of a word.

In counting word families, what types of word are included within the family and what forms are left out? Once again, there are no hard and fast rules for doing this, but two broad conventions have emerged. One is called *lemmatisation*. A *lemma* includes a headword and its most frequent inflections, and this process must not involve changing the part of speech from that of the headword. In English, the lemma of the verb *govern*, for example, would include *governs*, *governed* and *governing*, but not *government*, which is a noun and not a verb and, by this method of counting, would be a different word. Again, the lemma of *quick* would include *quicker* and *quickest*, which remain adjectives, but not *quickly*, which is an adverb and is also a different word in this system. The frequency criterion in English often uses a count made by Bauer and Nation (1993) of the occurrence of affixes. They divide these affixes into nine bands by frequency, and in lemmatising wordlists it is common to include the inflections that use affixes found only in the three most frequent bands. Table 1.1 lists some frequent headwords and the words that could be included under the lemma definition. This convention is not restricted to English. While language rules will vary in different languages, and affixes will differ in both their forms and the frequency of use, it is now convention to construct wordlists in other languages which have been lemmatised and which are as equivalent as they reasonably can be to English and to each other (e.g. Baudot [1992] in French and the

Table 1.1 Some examples of common words and forms included under the definition of lemma and word family

Base form	Forms that might be included in a lemma	Forms that might also be included in a word family
week	weeks	weekly, mid-week
govern	governs, governed, governing	government, governance, governess, governor, ex-governor, governable, misgovern
wide	wider, widest	widen

Hellenic National Corpus in Greek). This raises the enticing, but as yet little investigated, possibility of comparing language knowledge in different languages rather more meaningfully than has been possible before.

This type of count has proved useful in making estimates of the vocabulary knowledge of foreign language learners who are at elementary or intermediate levels of performance. The reason is often a practical and pragmatic one; it seems to work. As Vermeer (2004) points out, the lemma is the most reliable unit of counting words. The presumption is that learners at this level are likely to have mastered only the most frequent inflections and derivations, but will not know the more infrequent and irregular ways in which words can change. By using lemmatised wordlists as the basis for tests at this level, we get believable and stable results. Vocabulary tests, such as Nation's Levels Test (Nation, 1990; revised Schmitt *et al.*, 2001) and X-Lex (Meara & Milton, 2003), use this kind of definition of a word in their counts and estimates of vocabulary knowledge.

The second convention is to include a wider range of inflections and derivations, and uses a *word family* as the basis of word counts. Again, in English, it is now usual to apply a frequency criterion on the basis of Bauer and Nation's (1993) list of affixes; in this case, inflections and derivations using affixes in the first six of the levels they define. There is no requirement, as with lemmas, for words in a word family to remain the same part of speech. Table 1.1 also lists some frequent headwords and the words that could be included in the word family definition. The table is not intended to be a complete list, which could be very long in the case of the word family, but is intended to give an idea of the process of lemma and word family formation.

Not surprisingly, this type of count will produce smaller figures for vocabulary size than calculations made using a lemmatised count. Words that would be treated as separate in a lemmatised count now fall under a single headword. This is the type of count used by Goulden *et al.* (1990) and Diack (1975) for their tests and the reason is not hard to see. In both cases, they are attempting to estimate the vocabulary knowledge of native speakers who can reasonably be expected to be familiar with almost all the ways of deriving and inflecting words (even if they do not know they can do this). The *word family* has also been used in deriving wordlists for advanced users of English as a foreign language. Coxhead's Academic Word List (2000) is one such example, and the presumption must be that the users of this list, who intend to study at university through the medium of English, will have the kind of knowledge of word formation to make them comparable with native speakers. The drawback of this convention is that the estimates of the vocabulary size it produces are not directly comparable with the estimates of foreign language learners' knowledge that often uses the lemma as the unit of measurement. There is a rule of thumb that can be used to multiply the word family score to give an equivalent score in lemmas, but this is very crude.

Rule of thumb

To compare a vocabulary size measurement made using word families with one made using lemmas, multiply the score in word families by 1.6 to get a rough (very rough) equivalent score in lemmas.

There is one further convention which can confuse the business of deciding what a word is. There is often a distinction made between structural vocabulary, usually very frequent words like prepositions (*of*, *up*, *in*) and auxiliary verbs (*is*, *have*), and lexical vocabulary, usually less frequent words which appear to carry more weight of meaning. These, highly frequent, structural vocabulary items, in English about 150–200 words, are often referred to as level 0. There is an implicit assumption that these two types of words, level 0 and everything else, are different and the level 0 words are somehow less word-like than most other words. Word counts can be made which exclude these level 0 words, or count them separately, and examples of this will be found in later chapters. Often, when the term level 0 is being used, it is in a context where other groups of words are being analysed, such as 1000 word frequency bands or specialised wordlists. This is to be seen particularly in the efforts academics make to characterise and measure productive vocabulary knowledge.

There is no single, simple definition of a word that is used in the creation of tests that measure vocabulary knowledge and learning. Investigators can change the unit of measurement according to the circumstances and the learners they are investigating. The result of this can be quite surprising. For example, both Nation (2001) and Schmitt

(2000) report estimates of the number of word families in *Webster's Third New International Dictionary*. One reports 54,000 and the other 114,000 respectively. It is important to be clear at all times what the unit is.

What is Word Knowledge?

There are many types of knowledge involved in being able to use a word properly and effectively in a foreign language. In the same way that we must be clear what we mean by a *word* in making estimates of vocabulary size and knowledge, we must also be clear what we mean by *knowing*. The choice of definition is likely to greatly affect the size of any estimate.

One common convention is to divide word knowledge into *receptive* or *passive* knowledge and *productive* or *active* knowledge. It is generally thought that a learner's *receptive* knowledge, the words that are recognised when heard or read, is greater than a learner's *productive* knowledge, the words that can be called to mind and used in speech or writing. This is often a useful convention and some educational ministries and materials designers divide their wordlists into words they expect learners to know passively and those they expect learners to know actively. The Hungarian National Core Curriculum, for example, suggests that learners should learn some 1600 words by the 8th grade, of which 1200 should be known actively and a further 400 passively (Krizsán, 2003). It is not clear how these proportions have been arrived at. The passive and active distinction may not be as clear cut as it might at first appear, since good passive skills often require the reader or listener to actively anticipate the words that will occur.

Another convention, suggested by Anderson and Freebody (1981), which researchers in vocabulary acquisition find useful, is to distinguish between *breadth* of word knowledge and *depth* of word knowledge. The distinction is deceptively simple. Breadth of knowledge refers to the number of words a learner knows and depth of knowledge refers to what the learner knows about these words. This allows a distinction to be made between learners who may have learned lots of words, perhaps through the rote learning of translation lists, but do not really know how to use them, and learners who have also learned how the words they know associate with other words or the nuances of meaning they carry. While this is a great convenience in characterising the different qualities of learners, the terms breadth and depth turn out to be ambiguous words that can carry a variety of meanings, and their use can cause confusion. Vocabulary breadth, for example, might involve the passive recognition of word forms quite separate from meaning; the kind of recognition where you know a word is a word in a foreign language, you can remember seeing or hearing it, even if you cannot think what it means or provide a translation. Equally, vocabulary breadth might be measured by a translation test where the learner must provide a translation equivalent or some kind of explanation. A measurement of vocabulary knowledge using a productive translation requirement is likely to provide a smaller estimate than one that uses a passive recognition criterion only. The concept of vocabulary depth is even more difficult to pin down, as it might involve knowledge of word associates, collocation, colligation or word function. Meara (1997: 118) implies that this aspect might be brought together within a framework of links between words, regardless of exactly what that link is.

Simple binary divisions like receptive and productive, or breadth and depth do not really do justice to the complexity of word knowledge. In Table 1.2, Nation attempts a more complete and systematic summary of what the various types of word knowledge are.

Nation divides word knowledge into three areas: knowledge of *form*, knowledge of *meaning* and knowledge of *use*. Each of these areas is then further subdivided.

Knowledge of word *form* might involve knowing what a word looks like, the written form of a word; or of what it sounds like, the phonological form. Nation adds to this area the knowledge of word parts by which he means knowledge of the prefixes and suffixes we use to add or change meaning in a word. These are the additions and changes that were considered in the previous section on lemmatisation and word family creation. For example, it includes understanding that you can make an opposite of many words by adding the prefix *un-* at the beginning, as in *known* and *unknown*.

Knowledge of word *meaning* is likewise divided into three parts. The first sub-division, *form and meaning*, is the part most of us will think of in terms of knowing a word. It involves being able to link the form, however it occurs, to a meaning, and often in a foreign language this involves forming a link between a foreign language word and its translation in the native language. Languages are not exactly parallel to each other in the way they use their vocabulary, however. The other sub-divisions, *concepts and referents* and *associations*, indicate, therefore, that a word in one language might require several translations or carry subtly different meanings and associations in another language. A word such as *fat* carries very negative connotations in English when describing a person, and native speakers should use this word with some care. But, in parts of southern Nigeria, the concept has historically had very positive connotations; there used to be fattening houses in old Calabar, for example, where women would go to put on weight in order to look beautiful. Users of English from this background might expect the term to be almost complimentary. Language learners often need to know this

Table 1.2 What is involved in knowing a word

Form	Spoken	R	What does the word sound like?
		P	How is the word pronounced?
	Written	R	What does the word look like?
		P	How is the word written and spelled?
	Word parts	R	What parts are recognisable in this word?
		P	What words parts are needed to express meaning?
Meaning	Form and meaning	R	What meaning does this word form signal?
		P	What word form can be used to express this meaning?
	Concepts and referents	R	What is included in the concept?
		P	What items can the concept refer to?
	Associations	R	What others words does this word make us think of?
		P	What other words could we use instead of this one?
Use	Grammatical functions	R	In what patterns does the word occur?
		P	In what patterns must we use this word?
	Collocations	R	What words or types of word occur with this one?
		P	What words or types of words must we use with this one?
	Constraints on use	R	Where, when and how often would we meet this word?
		P	Where, when and how often can we use this word?

Source: Nation (2001: 27)
Note. R = receptive, P = productive

kind of information if they are not to cause confusion or offence by the wrong choice of words.

Knowledge of word *use* is also divided into three parts. *Grammatical functions* concerns knowing what part of speech a word is and how it will link with other words as a consequence. If you know the word *yellow*, for example, and know that it functions as an adjective, then in English it should be placed before the noun it qualifies and not after: *a yellow door* is right, therefore, but **a door yellow* is not. English learners of Romance languages such as French and Spanish have to modify this rule because adjectives commonly come after the noun in these languages. The *collocations* sub-section refers to the company words like to keep. Some words occur very frequently alongside certain others and these words are said to collocate with each other. A frequent English verb such as *do* forms many phrasal verbs with prepositions (*do up, do in, do away with*), and links with nouns and noun phases (*do my head in*). Some words are highly restricted in their company, for example, *kith* almost never occurs outside the phrase *kith and kin*. Other words do not show this kind of preference and can mix with other words much more widely according to the meaning the speaker or writer is trying to express.

The receptive and productive distinction maps onto this model easily. Nation divides each of the sub-divisions in his table into *receptive* knowledge (shown with an R) and *productive* (shown with a P) and retains the convention that there is a measurable distinction between these two types of knowledge. The breadth and depth distinction is less clear cut. Vocabulary breadth would include the *Form* category, but might also involve the *form and meaning* sub-category from the next section. Vocabulary depth would, by implication, be everything else left in the table.

Daller *et al.* (2007) have attempted to summarise these aspects of knowledge in a theoretical three-dimensional space that contrasts *breadth* and *depth* against a quality of *fluency. Fluency* distinguishes the ease and speed with which a learner can access and use the words they know, from simply recognising the words and knowing about how to use them. The idea is that some learners have high fluency and can use whatever language knowledge they have easily and without hesitation and can be highly communicative, while other learners have difficulty accessing the words they know and attempts at communication are characterised by frequent pauses and hesitations while the learner delves into their memory for the word or expression they are trying to use. Details are lacking in this model, but one way of operationalising it is to assume that breadth and depth are aspects of passive word knowledge, while fluency refers to the productive word knowledge a user has.

One thing that seems obvious in this discussion is that a single test could not possibly hope to measure every aspect of word knowledge. It is hard to imagine how to elicit language for the assessment of productive vocabulary while simultaneously priming learners with foreign language lexis to assess receptive knowledge, for example. It is usually thought necessary to use multiple measures, different tests and measures, in order to garner the information that can characterise a learner's vocabulary knowledge comprehensively (e.g. Nation, 2007: 39). In attempting to measure word knowledge, therefore, researchers tend to choose a workable method that may characterise one or more elements of the complex mixture described above. It often proves hard to find a method that can unambiguously measure just a single element of vocabulary knowledge. Because language knowledge has to be assessed indirectly, a variety of elements of vocabulary knowledge are often assessed at one time, and other types of knowledge and skill may be required by the learner, which may colour the vocabulary produced.

What Makes a Good Vocabulary Test?

It cannot be emphasised strongly enough just how careful the user has to be in dealing with estimates of vocabulary knowledge, particularly where the papers and data are rather old. For a long time, there were no standardised tests in the field of vocabulary testing, and tests had to be created *ad hoc*. It was often impossible to compare the results of one experiment with another in any meaningful way. The conventions and the system for describing word knowledge considered above are a fairly recent phenomenon, within the last 20 years or so, and even now researchers may vary in the vocabulary items they exclude from counts or how they define a word if circumstances seem to demand a change. We do not yet have a comprehensive set of tests which allow us to easily and reliably test every aspect of a learner's vocabulary knowledge, but we do have a small number of well-established tests in some areas, which allow large-scale studies, comparisons over time and even inter-language comparisons to be made. How are such tests created? Usually, there are two main issues to be considered in the creation of any test. One is *reliability* and the other is *validity*.

Reliability, very broadly, is the ability of a test to measure something consistently and accurately. This includes whether the test is stable over time, so if, for example, a vocabulary test is administered to a learner twice in the same afternoon when the learner's vocabulary cannot have changed significantly, then it should give the same score on each occasion. If it does this it is said to be reliable and if does not then it is thought to be unreliable. Judging the reliability of a test might also include equivalence estimates; whether different forms of a test compare well and produce equivalent results. If the learner taking two vocabulary tests in an afternoon were to take two different forms of a test, they should produce scores that show the same level of knowledge or ability and not different estimates. Equivalence estimates are becoming a major concern in language testing, particularly in the UK but also elsewhere, with accusations that standard examinations are becoming easier to pass. As a general rule, so-called objective testing of vocabulary, multiple-choice and forced answer tests, have good reliability as measured by test and retest methods, and some methods can also produce good equivalence scores. Subjective testing is much less satisfactory, and language testing makes extensive use of this through essay writing questions and open-ended comprehension questions. Writing an essay in a foreign language, for example, requires the learner not merely to demonstrate whatever knowledge of the foreign language he or she has, but also to choose a style and register, and make a choice of content and intended readership. If these were not enough to destabilise a test, then during the marking process, the assessor has to make a subjective judgement about elements such as the vocabulary used; is it extensive or limited or appropriate for the task? Much effort is currently going into making objective measures of the language produced by learners in written essays or oral examinations, using vocabulary richness scores for example, but even these methods cannot compensate entirely for the fact that essays and oral interviews are very indirect ways of measuring language knowledge and vocabulary, and are not always very good ways.

Validity addresses the question of whether a test measures what it is supposed to measure and not something else. This can be a complex area with various issues to be examined.

Content validity considers whether a test has the necessary and appropriate content to measure what it is supposed to. Frequently, tests of vocabulary breadth make use of frequency information as the basis of word selection for testing. Nation's (1990) Vocabulary Levels Test, for example, draws words from the second, third, fifth and tenth 1000 word frequency bands in English and from the University Word List (Nation, 1990). The assumption is that learning will be concentrated in these areas and that a test of this material will provide a good overall measure of vocabulary knowledge and general ability. It also uses lemmatised wordlists as the basis of its selection, which reflects the belief that lemmas have some reality as the unit of storage in the minds of learners (Levelt, 1989: 187). The test is generally thought to have good content validity as a result of these choices. Deciding what constitutes good content validity for other aspects of vocabulary knowledge can be more difficult. Vocabulary depth is a term that covers a number of separate constructs and it is unclear how these are related to each other or to vocabulary breadth. One writer, Vermeer (2001), suggests that depth may not really exist as a separate construct and is an extension of breadth of knowledge, as tests of the two correlate so well. Individual aspects of vocabulary depth, such as knowledge of collocations or idioms, tend to be measured separately as a result.

Construct validity, which is often closely associated with content validity, considers whether the test measures the construct or skill it is supposed to. In a language-based measure, this is where testing becomes highly challenging. Language knowledge is not a directly accessible quality, therefore our measurements have to be inferred from language production that may involve other knowledge and abilities. The difficulty of inferring language, and especially vocabulary knowledge, from written essays or general speech has already been raised in the previous paragraphs, and these concerns challenge the construct validity of vocabulary measures made in this area. But, for the measurement of productive knowledge, learners have to produce something, and if it is not to be a piece of writing or speech, what can it be? The requirement for researchers working in the area of testing productive vocabulary knowledge is to elicit language that is truly representative of the learners' productive vocabulary and which can, therefore, be argued to have good construct validity. Measures of productive knowledge also need a method of analysing this output that fairly and accurately describes vocabulary knowledge. Much work in this area is still idiosyncratic, where learners produce different types of output in different registers that are analysed using different tools. As a result, comparison of the results and conclusions is difficult. Measures of receptive vocabulary knowledge can avoid much of this difficulty because the test creator can choose the words for investigation and has the, apparently, less demanding task of designing a suitable means of allowing the learner to show which of these words they know.

In order to test whether a newly created or problematic test of a quality, such as productive vocabulary, really is working well, two different tests of the same quality are often tried on the same learners. If the test is working properly, the results of one test should compare well with the results of the second. This is like the equivalence measure described above, but in this context it becomes what is known as a test of *concurrent validity*. It is a frequently used method to help validate a test's construction and content. But where both tests use fairly indirect methods to access language knowledge, and performance is influenced by other areas of knowledge, then the correlations between the two can be modest and it can be hard to conclude just how well either test is really working (Fitzpatrick, 2007).

Finally, there is the question of *face validity* that is, whether the test is credible to users as a test of what it is supposed to measure. Vocabulary tests can excite surprising passions in users, and even tests with good construct and content validity can be challenged by learners. Learners can have very firm ideas as to what a language test should be like, and these tests do not always involve explicit vocabulary measurement. Where test writers have used frequency data and produced carefully targeted tests of vocabulary knowledge, the comparatively small scale and simplicity of the tests can often raise doubts in the minds of users. The potential benefits of a short and simple test – it avoids loss of concentration and other complications – can be lost on users. Even academics from fields outside vocabulary studies report a credibility problem with these tests. A Dutch colleague once reported to me that he just did not believe a vocabulary test could be useful especially as a general indicator of language level. Language measurement should not be a matter of belief, however, but of collecting and evaluating empirical evidence, and one of the reasons for writing this book is to try to marshal this kind of evidence to show just where and how vocabulary measurement can be useful. It can take quite some time to change attitudes and practices in an area as conservative as testing. I dare say that in medicine, many doctors and patients clung to the practice of leeching long after evidence began to emerge that other treatments were much more helpful to the patient.

How is Vocabulary Knowledge Measured?

How are vocabulary tests to be made so that they can be both reliable and valid, and gain greater face validity? There are two main issues to be considered in vocabulary test construction. One is, which words are to be selected for measurement, examination or counting? The second is, what method is to be used to check whether learners know or can use these words? Researchers are approaching something like a consensus in tackling the first question, and vocabulary tests and other assessments make use of word frequency data and test the most frequent vocabulary. This is the subject of the next two chapters and will be dealt with in detail there.

There is less consensus in answering the second question, partly because in order to test different aspects of word knowledge, different methods will be needed. A test of a learner's receptive vocabulary knowledge, for example, will require the test writer to select words that can be presented to the learner who may not need to productively use the foreign language at all. A test of productive knowledge, however, will require a technique that can elicit vocabulary in the foreign language from the learner. Eliciting language that can tell the researcher something useful about a learner's vocabulary knowledge has proved remarkably difficult. The chapters later in this volume will examine measurements of a variety of aspects of language knowledge and the testing techniques relevant to each will be considered there.

Conclusion

This chapter has attempted to summarise, by way of background, what is meant by a word and what is word knowledge. It is essential for the construction of any good test that measures vocabulary knowledge, to be sure exactly what is being measured. It has also considered questions concerning how vocabulary knowledge can be measured and the qualities that a good test should have. The next two chapters will consider in rather more detail the words which are examined in measuring vocabulary knowledge; essentially examining the content validity of most modern measurement techniques in this area. On the basis of this, the later chapters will consider the details of constructing tests for particular qualities of vocabulary knowledge, their construct validity, and will apply these tests to learners of foreign languages.

Chapter 2
Word Difficulty, Word Frequency and Acquisition: Lexical Profiles

Much of our understanding of which words are learned, how they are learned and how to test for word knowledge, is governed by our understanding of word frequency. This chapter will

- *examine the frequency model of vocabulary learning;*
- *illustrate the lexical profiles that groups and individuals possess;*
- *show how these profiles develop over time and as overall language knowledge increases;*
- *consider how word difficulty might also influence learning.*

Because word frequency and learning are so closely connected, it is generally thought necessary to target knowledge of the most frequent words in a language for assessment. This enables a good measure of vocabulary knowledge to be constructed that works accurately yet efficiently.

Words can vary in all sorts of ways. They can vary in the sounds and letters that make them up. They also differ in their length, how the sounds and letters are allowed to combine and how similar they are to a learner's native language. They can differ in how they are allowed to change and make derived or inflected forms, such as plurals and past tenses. And they can vary in the range of nuance and meaning they convey and, consequently, in what situations you can use them. Unquestionably, these can all influence whether, and how completely a word is learned. These kinds of differences between words have been investigated at some length, usually under the umbrella idea of the learning burden; what makes a word difficult or easy to learn.

Perhaps the most important way in which words differ, however, is the frequency with which they occur. It is important because frequency determines which words a learner is likely to encounter and how often they are encountered. It is thought that this factor, in turn, creates general differences in when a word is likely to be learned: some words tend to be learned at the beginning of language learning and others are more likely to be gained later. It is central to understanding the vocabulary learning process and to how much of this process can be investigated and measured. If we know which words are likely to be learned and which words are not, then it is possible to construct much better tests of vocabulary knowledge than would otherwise be possible. I want to begin this chapter, therefore, by examining the relationship between the frequency of occurrence of a word and learning. Towards the end of the chapter, other factors, such as word difficulty, can be considered and their effect on the overall process of learning measured.

Differences in Word Frequency

In normal language, we use some words much more often than others, and a brief scan of any page of text, including this one, will usually serve to illustrate this. Words such as the articles *the* and *a/an*, prepositions such as *in* and *of*, conjunctions such as *and*, and pronouns such as *it*, occur very frequently. They occur millions of times in most large corpora. Other words such as *curiosity* and *gravel* are much less frequent. Table 2.1 lists, in frequency order, the 20 most frequent words in the British National Corpus (BNC) and another 20 words from the beginning of the 5000 word frequency band, to help illustrate the difference.

Table 2.1 also helps to illustrate that the most frequent words are almost always function or structure words, which appear to carry little weight of meaning themselves, but are crucial to making grammatical and meaningful language. Less frequent words tend to be content or lexical words, nouns, main verbs and adjectives that, it might be thought, appear to carry a greater burden of meaning in any sentence. Both are important, of course, and both are essential to mastery of a foreign language. The most frequent words in English also tend to interconnect much more frequently. A very frequent verb such as *get*, for example, will link frequently with pronouns (*I get*, *you get*, *she gets*), will link frequently with prepositions to make phrasal verbs (*get up*, *get off*, *get on*, *get by*) and will link with noun phrases (*get married*, *get divorced*, *get a take-away meal*). By contrast, less frequent words, such as *gravel* and *cylinder*, are much more restricted in their use and will not collocate so widely, or may not appear to associate in the same way as *get*.

What Table 2.1 also shows is just how different words can be in their frequency of occurrence. Frequent words, those at the top of the list in Table 2.1, are much more frequent than those at the bottom or even half way down the list. The most frequent words occur millions of times in the BNC, while the selection of words from the 5000 word band occur about 1200 times. I have tried to illustrate the scale of the difference in Figure 2.1. In this figure, I have drawn on Baudot's (1992) corpus of modern French (about 1.1 million words) and calculated the average number of times that words in the first five 1000 word frequency bands occur.

What emerges from this is that words in the first 1000 word band are roughly 11 times more frequent, on average, than words in the second band, and 40 times more frequent than words in the fifth frequency band. Words in the first band occur, on average, about 800 times in the corpus,

Table 2.1 The most frequent words, and words from the 5000 word band, and their occurrences in the BNC

Order	Occurrences	Word	Order	Occurrences	Word
1	6,187,267	the	5001	1188	regulatory
2	4,239,632	be	5002	1188	cylinder
3	3,093,444	of	5003	1187	curiosity
4	2,687,863	and	5004	1185	resident
5	2,186,369	a	5005	1185	narrative
6	1,924,315	in	5006	1185	cognitive
7	1,620,850	to	5007	1184	lengthy
8	1,375,636	have	5008	1184	gothic
9	1,090,186	it	5009	1184	dip
10	1,039,323	to	5010	1184	adverse
11	887,877	for	5011	1184	accountability
12	884,599	I	5012	1183	hydrogen
13	760,399	that	5013	1183	gravel
14	695,498	you	5014	1182	willingness
15	681,255	he	5015	1182	inhibit
16	680,739	on	5016	1182	attain
17	675,027	with	5017	1181	specialise
18	559,596	do	5018	1180	steer
19	534,162	at	5019	1180	selected
20	517,171	by	5020	1180	like

Source: Kilgariff (2006)

words in the second band 74 times and words in the fifth band only 20 times on average. Even these differences disguise just how frequent the few most frequent words are. The most frequent word in the corpus, *de*, occurs over 40,000 times and the second, the definite article *le*, over 25,000 times. The majority of words in this corpus occur only once or twice. With differences of this order, it is not surprising that learners very quickly become familiar, at least to some degree, with some of the most frequent words in a language.

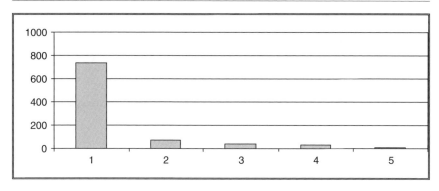

Figure 2.1 Mean frequency of words in frequency bands (Baudot, 1992)

The Frequency Model: Drawing a Frequency Profile

It is generally assumed that there is a strong relationship between a word's frequency and the likelihood that a learner will encounter it and learn it. This is a very important idea in the measurement of second language (L2) vocabulary acquisition because it is a principle on which the most commonly used vocabulary breadth tests are based. The idea is not a new one and goes back 100 years or so to the pre-structuralist, scientific method in language teaching. Palmer (1917: 123), for example, wrote that '...the more frequently used words will be the more easily learnt...'. Later writers accept this as self-evident; for example, both Mackey (1965) and McCarthy (1990) repeat Palmer's idea without reservation. However, despite the widespread use of the idea over recent years, this frequency model or frequency hypothesis has, as Wesche and Paribakht (1996: 14) point out, only been an assumption and it seems not to have been demonstrated until very recently.

Fortunately, one of the advantages of this idea is that it can be turned into a model that can then be tested empirically. Meara (1992) does this by graphing the relationship and producing a frequency profile that, he suggests, should look like Figure 2.2.

Column 1 represents knowledge of the first thousand most frequent words in a language, column 2 the next most frequent 1000 words, and so on. A typical learner's knowledge, Meara suggests, is high in the frequent columns and lower in the less frequent columns, giving a distinctive downwards slope from left to right. Learners will tend to know more of the high frequency words than the lower frequency words. As the learner's knowledge increases, the profile moves upwards until it hits a ceiling at 100% (all the words in this frequency band are known) when the profile flattens out at the most frequent levels and the

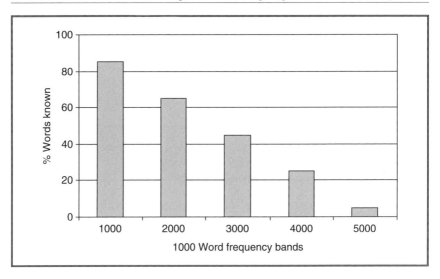

Figure 2.2 Vocabulary profile of a typical learner (Meara, 1992: 4)

downwards slope, left to right, shifts to the right into less frequent vocabulary bands.

Testing the Model and Drawing Real Frequency Profiles

Recent studies have tested this model and found that it seems to be extremely robust, at least in terms of the characterisation of populations of learners. Milton (2006a) conducted a study of all 227 learners at a language school in Greece, with abilities ranging from beginner to upper-intermediate learners of English, expressly to test the frequency hypothesis. The learners were given an orthographic vocabulary recognition Yes/No test with 20 test words taken from each of the first five 1000 word frequency bands which Meara included in his model. The test used was X-Lex (Meara & Milton, 2003), which uses frequency lists drawn up by Nation (1984) and Hindmarsh (1980). The words that the learners identified as known in each band were calculated separately and mean scores for each frequency band produced. The results, when graphed produced a profile, high on the left and tapering off to the right, as the Meara model suggested it should. This is shown in Figure 2.3.

An ANOVA confirms that there is a statistically significant relationship between the frequency bands and vocabulary size scores ($F = 93.727$, $p < 0.001$). This type of evidence provides considerable support to the frequency model of learning and the idea that the more frequent a word is, the more likely it is to be learned, as a general rule.

This effect is not restricted to learners of English as a foreign language (EFL), but has also been observed in learners of French in British schools. Richards and Malvern (2007) report data collected by Helen Bradley from a small sample of 17-year-old students of French and this is shown in Figure 2.4. The data were collected with a French adaptation of the X-Lex test (Meara & Milton, 2003) used in the Greek study and designed to be structured in the same way using frequency information drawn from Baudot (1992).

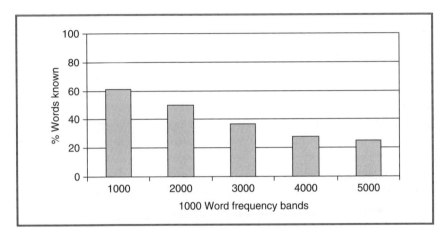

Figure 2.3 Frequency profile for Greek learners of EFL (Milton, 2006a)

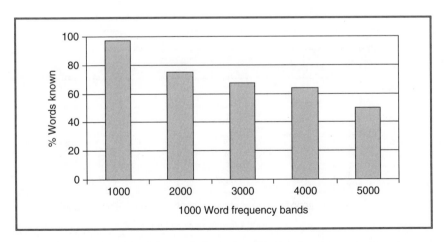

Figure 2.4 Frequency profile of British learners of French (Richards & Malvern, 2007: 79–80)

On the basis of these graphs, it might be argued that the profiles, which are not straight lines, are steeper to the left between bands 1 and 2 and are flatter on the right. This ought to reflect the differences in the frequencies of the words within each different band. The words in column 1 are comparatively much more frequent than the words in column 2, and so on, and in the less frequent bands this difference evens itself out and the frequency of words becomes much more similar. This effect is most evident in a third example, shown in Figure 2.5, taken from Aizawa (2006) who tested 363 Japanese learners of English at university in Tokyo. Aizawa used the Japanese JECET 8000 wordlists and was able to extend his profile to eight 1000 word frequency bands.

While the sloping left to right profile that Meara describes is clearly evident in the first four 1000 word bands, the profile clearly flattens out in the frequency bands beyond this point. This has led Aizawa to suggest that after about the 5000 word frequency level, the variation between levels is not only slightly inconsistent, but also too small to be statistically significant. Notwithstanding this caveat, the conclusion to be drawn from these studies is that the assumption we have always made about frequency is fully borne out by the evidence of real learners. There is a tendency, at least in learners taken as a group, for the most frequent words to be learned earlier in the process of learning.

Rule of thumb

The most frequent words in a language tend (but only tend) to be learned earlier than less frequent words.

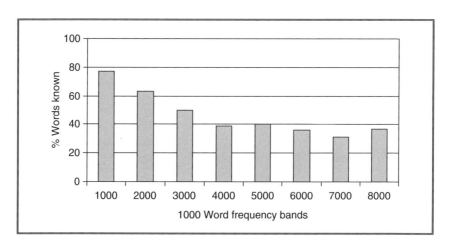

Figure 2.5 Frequency profile for Japanese learners of EFL (Aizawa, 2006)

Two notes of caution should be made here. One is that this is a tendency and not an absolutely rigid rule. A more frequent word will not inevitably be learned before a less frequent one. Materials for learning language are usually thematically arranged and words for teaching cannot be selected purely by frequency. Inevitably, learners will learn the thematically important words in addition to the highly frequent function words. Thus, young learners tend to learn words such as *giraffe* and *tiger* at the outset of learning, even though these are highly infrequent in adult corpora. They are part of the child's world picture and the learning of animal names is a common starting point for many language courses aimed at young learners. The second point is that frequency information does not provide information about difficulty. In fact, it is possible to make a good argument that some of the most frequent words are, in many ways, the most difficult words for English learners to use with complete fluency. This is because they often combine so idiosyncratically with other words (ask any learner of English how hard it is to learn to use prepositions in English accurately) or take irregular inflections. What frequency information does tell us is, what is the likelihood of a learner encountering a word, and having it repeated often enough, for it to be learned.

How Profiles Develop over the Course of Learning

The evidence suggests, therefore, that Meara's (1992) model of a frequency profile is accurate in the way it characterises vocabulary growth in groups of learners, with word knowledge concentrating in the more frequent bands. Is his idea also correct that the profile will be similar at all levels and will move upwards with increased knowledge and level until it reaches 100% knowledge of any one band, when a plateau will emerge? It is not inevitable that this will be the case. The vocabulary profile has its frequency bands drawn from very large language corpora. But individual texts within each corpus can vary from one to another and from the overall frequency list that a corpus produces. Individual texts will vary because they are likely to be about different topics and different themes. Lexical items present in a text on animals, for example, are likely to be absent in a text on car mechanics. When lots of these items are put together in a corpus, the effect is for structural vocabulary items, which occur in all or many texts, to work their way to the top of the general frequency list, while the animal names and car parts, absent from most texts, sink to somewhere near the bottom. The effect can be seen in Table 2.2.

While the BNC is a bigger corpus than the other two, which is likely to exaggerate the tendency for function words to preponderate in materials drawn from across thematic areas, the individuality of the other two sets

Table 2.2 Comparing the most frequent lexis from children's books (Vassiliu, 2001), from car texts (Milton & Hales, 1997) and from the BNC

Order	BNC	Car manuals	Children's EFL books
1	the	and	is
2	be	the	the
3	of	to	a
4	and	of	your
5	a	in	no
6	in	is	look
7	to	or	where
8	have	with	for
9	it	remove	but
10	to	a	did
11	for	replace	from
12	I	for	say
13	that	oil	as
14	you	be	very
15	he	valve	dog

of materials is very clear. The car manuals corpus, of about 100,000 words, includes vocabulary such as *oil* and *valve* with very high degrees of repetition that would not be expected outside this register. Working within this genre also involves high repetition of particular actions, hence the remarkable frequency of *check, remove* and *replace.* These words, of course, have no place in EFL teaching texts designed for young learners, and Vassiliu's sample of such materials produces very different lexical words. Words such as *look* and *say* are clearly part of the rubric of course books and give instructions to learners telling them what to do. *Dog* is a product of the thematic content of the material that focuses on ideas appropriate for very young learners, in this case animals. Nonetheless, it is clear too that even in these small samples of very subject-restricted texts, the function words of English are still beginning to preponderate.

It seems possible, therefore, that at the outset of learning, the profile may change from Meara's profile because language exposure will only have been to one, or a small number of, language texts. Language exposure may not have been sufficient for the characteristics of normal language to emerge. Does this variation occur and, if it does, at what point has sufficient language exposure been achieved for the normal profile to reassert itself? To answer this question, the data from 227 Greek learners of English (Figure 2.3) have been reanalysed and vocabulary profiles drawn for each of the seven classes from junior, the beginners, up to First Certificate in English (FCE), taking the Cambridge examination. The results are shown in Figure 2.6.

Perhaps surprisingly, this data suggests that Meara's frequency profile can emerge even at the earliest stages of learning. After only 100 classroom hours in this case, and when input might be expected to be at its least typical, the frequency profile is almost complete. From this low level, the profile does move up the graph, very much as Meara predicted. It is not clear from this data at what point or whether a plateau is reached at 100% of knowledge in any frequency band. Even the top group have a mean in the most frequent bands someway short of the maximum.

In order to examine whether learners do routinely achieve 100% in the most frequent bands, the individual profiles for the 10 highest scoring students in Milton (2006a) have been drawn up and are shown in Figure 2.7.

This figure is, in many ways, highly unsatisfactory, confused and unclear with many overlapping lines, but it serves its purpose. What emerges from this jumble, is that the most able learners appear to reach a plateau in the most frequent bands, not at 100% as anticipated, but at a rather lower level, about 85–90% in these cases. It is not obvious why the profile plateaus at this point. It may be that some of even the most frequent words have qualities that make them impervious to the effects of the normal teaching and learning processes. Alternatively, there may be an issue in the selection of vocabulary for inclusion in textbooks,

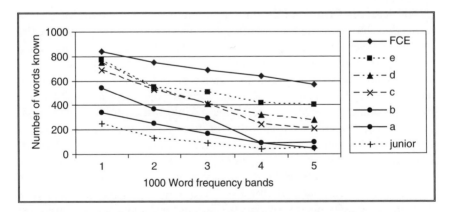

Figure 2.6 Frequency profiles for Greek learners of EFL divided by class

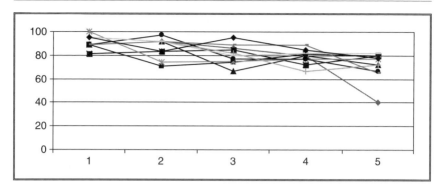

Figure 2.7 Individual profiles for the 10 highest scoring students in Milton (2006a)

which means that some highly frequent vocabulary has to be omitted and cannot, therefore, be learned. Or it may be that this observation is simply the by-product of learner idiosyncrasies and that each learner manages to avoid encountering and learning a different set of words. A more detailed examination of the unknown words in these frequency bands is required to answer this question.

The trend seen in the English learning data is repeated in the learning of other languages. A study of French as a foreign language in a British school (Milton, 2006b) reported learning over all seven years of the school curriculum, from beginners at the end of their first year in school, to more able language learners at the end of seven years tuition taking 'A' level examinations. The profiles for year 3, 5 and 7 are reported in Figure 2.8. Profiles from levels 1, 2, 4 and 6 have been omitted only because their inclusion made a cluttered figure, which is difficult to interpret visually.

The learners in this study had the benefit of fewer hours of formal input than the Greek learners of English, about 60 hours per year for the first five years, and progress in vocabulary learning is smaller as a result. In frequency bands between 1000 and 4000, the frequency profile emerges and moves upwards as expected. But level 5 is different; a comparatively high level of vocabulary knowledge appears in this band from the outset of learning, producing a kink in the profile. Learning at this frequency level remains static for four years and only by year 5, after some 300 hours of input, does the complete profile assert itself. Work on these data is still in progress, but the kink at level 5, and the time it takes for the complete frequency profile to develop, may well be the product of the materials the learners have to learn from. It appears that an extremely narrow range of themes and materials is provided to learners in the early years of learning, and even though the materials

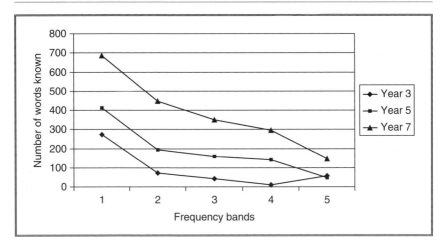

Figure 2.8 Frequency profiles for UK learners of French divided by class (Milton, 2006b)

are meant to be 'authentic', they are possibly insufficient in variety and quantity to allow the normal distribution of French vocabulary to emerge.

Nonetheless, despite the small range of input that beginners are likely to encounter at the outset of learning, it appears that learning is still concentrated among groups of learners, as Meara predicted in the most frequent bands as identified in large, general corpora. The frequency profile is a feature of learning across the range of abilities and the profile rises to around 85–90% before it begins to plateau. This should imply that vocabulary tests concentrating in these frequent bands will provide useful data at all stages of learning after the first 100 hours of tuition and provided input is of good quality.

Vocabulary Profiles in Individual Learners

Thus far, this chapter has considered the frequency model of learning by drawing on data taken from groups of learners. The data suggests that learners, as a group, are sensitive to the frequency of occurrence of the words they encounter. However, groups are made up of individual learners, and it is by no means inevitable that every learner will be identical in their reaction to word frequency. Every teacher knows that while every pupil in a class receives the same amount of classroom time, follows the same course books, hears the same teacher talk and does the same exercises, the pupils will vary in what and how much they learn. If word frequency is to be used as the basis for vocabulary test construction and for the measurement of knowledge, then this individual variation is potentially important. There is a danger that tests may work well for some or most learners who are sensitive to frequency, but work poorly with those who learn differently. It is worth asking the question whether some learners are less sensitive to word frequency than others, and if there are such learners, how widespread is this tendency in a population. The answers to these questions will suggest how strong the content and construct validity of vocabulary measurements based on frequency information will be.

A Friedman test on the results from Greek learners of English in Milton (2006a), shown in Figure 2.3, confirms the impression that individual learners tend to be influenced by word frequency and that the overall trend is very strong indeed in a population as a whole ($\chi^2 = 512.55$, two-tailed $p < 0.001$). But even strong relationships of this kind can disguise some systematic variation and do not imply that every learner's vocabulary up-take produces a perfectly regular vocabulary profile. To try to illustrate how usual the frequency profile is among individuals, I have reworked the data from Milton (2006a) and examined the individual profiles of the 227 Greek learners of English. Learners whose results show the frequency profile (the score in the first 1000 word frequency band is higher than the score in the second which is higher than the third) have been grouped separately from learners who do not. The results of this division are shown in Figure 2.9, where the data is presented class by class; the junior group are beginners with one year of English and the FCE group is completing seven years of instruction and undergoing preparation for the Cambridge FCE examination.

It appears that about 60% of learners, 132 of 227, in this group have exactly the kind of frequency profile which the group as a whole displays. Only in the lowest and highest classes do the learners with

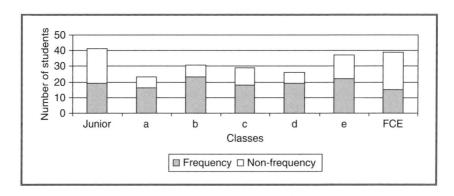

Figure 2.9 Proportions of learners of English in Milton (2006a) displaying regular frequency profiles

non-frequency profiles out-number those with more regular profiles. Among the beginners, the presence of the frequency profile at all is something of a surprise given the small amount of input these learners will have received and the way small corpora, such as beginners' textbooks, differ from the very large corpora where we take our frequency information from. In the highest class, it appears that ceiling effects are influencing the profiles. The most able learners have scores in the most frequent bands that have reached a maximum and the frequency profile is no longer observable as learning moves to the less frequent bands. Notwithstanding these considerations, it seems that a minority of learners, perhaps one in three or one in four, do not display the frequency profile in the words they learn. It is possible that this variation may indicate some systematic differences in the way learners acquire vocabulary, and Meara *et al.* (2001) suggest two possible profiles in addition to the frequency profile which might emerge from differences in learning style and aptitude. This kind of individual variation is considered in more detail in Chapter 11.

Word Difficulty and how this Influences the Frequency Model

At the opening of this chapter, I suggested that word frequency was the most important factor in helping us understand which words are likely to be learned and when. The evidence that has been collected in this chapter confirms how influential word frequency appears to be. At the same time, it was suggested that there are a number of other factors, associated with word difficulty and learning burden, which will also help influence which types of word are learned. Potentially, these factors could destabilise the frequency model. What are these factors and what influence do they have on vocabulary learning? Is it possible, or necessary, to build word difficulty features into a general model of word learning to create a better directed test of vocabulary knowledge and enable better understanding of the measurements which come out of such tests?

Perhaps the most obvious source of potential difficulty for a learner is the form of the word itself. If the new word contains unusual combinations of letters or sounds, or is difficult to pronounce, then it would seem less likely to be retained in memory and recalled for use, than a new word that does not possess these features. There is some research evidence to support this idea. Rodgers' (1969) study of English-speaking students of Russian, for example, reported that words with non-English sound combinations and which were difficult to pronounce, were not learned as well as words which were easier to pronounce. Speakers of semitic languages, such as Arabic, tend to focus on consonants in reading and consequently find difficulty in other languages where vowels are important. Ryan (1997, 186) points to writing confusions in English, such as *wells* and *wheels*, *left* and *lift*, and *present* and *prison*, where the consonants remain relatively unaffected by error, but the vowels are often mis-positioned, omitted or substituted for each other. Words that are similar in form, or at least appear similar to the learner can thus be confused. Laufer (1990: 148), for example, recalls from her experience of learners that *available* is often misinterpreted as *valuable*, *embrace* as *embarrass*, and *simulate* as *stimulate*. In production, she points out that pairs such as *thinking* and *sinking*, *price* and *prize*, and *cute* and *acute*, may convey in production a message very different from that which was intended.

Another widely considered factor is how similar the target word in a new language is an equivalent in the learner's own language. Gairns and Redman (1986: 67) illustrate this idea with cognates such as *taxi*, *bar* and *hotel*. These are common vocabulary items in many European languages and French, Spanish or Italian learners of English would have little difficulty recognising these words if they encountered them in written form. The pronunciation may be different in these languages, and this may cause difficulty in learning correct pronunciation, but the written form is often identical and learning should, it might be thought, require very little effort from the student. Tharp (1934: 129–130), reporting the findings of a dissertation written by Limper, sounds a note of caution in generalising too widely about the effect on learning of cognates. It appears that learners can be highly idiosyncratic in their reactions to these and not just in the way two words can appear cognate to one learner, but completely unconnected to another. It seems learners are also unpredictable in the way one derivation of a word can be recognised as a cognate while a different derivation of the same word is not recognised.

Gairns and Redman (1986: 68) also suggest that concrete items that can be represented visually, or demonstrated simply, may also be more economical to teach and learn than abstract items and ideas. An item such as *table*, which can be seen and touched, might be more easy to learn than, say, *philosophy* or *intuition*. Part of the issue here may be whether a direct translation equivalent exists between the target and the native language. A gap where this does not exist is a *lexical void*, and a question affecting difficulty is whether the learners are aware of the ideas and concepts they are learning in their native language. Language teachers, especially those teaching a language for specialist or academic purposes, will be familiar with the experience of coping with learners who do not know the subject matter of the language they are learning. Teaching words such as *carburettor* and *transmission* can be relatively straightfor-ward if the learners are car mechanics, they know exactly what is being talked about, but to someone with no knowledge of car engines these terms become meaningless jumbles of letters or sounds, and so, very forgettable.

Laufer (1997: 144) reports that, intuitively, it would seem that longer words should carry a greater learning burden than shorter words. The evidence is ambiguous, and some studies fail to find such a link (e.g. Rodgers, 1969). As Laufer points out, length is a factor that is difficult to isolate in studies as it often conflicts with the morphological transparency of longer words. Words such as *mismanagement*, she suggests, despite being longer, comprises several familiar morphemes which enables learners to recognise it more easily and, presumably, to memorise it.

Part of speech can also play a role in influencing the learning burden of a word. Nouns, it seems, are easier to learn than verbs, which are easier than adjectives. Horst and Meara's (1999) study of a single learner making multiple readings of a comic book investigated the classes of the words that the learner acquired and these findings are summarised in Table 2.3.

While these results appear to support the idea of the influence of word class on take up, it must be borne in mind that the learner in this case was deducing the meaning of new words from picture cues in a comic book. While nouns often lend themselves to being pictured (the learner in this case referred to the picture which enabled him to work out that *hooivork* was a pitchfork), adverbs may be much harder to illustrate. The results may have been different had the learner been studying translation pair wordlists, for example.

Rule of thumb

A foreign language word is thought likely to be easier to learn if:

- it is like its first language translation;
- it is relatively short;
- it is concrete and imagable;
- it is different in sound and appearance from other new words.

All these factors may affect which words are likely to be remembered as words, so that a correct foreign language form of a word can be matched with an item, a concept or a first language (L1) translation. They

Table 2.3 Uptake of vocabulary by word class

Nouns	*Verbs*	*Adjectives*	*Adverbs*
$n = 51$	$n = 32$	$n = 20$	$n = 8$
63%	38%	35%	13%

Source: Adapted from Horst and Meara (1999: 324)

might well have an impact on the effects of frequency in the manner they have been measured so far in this chapter. A cognate word, even if it is highly infrequent and is encountered only once, might be learned because it is so similar to the native language item, while highly frequent items, if they are long or completely different from the native language, might take many more encounters before being memorised correctly. There are other potential causes of difficulty, such as differences in connotations, associations and collocations between first and target language words, which would not be picked up by a passive knowledge Yes/No vocabulary test of words in isolation. These kinds of factors tend, as Laufer (1990: 574) points out, to be researched separately and in isolation from each other, so we have very few studies that attempt to coalesce these factors into a comprehensive picture of word learning difficulty in order that the cumulative effect of these factors can be seen. Very often too, investigations in this area are based on analyses of very small numbers of words and with a small number of students, and it is not clear how the conclusions they reach are generalisable in the process of building a whole lexicon with, potentially, many thousands of words. Even Laufer's own considerable contribution stops short of trying to build the measurement of these factors into a single model of word learning.

It ought to be possible to take all these separate factors, however, and operationalise them in a single model. Milton and Daller (2007) have attempted to build some of the factors listed above into such a model, with frequency, to calculate how much each factor contributes to whether a word is likely to be learned or not. This attempt is something of an experiment, so in addition to frequency they have added only target word length and degree of cognateness into the model. In order to do this, 106 British learners of French, ranging in ability from beginner up to degree level, were tested using a 100 item Yes/No orthographic test of the most frequent 5000 words from Baudot's (1992) lemmatised French vocabulary list. Four sets of data were collected.

The test words were given a score for their frequency. This was done in a number of ways. One way was to group the test words into their frequency bands, and words thus gained the score for their band: 1 for words in the 1000 most frequent word band, 2 for words in the second 1000 word band, and so on. The test contained 20 words randomly selected from each of the first five 1000 word levels. A second way to score frequency was to use the number of occurrences in Baudot's corpus. The third method was to use the frequency scores in Baudot's corpus, but to omit level 0 words from the test, thus examining the effect of frequency when only lexical vocabulary is tested.

Word length was measured by counting the number of syllables in each test word. The assumption is made that the more syllables a word possesses, the harder it is likely to be. Test words in French varied between one and five syllables and were not equally distributed across the frequency levels. The mean length of syllables for the words at each frequency level is shown in Table 2.4.

Measuring the cognateness of a word is a bit more complicated. When this is discussed, by teachers or academics, there tends to be an assumption that a word is either cognate or it is not. However, a binary division does not make this kind of modelling work very well and fails to reflect the fact that L2 words may vary in how similar they are to L1 equivalents. Some L2 words are more like the L1 than others. For English-speaking learners of French, the word *moment* is identical in spelling and appearance to an L1 equivalent, but the word *heure* is not identical, although it is pretty similar. For the purpose of measuring this degree of similarity, a calculation has been made according to how many letters in the correct sequence occur in the target word, as a proportion of the original L1 word. MOMENT has six out of six letters in common between English and French and scores 1. By contrast, *heure* has three out of five letters in common, *HeURe*, and scores 0.6. The assumption is being made that the more letters a word has in common, the more cognate it will be and the easier it will be. The test words in French varied between 0 and 1 according to their degree of cognateness and were not equally distributed across the frequency levels. The mean cognateness score for the words at each frequency level are shown in Table 2.4.

In order to assess the impact of these variables on the learning process, the number of Yes responses to each word was totalled to give a measure of how likely a word is to have been learned by the subjects. Words that are easy should score well, approaching 106, while words that are hard will score low, closer to zero. I do not think there is a name for this kind of calculation, but for the purpose of this chapter it will be called a learnability score. The mean learnability scores for the words at each frequency level are shown in Table 2.4.

Table 2.4 Mean syllable length and cognateness scores per frequency level

Frequency level	Mean number of syllables	Mean cognateness score	Mean learnability score
1	1.9	0.4	23.70
2	2.4	0.6	10.85
3	2.6	0.6	11.80
4	2.4	0.5	9.40
5	2.6	0.7	8.65

At first glance, it appears these factors may not be acting entirely independently of each other. Words in the most frequent band appear on average to be shorter, which should make them easier, but less cognate, which should simultaneously make them harder. For words in the least frequent band, the opposite is true. These words appear to have more syllables, which should make them harder, but to be more cognate, which should make them easier. Appearances may be deceptive, however, and calculation of the correlation between these factors suggests there is little or no systematic relationship, and none that is statistically significant. Correlations are given in Table 2.5.

What might we expect from testing a model of word learning in this way? It is, admittedly, a very crude model. Even rating words by their frequency in a corpus must suffer from some kind of ceiling effect as, beyond a certain level, if words are going to be learned at all, they will be learned and further repetition becomes redundant. The calculation that omits level 0 might prove more useful than the other frequency assessment methods as a consequence. The calculations for word length and cognateness might also be challenged and amended. Nonetheless, given that there is such a consistent relationship between frequency and word learning, it would be surprising if frequency did not make a quantifiable contribution to the outcome of which words are learned and which are not. The correlation results which are all in the region of 0.5 suggest that the relationship is quite strong. A regression analysis should show the degree of variance in the learnability scores which frequency can explain. But, if measures of difficulty, such as cognateness and syllable numbers, really do also impact on whether a word is likely to be learned or not, then this should also be visible in such an analysis. It might be hoped that these extra measures will refine the system and contribute additionally to explaining the variation in learnability scores. That would be the hope and expectation, but does this occur?

The results of a step-wise regression analysis confirmed that frequency does have a measurable impact on the learning of vocabulary. When words are placed in frequency bands to provide only an estimate of relative frequency, the frequency measure was able to explain about 20% of the variance in the learnability score. This is moderate to low in its

Table 2.5 Correlations between frequency level, number of syllables and cognateness

	Level	*Cognateness*
Syllables	0.182	0.135
Cognateness	0.167	

predictiveness. Using actual frequency scores, even this predictiveness disappears under the influence of the very highly frequent function words. Using lexical items only and excluding words from level 0 in the analysis, frequency's predictiveness returns and explains about 30% of variance in the learnability scores. This is still a moderate score, but no matter how the frequency measure is tinkered with, the figure of about 30% cannot be improved upon with this set of learners. This is probably quite an encouraging result, however, and might be improved in a better model that is able to take account of the real differences in frequency between the test items. There are several obvious ways in which the frequency aspect of the model might be changed and improved, not least by referring to the materials actually used by learners. The study included a large number of beginner level French learners, among whom it appears several years of study are required for the effects of frequency to appear.

The regression analysis tells a different story for the difficulty factors, cognateness and word length. In neither case, and in none of the analyses, could these factors be shown to have any impact on learnability. The expected effects for elements of word difficulty have not emerged in this analysis and there might be several reasons why this is so. One is that the systems used for measuring the elements of word difficulty are not appropriate in some way to capture these qualities of difficulty, and different forms of measurement might yield different results. Additionally, the choice of language for the study may have influenced the results. French and English have so many words which are cognate, that the effect might be lost in these circumstances. Words which are cognate between the two languages in this study might not be cognate in others and different results might be produced if the study were replicated with, say, Chinese learners of Icelandic, where far fewer cognates might be expected.

However, the possibility should also be considered that the effects of difficulty factors, such as cognateness and word length, are not as consistent across a whole lexicon, nor as great, as their prominence in the literature leads us to suspect. Both these factors may have been influenced by the effect of morphology in English and French. Many affixes in these languages are so similar that it may be possible to reduce an unknown long word to shorter component parts that are either known or are guessable. This is clearly a subject for further investigation. Nonetheless, this conclusion does serve to indicate the salience of frequency of occurrence as an influence on which words a learner is likely to encounter and learn. It serves to place in context the effect of the various different kinds of difficulty that may also influence whether a word is likely to be learned. Factors such as word length, the part of speech or concreteness of the words, and the idiosyncrasies of the textbook, do not seem to reverse the influence of general frequency. This is not to deny that factors like length and cognateness do not have an effect, but it appears that it is nothing like the effect of frequency. These difficulty factors may have an impact on the learning of small groups or individual words, but the kind of general effects which frequency creates appear to be absent with difficulty factors.

Conclusion

The conclusion that can be drawn from this chapter, and the point of the chapter, is that there is a system to learning vocabulary, or at least recognising foreign language vocabulary, and it is driven by word frequency. Factors like word difficulty may operate at the level of individual words, but do not appear to have anything like the impact of frequency and do not seem to destabilise the frequency model of learning. As Palmer pointed out, the most frequent words in language really do tend to be learned earliest. This conclusion allows vocabulary testing and measurement to be targeted. We can use frequency information to investigate knowledge of a careful selection of words which learners are likely to have encountered and had the opportunity to learn, without worrying that such measurements will be badly missing the point by not taking into account other factors and investigating large numbers of infrequent vocabulary. Measurements using only frequency-based data as the basis of an estimate of total vocabulary size are probably going to under-estimate and, for the most able learners, there will be a ceiling effect. The higher the level of the learners, the more likely it will be to under-estimate measures using only the most frequent words.

The frequency profile demonstrates that the vocabulary that L2 learners acquire tends to concentrate in the most frequent vocabulary bands. This helps the process of testing a learner's vocabulary knowledge because a test can focus on words in this area. If a test scatters its test items randomly across all the tens or hundreds of thousands of word forms in a language then, where knowledge is concentrated in this way, there is a danger that whatever words a learner knows will be missed. But, by knowing where learning concentrates, then the test can also concentrate test items in this area and form, hopefully, a good estimate of knowledge. It will only be an estimate, however. This is partly because even with this knowledge, not every word in the most frequent bands can be tested, only a sample will be used. But it is also because there will always be word knowledge outside the most frequent bands. Depending on the learner's individual experience of the themes covered in class, or on the learner's individual interests, knowledge of thematically related, content words will be scattered among the less frequent bands and a vocabulary test cannot reasonably hope to sample these adequately. Despite this, as Aizawa (2006) suggests, a test based on the most frequent bands should give a good estimate of vocabulary knowledge, which should, in turn, allow us to examine vocabulary development throughout the process of language learning.

For other purposes, this need not be such a problem. Aizawa concludes that for placement testing, the use of profiles and frequency data, as in, for example, Meara and Milton's (2003) X-Lex, might best be restricted to only the most frequent levels. The fact that such measures may not give a completely accurate absolute score for vocabulary knowledge does not prevent them from giving good indications of overall knowledge and accurate indications of comparative levels of knowledge. It seems inevitable that a measure of vocabulary knowledge that can be compared across learners, educational systems, languages and countries must draw on frequency information.

Chapter 3
Frequency and Coverage

This chapter examines the relationship between the most frequent vocabulary and text coverage – how much of a text a reader is likely to understand. It will introduce Zipf's law, which allows the relationship between word frequency and coverage to be graphed. This will suggest:

- *how much vocabulary is needed to read a text for basic, gist understanding;*
- *how much vocabulary is needed in listening to normal spoken text;*
- *how much vocabulary is needed for full comprehension in both reading and writing;*
- *whether specialist lexicons can reduce the learning burden and add to coverage and comprehension;*
- *whether vocabulary measurements can be a good indicator of general foreign language level.*

In the previous chapters, vocabulary has been considered with the particular concern that frequency can help explain much about which words are likely to be learned and when. By knowing the most frequent vocabulary in a language, we can construct well-directed vocabulary tests that can measure knowledge in an essential area of language. It was pointed out that this is not a new idea and that Harold Palmer described this relationship between frequency and learning. But Palmer's (1917: 123) observation that the most frequent words will be learned earliest, goes further and suggests that the most frequent words are also the most useful to the learner; they are the words that will enable the learner to understand and express himself/herself most efficiently. There is a second reason for wanting to test and measure knowledge of the most frequent words in a language, therefore, and that is that the information gained is likely to tell us about the learner's ability to function, and to communicate, in the foreign language. A learner who knows only highly infrequent words, it is suggested, will be less well equipped to function, than a learner who knows the most frequent words.

I have argued that Palmer's assumption that the most frequent words will be learned earliest has proved to be broadly correct. Does his second assumption, that the most frequent words are the most useful, also stand up to scrutiny?

The Relationship Between Word Frequency and Coverage: Zipf's Law

It has already been noted in Chapter 2 that the frequent words in a language, words like *the* and *and*, tend to be very frequent indeed and that there are comparatively few of these very highly frequent words. At the other end of the frequency scale, there are lots of words, like *maunder*, *ecumenical* and *Zipf*, which appear to be very infrequent and occur only a handful of times in a corpus of normal language. In between, there is a medium number of words with middle-of-the-road frequency scores somewhere between the two extremes. This kind of distribution is known as a Zipf distribution and has given rise to Zipf's law. Zipf's law allows the relationship between the rank of a word in a frequency list and the number of times it occurs, to be described more systematically and graphed up. Zipf's law states that in a corpus of natural language, the frequency of a word is roughly inversely proportional to its rank in the frequency table. So, the word that is ranked first in the table is likely to occur about twice as often as the word ranked second, which is likely to be twice as frequent as the word ranked fourth and so on. To help illustrate this, Table 3.1 shows the rank and frequencies of the eight most frequent words in both English and French corpora.

It is clearly not a perfect law, nor a perfect relationship. In both these examples, the second ranked word may be substantially less frequent than the first ranked word, but it is more than the 50% that Zipf's law suggested. Similarly, in both examples, the fourth ranked word has a frequency that is much greater than 50% of the second. In the English corpus, the frequency of the eighth ranked word, *have*, is nearly half that of the fourth, *and*, but in the French corpus this regularity is still missing.

Table 3.1 Ranks and frequencies of words in English and French

	English (Kilgariff, 2006)		*French (Baudot, 1992)*	
1	the	6,187,267	de	68,373
2	be	4,239,632	le	42,419
3	of	3,039,444	être	26,897
4	and	2,687,862	un	26,613
5	a	2,186,369	avoir	23,570
6	in	1,924,315	à	23,475
7	to	1,620,850	et	23,325
8	have	1,375,636	les	19,230

In other corpora, this relationship can be rather neater. In the Brown Corpus (Kuçera & Francis, 1967), for example, the most frequent English word, *the*, accounts for nearly 7% of the whole corpus (69,771 occurrences out of over one million words). The second ranked word, *of*, has 36,411 occurrences, almost 3.5%.

Zipf's law is not a perfect description of language, therefore, it is an empirical law not a theoretical one. Nonetheless, the relationship between a word's frequency and it position in the frequency table is quite clear and it has an important implication. It means that a small number of words tend to make up a very large portion of any normal text. In the Brown Corpus, some 135 words account for half of the entire corpus. A fuller list of frequency bands and the coverage they are likely to provide, in English, is shown in Table 3.2, which also shows that the most frequent words contribute very heavily to text coverage and the less frequent a word is, the less it contributes. This data is presented in graph form in Figure 3.1.

In Figure 3.1, the curve rises steeply on the left hand side, and in this area each additional word contributes significantly to text coverage. Knowledge of about 1000 words in English should mean that a learner would recognise and understand about three quarters of the words in normal text. Knowledge of about 2000 words in English should mean that about 80% of the words in normal text would be understood. So, if learners were to learn these words, then they would know a large proportion of the texts they read or hear and, it might be argued, stand a

Table 3.2 Typical coverage figures for different frequency bands

Number of words	Text coverage (%)
10	24
100	49
1,000	74
2,000	81
3,000	85
4,000	88
5,000	89
12,000	95
44,000	99
87,000	100

Source: Carroll *et al.* (1971, cited in Nation, 2001)

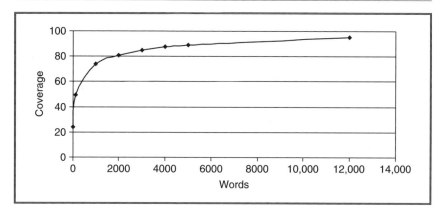

Figure 3.1 The most frequent bands in Table 3.2 presented in graph form

better chance of understanding them. The logic behind Palmer's claim that the most frequent words are also the most useful is very clear. Nation suggests that these 2000 most frequent words are so important to language learning and language ability that almost anything that can be done to make sure that they are learned is worth doing (Nation, 2001: 16). This might imply that they should be taught explicitly, despite the enormous commitment in classroom time that this would entail. After about 2000 words, the curve flattens considerably and each additional word contributes much less to overall coverage. If you already know the most frequent 2000 words in English, then for the effort of learning the next most frequent 2000 words, only an additional 7 or 8% of coverage might be gained.

Rule of thumb
The most frequent 2000 words in English are likely to be the most useful to a learner and knowing these will enable the learner to recognise about 80% of any normal text.

The Relationship Between Coverage and Comprehension

The suggestion is being made here that there is a strong relationship between text coverage and comprehension; that the more words you know, the better you will be able to understand when reading or listening in the foreign language. Also, the more words you know, broadly speaking, the better you will be able to express yourself in speech and writing. This may seem obvious. After all, if you know no words in the foreign language, you will not understand anything at all, while if you know all the words, you would hope that you would be able to access full meaning. It may not be so simple, however. As anyone who has read the great German masters of philosophy will know, it is possible to understand every individual word when reading a text and still take very little understanding from the experience. Also, the most frequent words are usually structure and function words, the words which are needed to make language grammatical, but which may contribute very little to the substance of what is being spoken or written about. It is possible, therefore, to be familiar with a large portion of a text and still have no real understanding of the content, through ignorance of the content words, the nouns and verbs, which carry so much of the meaning. Language, if it is to be meaningful at all, must have a topic, a theme or an idea to it, and the words associated with these do not fit easily into the most frequent bands in frequency listings. They are spread across the frequency bands. It seems that knowledge of some less frequent words is also essential for good language comprehension and language production.

Despite these reservations, there is more than an element of truth to the idea that coverage is important to comprehension and that knowledge of the most frequent words, which contribute so much to coverage, is also important. This is best appreciated with a series of examples that puts the reader in the position of a learner with varying amounts of vocabulary knowledge. The first example takes the first sentence of a well-known speech, and simulates how comprehensible it would be to a learner who knows only the most frequent 10 words of English. These words have been left in place in the text and all other words have been replaced with a series of XXXXs.

> XXXX XXXX and XXXX XXXX XXXX, XXXX XXXX XXXX XXXX on XXXX XXXX a XXXX XXXX, in XXXX, and XXXX to the XXXX XXXX XXXX XXXX XXXX XXXX XXXX.

Even though these 10 words give about 20–25% of coverage in normal text, which seems like quite a lot, it is impossible to take anything from this text. The speech this sentence comes from is unrecognisable. The second example raises the reader's knowledge to between 100 and 150 words, which is enough to give about 50% coverage. The additional words in this range have been inserted into the text and the remainder left as XXXXs.

> Four XXXX and seven years XXXX, our fathers XXXX XXXX on this XXXX a XXXX XXXX in XXXX, and XXXX to the XXXX that all men are XXXX XXXX.

Again, 50% coverage sounds like it should be quite good, but it is still impossible to gain much in the way of comprehension. Most people, when I present this material in lectures, cannot suggest what the missing words might be, unless they recognise the speech, as there is not enough information to give a clue as to the subject of the material. Even readers who do know this speech, in many cases, fail to recognise it at this level of coverage. The next example raises the reader's knowledge to about 2000 words, which is enough to give about 80% coverage, and these additional words have, again, been inserted in the appropriate places.

Four XXXX and seven years ago, our fathers brought forth on this continent, a nation, XXXX in XXXX and XXXX to the XXXX that all men are created equal.

At this point, most people, if they know the Gettysburg Address, will recognise this as the first sentence of that speech. The text is obviously much more comprehensible at this level of coverage, and readers who do not know the speech will now have a good idea of what it is about. But comprehension is far from perfect and the series of four unknown words in close proximity in the second half of the passage is a real barrier to taking the sense of the whole piece. It is still surprisingly difficult, even with so much contextual information, to guess the missing words if you do not already know them. The final example raises the reader's knowledge to about 6000 words, enough for over 90–95% coverage, in English and reinserts the additional words in this range.

Four score and seven years ago, our fathers brought forth on this continent, a nation, XXXX in liberty and dedicated to the XXXX that all men are created equal.

At this level of coverage, most readers feel they can understand just about everything. Ninety-five percent coverage leaves only a couple of unknown words in a passage of this length, and most readers have the ability to gloss over these and take the general meaning of the piece without needing to recognise or guess every single word. If the passage were to be intensively studied, for an examination for example, then the reader might worry about the unknown words, but for general reading, this level of knowledge seems to give quite good understanding. It is suggested from this information that large amounts of vocabulary and very nearly complete coverage are needed for anything approaching normal comprehension and language use.

It is worth considering what happens if only the less frequent words are known. It might be argued that if these infrequent content words are so important then perhaps learners might be better employed learning these. Can a learner function in a foreign language without the most frequent function and structure words? In the final example, therefore, I have removed the 150 or so most frequent words in English and substituted XXXXs as before.

XXXX score XXXX XXXX XXXX ago, XXXX XXXX brought forth XXXX XXXX continent XXXX nation conceived XXXX liberty, XXXX dedicated XXXX XXXX proposition XXXX XXXX XXXX XXXX created equal.

It is possible to get a flavour of what the speech is about with only this information but, because of the missing information, comprehension is fractured and the detail of the message is difficult to grasp. A reader might be able to work out that the text is about a nation or a continent and that freedom and liberty is involved; but which nation and whose liberty, and why this is important, remains a mystery. Knowing just a few words in a foreign language does not help a learner to complete understanding even if the words that are known are the lexical items that carry the most semantic weight. Whichever words you choose, almost all the words in a text must be known before the full message can get through to the reader or listener.

This challenges many of the assumptions that are made about how many words are needed for command in a language. They challenge the kind of assumptions that are ascribed to Ogden and the other champions of Basic English that a vocabulary as small as 850 words is sufficient for understanding and for sounding normal in speech. Most readers would be stretched to breaking point if required to function normally in their working lives with the kind of coverage which less than 1000 words provides. It suggests too that vocabulary tests that concentrate on the most frequent words of English may, indeed, provide useful information about how well a learner can function in the foreign language.

How Much Coverage is Required for Comprehension?

If there seems to be merit in the idea that the greater the proportion of a text that is known, the better understanding will be, then this begs the question of exactly how much coverage is needed before understanding is complete. This is a topic that has received some attention from researchers, and particularly Laufer (see below), who have been concerned with establishing the kind of proportions of a text, and the vocabulary resources, required to handle the reading needed in academic study in a foreign language.

Laufer and Sim (1985) investigated the knowledge needed to successfully comprehend an English for Academic Purposes text in the Cambridge First Certificate in English examination. The study reached the conclusion that vocabulary knowledge is the most important area of knowledge required for comprehension; more important than knowledge of the subject and more important than syntactic knowledge. Laufer (1989) took this further and calculated that students needed to know and understand at least 95% of the running words in a text in order to ensure 'reasonable' comprehension. Reasonable comprehension was assessed by the ability to gain at least 55% on a reading comprehension examination; the minimum required for a pass in the Haifa university system. While it not entirely clear what this means in terms of understanding, it suggests there is a figure for the vocabulary knowledge required to handle the demands of university study through the medium of English as a foreign language (EFL). Hu and Nation (2000) reported even more demanding levels of coverage required for other types of comprehension and suggest 98% coverage would be a threshold at which learners could understand enough of a text to be able to read it for pleasure. There need not be a contradiction between these two figures. Reading for study and reading for pleasure may simply require different levels of knowledge. Reading for study need not be inhibited by pausing once every 20 or so words to check a meaning, while reading for pleasure suggests the reader scarcely needs to pause at all (Carver, 1994).

A threshold of 95 or 98% might imply that there is an all-or-nothing quality to this kind of knowledge, and that learners without this kind of knowledge can take little from a text and would fail the Haifa university examinations. However, Laufer's (1989) results indicate that there is some flexibility around this figure. There were some learners who had less than 95% knowledge and still managed a reading comprehension score, which suggested they could understand the texts being used. Possibly, this is an artefact of the tests that are unlikely to have measured either the words the students knew, or their comprehension, with absolute accuracy. Students with large vocabularies may have recorded low vocabulary scores and passed the comprehension examination, or students with low vocabularies may have been lucky in the comprehension examination and gained a pass they did not really merit. No test is perfect. But possibly too, this may simply reflect differences in how well individuals can infer meaning from partial knowledge of a text. Some readers may be particularly good at this and can manage with slightly smaller vocabularies than other readers require. It is unclear how large this variation is likely to be. Nation (2001: 147) suggests that these thresholds at 95 and 98% are probabilistic, therefore, and are not all-or-nothing levels of knowledge required for understanding. Comprehension, as Ward (1999: 309) points out, is likely to depend as much on the importance, exact position, guessability and reoccurrence of the unknown words, as it does on the percentage of words which are known.

Rule of thumb
For full understanding of a text, almost all the words, probably 95% or more, will need to be known.

Laufer (1989) goes on to try to calculate how many words are needed in a learner's vocabulary to achieve 95% coverage. Using evidence from Dutch school books, she reaches the conclusion that approximately 4800 lemmatised words (the most frequent words, that is) would be required for this. In a later study (Laufer, 1992), using the Eurocentres Vocabulary Size Test (Meara & Jones, 1990), which is designed to estimate the proportion of the most frequent 10,000 English words a learner knows, estimates that 3000 word families are required before learners achieve a level of reading comprehension ability needed to enter the Israeli university system.

Nation (2001: 146) suggests analysis of corpora might well produce better results and more insights. Graphs that plot frequency against coverage show their value here and allow estimates of the coverage produced by different volumes of vocabulory to be easily made. In Figure 3.2 coverage is drawn up and the figures from Carroll *et al.*'s (1971) corpus suggest how many of the most frequent words of English a learner would need to know before 95% coverage of normal text could be expected.

The figure this corpus suggests is about 12,000 lemmatised words, substantially more than Laufer estimated. But, as Nation points out, corpus analysis suggests an explanation for this, which is that the numbers of words needed for coverage and comprehension may vary according to a number of factors. One is the type of text. Newspaper articles, for example, will differ in the words they use, from academic essays and from informal letters written home. Some types of text are likely to require bigger vocabularies for comprehension than others. A second factor is the length of the text being read. A brief note for the milkman will not only have fewer words, but fewer different words than

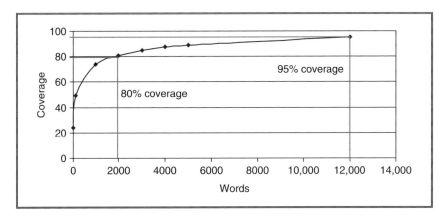

Figure 3.2 Word knowledge implied by corpora for 80 and 95% text coverage

a library of texts on business marketing. Finally, there is the homogeneity of the text. A collection of writings on different topics and by a number of different authors may well employ a wider variety of words than writings on a single topic by a single author, even if the total length of the collection is the same. Very large corpora, drawn from disparate sources such as that used in Figure 3.2, therefore, may suggest a much larger vocabulary size is needed than would be the case for a more specialist subject area. Laufer's interest in academic texts, in particular, may mean that a different and smaller vocabulary knowledge is needed to reach the kind of levels she suggests for comprehension. This possibility is investigated later in this chapter.

There may, of course, be a difference between what teachers and academics consider reasonable comprehension and how learners themselves view their ability in a foreign language. Seaton (2004) collected data from his students of Academic English, where he tested their knowledge of the 5000 most frequent words in English (using Meara & Milton, 2003) and also asked them to rate on a scale of 1 to 5 how good they felt their comprehension was, separately, in reading and in oral communication. A score of 1 meant they understood nothing and 5 indicated they thought they understood everything. I have summarised the results he obtained in Figure 3.3.

Very broadly, this suggests, not surprisingly, that the more vocabulary the learners know, the more they think they understand both in reading and in speech. However, there is considerable variation that mean scores of this kind disguise, and self-reporting seems an inherently unreliable means of assessing comprehension. Nonetheless, there are a number of insightful observations that Seaton is able to draw. One is that learners who scored less than 1000 words in the vocabulary size test always reported themselves at level 1 in comprehension, and learners scoring

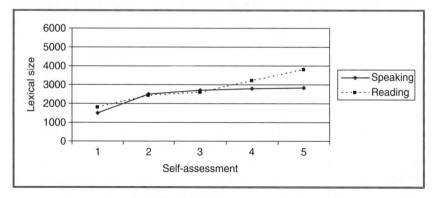

Figure 3.3 Student self-reports of comprehension and vocabulary knowledge

under 2000, predominantly did the same. Seaton had no absolute beginners in his sample and the variation in scores among these non-comprehenders was very small compared with the other self-assessment grades. This implies that the progress of comprehension may not always be smooth and incremental as vocabulary knowledge increases, but rather there is a real threshold at around the 2000 word level which Nation (2001: 147) identifies. Below that level, learners overwhelmingly feel they can take nothing from a written or spoken text. If learners progress above that level, then some degree of comprehension becomes possible. Such is the variation in vocabulary knowledge at comprehension levels 2 and above, that a few learners feel they can understand almost everything they need to with only just over 2000 words. Seaton suggests these learners are gauging their ability on the basis of their ability to perform in class, where texts and language tend to be graded, and have little interaction with native speakers outside of class. More generally, learners at this level of vocabulary knowledge tend to report that they understand only a little. This 2000 words level represents about 80% coverage in English and it has been marked on Figure 3.3.

Rule of thumb

There is a threshold for gist understanding at about 2000 words. At around this level of knowledge, learners pass from feeling they can take nothing from a text to picking up some general ideas and having moments of lucidity.

A second point that emerges from this data is at the other end of the comprehension scale, among those who report they understand everything they read and hear. Here, there is an obvious discrepancy between the mean vocabulary sizes in reading and listening. Learners appear to require a larger vocabulary between 3500 and 4000 on this 5000 word test before they consistently report full understanding of the materials they read. This figure probably fits with Laufer's estimate of about 5000 lemmatised words overall being required for comprehension. Learners at this level of ability will have some knowledge of vocabulary outside the 5000 most frequent words being tested in Seaton's experiment. Learners with somewhat smaller vocabularies are able to report full understanding in speech. A knowledge of 2500–3000 lemmatised words is consistently reported by learners to be sufficient in this area of language. It is possible that this reflects differences in coverage which corpora drawn from written only and from spoken only sources describe. In spoken language, the most frequent words are generally thought to be even more frequent than they are in written language, and fewer words produce greater coverage in speech than would be the case in writing.

> **Rule of thumb**
> Learners, by and large, feel they can do well with fewer vocabulary resources in speech and listening, than they can when dealing with language in written form.

Coverage in Written and Spoken Corpora

An explanation for the differences in vocabulary knowledge of learners reporting full oral and reading comprehension may reflect the fact that frequencies of words in oral and written English vary. The difference may also be a reflection of the things Nation was talking about above. Much conversational speech tends to be less formal, less academic, than writing, so the words we use will vary accordingly. Conversation, for example, the greetings we exchange every day with friends and colleagues, can be more formulaic and repetitious than anything we would put in writing. Spoken conversation, in particular, can also draw heavily for communication on gestures, facial expressions and other non-linguistic cues that should reduce the burden on the vocabulary knowledge needed. These are likely to affect word frequency distributions in written and conversational language, which reinforces the idea that the words needed for comprehension will vary according to what the learners want to do with language. Will the learners be required to read and write, or speak, extensively in the foreign language?

Thus far, the discussion of coverage has largely concerned itself with the ability to comprehend written text and the frequency lists used have been derived from corpora that are heavily reliant on fairly formal written material. Perhaps this is not surprising when most learners we investigate are learning in a formal academic environment that lays a heavy emphasis on being able to interact with and learn from written language. The differences can appear very great indeed and a single, now rather old, study has done much to foster this idea. Schonell *et al.* (1956) collected data from the spontaneous speech of about 2800 unskilled and semi-skilled workers in Australia, and from interviews with them. Just over half a million words were manually recorded and transcribed. The words in the text were then organised under headwords and the coverage these headwords produced were calculated. A summary of the results this data produced is given in Table 3.3.

This appears to suggest that it is possible to gain significant levels of coverage in spoken English with remarkably few words. Some 200 words would provide about 80% coverage and about 800 or so words would provide 95% coverage, which might imply pretty good comprehension on the basis of the figures outlined above. However, this data is rather

Table 3.3 Comparison of coverage from spoken data in Schonell *et al.* and CANCODE

Word families	Schonell et al.	CANCODE
89	71.22	71.96
145	78.69	77.23
209	83.44	80.60
451	91.21	86.57
674	94.22	89.23
990	96.38	91.52
1281	97.48	92.85
1623	98.31	93.93
2000	–	94.76

Source: Schonell *et al.* (1956) and Adolphs and Schmitt (2003: 431)

old and follows a methodology different from the most recent work in this area. Schonell *et al.* used a headword system, something like the word families described in Chapter 1, for their definition of what a word is, and this is more inclusive than the lemmatised lists which are generally used today. The data they collected appears very narrow in focus: spontaneous speech and interviews of a very general kind. It seems likely that this kind of data would be unrepresentative of much spoken language; the kind many language learners would need comprehension of, such as lectures and discussions in seminars. The corpus is also, by modern standards, rather small.

Adolphs and Schmitt (2003) have attempted to update this study and bring it into line with modern practice, so the results are more comparable with information drawn from other corpora, and to draw on a larger corpus. One corpus they use is the CANCODE corpus of spoken conversational material (described in McCarthy, 1998), which should provide more up-to-date material analogous to that which Schonell *et al.* collected. A frequency list and figures for coverage were derived using a word count based on word families, not lemmas, in order to be as similar as possible to Schonell *et al.* The results they obtained are given in Table 3.3 alongside those of Schonell *et al.* The results suggest that rather more vocabulary is required for oral communication than is often assumed, but still suggest that higher levels of coverage can be obtained with smaller vocabulary sizes than is possible with written language. A few hundred word families are enough to provide about 80% coverage, but over 2000 word families are needed for 95% coverage or better, which might be expected to give something like reasonable comprehension of a normal, non-technical, conversation. This conclusion, 2000 word families needed for communicative levels of knowledge, appears to fit well with the figures of 3000 to 3500 lemmas that learners reported for their own comprehension in Seaton's study reported above.

General conversation is not necessarily typical of every piece of spoken discourse. As Adolphs and Schmitt (2003: 433) point out, if a non-native speaker was listening to an academic lecture on a fairly technical subject without visual support and without the opportunity to interrupt the follow of speech to ask questions and confirm comprehension, then there would be a much greater burden placed on vocabulary knowledge than in a general conversation. Most large, modern corpora, however, generally contain sizable sub-sections of text transcribed from a variety of spoken sources. The frequency information these sub-corpora provide can differ from each other and from the written corpus. This is noticeable even in a few of the most frequent unlemmatised words. To illustrate the difference, Table 3.4 lists the eight most frequent unlemmatised words from the written, the 'demographic' spoken and the 'context-governed' spoken sections of the British National Corpus (BNC) with their

Table 3.4 BNC lists of the most frequent unlemmatised words from spoken and written corpora

	Written		*'Demographic'*		*'Context governed'*	
	Word	*Coverage*	*Word*	*Coverage*	*Word*	*Coverage*
1	the	6.43	I	3.99	the	4.76
2	of	3.10	you	3.21	and	2.75
3	and	2.69	it	3.05	I	2.20
4	a	2.16	the	2.74	you	2.16
5	in	1.89	's	2.19	it	2.03
6	to	1.63	and	2.16	and	1.90
7	is	0.99	n't	1.84	of	1.88
8	to	0.94	at	1.63	to	1.69
	Total coverage	19.83	Total coverage	20.81	Total coverage	19.37

Source: Kilgariff (2006)

respective frequencies and coverage. The demographic sub-corpus contains conversational material and is similar in make-up and the coverage it produces to the CANCODE material (Adolphs and Schmitt, 2003) summarised in Table 3.4. The context-governed sub-corpus has rather different oral material in it and contains transcripts of lectures, meetings and sermons.

Even this small sample begins to suggest the nature of the differences that the different spoken corpora produce. The total coverage of the most frequent eight unlemmatised words in the demographic spoken corpus is about 1% higher than the eight most frequent words from the written corpus. These are the differences that produce greater coverage with fewer words in spoken rather than written text. The coverage of the eight most frequent context-governed words is less than in the demographic corpus. It is also, surprisingly, smaller than that of the written corpus. In this sample, the context-governed coverage appears closer to the written corpus than the demographic material, but this is probably misleading due to the small number of words in this example, and a larger sample suggests that, while they are still clearly different, the two spoken corpora are more like each other than they are like the written one. Nonetheless, coverage in the context-governed corpus is consistently 7–10% less than in the demographic corpus. In order to demonstrate this, Figure 3.4 graphs up the coverage of the first 3000 entries in each sub-corpus of the BNC.

The conclusion to be drawn from this is not just that the comprehension of oral materials can require fewer vocabulary resources than understanding written text. It is also that the ability to understand well both written and spoken text, if it is remotely normal, requires very considerable vocabulary knowledge. Knowing less than 1000 words of a foreign language is probably insufficient for comprehension, even in spoken language, unless communication is of the most formulaic kind, such as greetings, and lacking in any specific or specialised content. Once

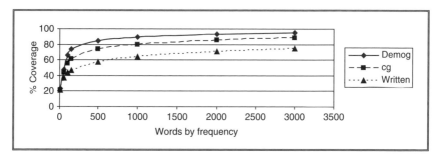

Figure 3.4 Coverage from written and spoken corpora in the BNC

a learner gets into a lecture or any kind or detailed engagement, then the learner needs more specialised and less frequent vocabulary. Most learners in formal educational settings will need both written and oral language in class and for examinations, and they will need substantial vocabulary resources to cope in most cases. However, some learners, people who take evening classes before going on holiday for example, may want something quite different, where a few spoken sentences to be polite and order a meal would be sufficient. Much will depend on the types of communication a learner will need to engage in and the degree to which the vocabulary these will need can be predicted with any degree of certainty. The subject of specialist lexicons, anticipating the words needed for a particular activity rather than obliging the learners to acquire large amounts of general vocabulary they will never need, has recently attracted some attention and this is the subject of the next section.

Rule of thumb

In speech and listening, beyond the most predictable and formulaic exchanges, learners will still need 3000 words or more to approach full comprehension.

Coverage in Specialist Lexicons

The figures for coverage and comprehension discussed thus far have relied on general language corpora and have assumed, therefore, that learners will need the ability to use their language in a wide variety of domains and registers in order to be fluent. It is partly this breadth of material in corpora which gives rise to the large volumes of vocabulary required for something like full coverage. Learning these large amounts of words is time consuming and, for the learner, a daunting task. Many language users, however, may not need to function in a variety of settings. The holiday traveller to the Mediterranean will probably not need the foreign language names of birds and trees, the names of chemicals, or the academic vocabulary needed to write an essay at a university, in order to function and to survive. If these things are not needed, then there ought to be no need to learn them. Much of the interest in specialist and technical lexicons lies in the prospect of identifying the particular words that learners in various kinds of activity will need to use so that, in these specialist areas, high coverage can be maintained and comprehension of this specialist material achieved, but with smaller overall vocabulary. There is much to be gained by reducing the learning burden in this way; it is less intimidating and time consuming for learners and less expensive for their parents or sponsors.

One such specialist list that is widely used is the Academic Word List (Coxhead, 2000), which is intended for use by university students studying through the medium of English. Coxhead derived this list of 570 headwords from a corpus of 3.5 million words of academic material drawn from a variety of academic disciplines in arts, law, commerce and natural science. These four broad subject areas were made up of 28 specific disciplines, such as history, economics, geography and biology. The headwords include all derived and inflected forms, and is, therefore, an analysis based on the word family rather than the lemma, and includes about 3100 word forms altogether.

To be included in the Academic Word List these words had to fulfil a number of criteria:

- They had to be outside the 2000 most frequent words of English as defined by West's *General Service Word List* (West, 1953).
- They had to occur at least 100 times in the whole 3.5 million word corpus (the frequency criterion).
- They had to occur in at least 14 of the 28 specific disciplines (the range criterion).
- They had, further, to occur at least 10 times in each of the four broad subject areas.

The Academic Word List when combined with the most frequent 2000 words proved to have surprisingly good coverage of a wide variety of academic texts, equivalent to a far greater number of words drawn from a more general written corpus. Table 3.5 gives the figures provided by Coxhead (2000: 225) for the coverage provided by these two lists in her corpus (The General Service Word List is divided into two; the first 1000 most frequent words and the second 1000 most frequent words).

Depending on the academic text, the two wordlists can give about 85.5–91.4% coverage (Nation, 2004: 8), a figure which would require 4000 to 5000 word families from Carroll *et al.*'s (1971) figures of coverage in a general corpus. While this would provide a learner with the knowledge to read and recognise most of the words in a text, it still falls some way short of the 95 and 98% coverage figures that would be required for

Table 3.5 Coverage of academic texts provided by the GSL and AWL

GSL 1 k	71.4%
GSL 2 k	4.7%
AWL	10.0%
Total	86.1%

satisfactory comprehension. There may be two reasons for this. One is that this particular genre, academic text, may be especially demanding in vocabulary knowledge and it would be impossible to explain or understand the depth and complexity of many academic ideas without access to a very large number of words to express these ideas. The second reason may be that the Academic Word List draws from a wide variety of texts and specific academic disciplines may require their own specialist vocabulary. Students of a particular specialism would need this vocabulary in addition to the academic and general wordlists in order to comprehend specialist texts. Dictionary compilers and EFL textbook writers often create such wordlists or provide glossaries, and a typical example might be the *Oxford Business Dictionary of English*, which identifies a basic list of 1000 items which are claimed to be 'particularly important in Business English' (Parkinson, 2005: Preface). It is not always clear exactly how these lists are constructed nor how much extra coverage they offer, and therefore how useful they are. It might be hoped that they would add sufficient extra coverage for something over 95% coverage in relevant specialist texts to be achieved.

Konstantakis (2007) attempts to construct exactly such a specialist or technical wordlist in the domain of business studies in order not only to provide a potentially useful list, but also to test how large such a list has to be before it can reach the 95% threshold in coverage. Using a combination of range and frequency criteria and a methodology similar to Coxhead, Konstantakis derives 498 words with unusually large coverage in business English textbooks and then derives word family lists for each of these to create a Business Word List. The words are demonstrated to be part of a specialist domain by comparing their coverage in a corpus of one million words taken from academic business texts, with coverage in literary texts unrelated to business. In non-business texts, the coverage provided by this list is much lower. The figure for coverage in these different domains are provided in Table 3.6.

In academic business text, both the Academic Word List and the Business Word List have considerably larger coverage than in text drawn from fiction. Words from the Academic Word List are 10 times more frequent, and from the Business Word List six times more frequent, in the business texts than in *The Lord of the Rings*. Overall coverage from these lists, in this specialist domain, is larger too; some 5% greater than in either of the two fiction corpora. Nonetheless, the extra coverage provided by even a very carefully constructed specialist wordlist such as the Business Word List appears quite modest at about 2.5%, and while overall coverage is approaching 95%, it is still just under this figure. Konstantakis has removed, as did Coxhead, abbreviations, proper names, hyphenated items and other oddities that are normally considered fairly transparent in meaning for readers. With these included in the

Table 3.6 Coverage in academic business and literary

	Business text *(1 m words)*	*General fiction* *(2.5 m words)*	*Lord of the Rings* *(624,000 words)*
GSL 1 k (%)	73.70	82.01	82.95
GSL 2 k (%)	6.13	5.23	5.41
AWL (%)	11.15	1.31	0.52
BWL (%)	2.60	0.71	0.41
Sub-total (%)	93.58	89.26	89.29
Abbreviations etc. (%)	0.83	0.01	0.00
Total (%)	94.41	89.27	89.29

Note. Konstatakis calculates the coverage of proper names, abbreviations and other anomalies separately from the rest of the wordlists and these have, in places, to be added in separately to obtain figures for coverage equivalent to other calculations in this chapter.

count, this figure rises to over 95%, but if these items are systematically omitted, then Konstantakis's work, which is still in progress, suggests that some 2000 additional business-related word families might be required to raise coverage in the area significantly above 95%. It does appear that a large vocabulary, in the thousands, can be required for comprehension even in what appears to be a restricted and discrete domain.

Not all specialist domains may be the same, of course, and some may require much more vocabulary than others. Engineering disciplines often require less demanding English language university entry requirements than other disciplines and this might imply, among other things, that these subjects carry a comparatively light vocabulary burden. Ward (1999) investigates the vocabulary of engineering textbooks and the number of word families required to achieve 95% coverage. He follows a different methodology to that of either Coxhead or Konstantakis in that he does not attempt to create a wordlist which would be additional to the General Service Word List, pointing out that this list accounts for rather less coverage in science and technical texts (78.5%) than in humanities (83.6%) (Ward, 1999: 314). Ward points to words in the General Service Word List which appear to have little relevance and cannot be found in his engineering texts, for example, *east*, *toe* and *stolen*. Ward constructed a corpus of approximately one million words from five, first year university engineering texts, excluding a wide variety of non-standard elements of the text, such as diagrams, rubrics, footnotes, variable names, equations, proper names, units of measurement and abbreviations. The

Table 3.7 Coverage of engineering texts provided by engineering vocabulary lists

	1 k List	*2 k List*	*2 k Total*	*3 k List*	*3 k Total*
Thermodynamics	92.9	2.9	95.8	0.7	96.5
Fluid mechanics	91.7	4.2	95.9	1.1	97.0
Mechanics of materials	93.2	3.1	96.3	0.5	96.8
Statistics and probability	90.2	4.5	94.7	1.2	95.9
Vector mechanics	92.7	3.1	95.8	0.8	96.6

Source: Ward (1999: 312)

words in this corpus were grouped according to word families and vocabulary lists appear to have been derived using a frequency criterion only. These lists are arranged in 1000 word (or word family) frequency bands and the coverage of the five elements of the corpus they provide are shown in Table 3.7.

These lists suggest that a smaller vocabulary, and rather different vocabulary resources, are needed for comprehension in this domain of engineering than in that of business studies. In four out of the five subject areas, the desired level of 95% coverage can be achieved with 2000 of the most frequent word families. This table applies the lists to texts from which they were derived, but Ward also demonstrates that these lists work equivalently across a variety of other engineering sub-disciplines. Ward's intention of reducing the learning burden of his engineering students to manageable proportions looks like it may hold water.

Details of the words in the lists are lacking, but this is a most interesting set of calculations and further work on this list could prove fruitful. I would wonder, for example, how coverage would be affected if the excluded material, the tables and the footnotes for example, much of which appears quite important, were included in the calculation. I would wonder too, how good comprehension will be with learners who have only a couple of thousand words when the calculation for coverage, using word families, assumes quite considerable knowledge of English morphology. Recognising and being able to use the verb *vary*, for example, in its more frequent inflected and derived forms, such as *varies* and *varied*, may be within the realms of learners with small vocabularies, but being able to recognise and use the much less frequent forms, such as *invariability*, might prove much more difficult. Familiarity with this information is usually the preserve of more advanced foreign language users, which Ward's learners are not. To be useful to learners with little knowledge of English outside this list, it would be essential to provide extensive training in English morphology, provided, of course, learners are capable of mastering infrequent derivational affixes separate from the growth of a larger vocabulary. This question of how the learning of word parts progresses in relation to the growth of a foreign language lexicon, is tackled in Chapter 5.

A final concern regarding Ward's conclusions is that this figure of 2000 is 2000 word families and may not be directly comparable to the figures for coverage discussed at the beginning of the chapter, such as the BNC lists, which used lemmatised corpora. This figure might represent 3000–3500 lemmatised words, which is a good reduction from 5000 words that Laufer calculated might be needed from a general list for such coverage, but is still, also, a considerable learning burden. This does raise doubts as to whether it is always possible, or even generally possible, to very substantially reduce the learning burden of vocabulary by carefully narrowing the domain of language to be studied. Building a large vocabulary of several thousand words appears to be an absolute condition of being able to function well in a foreign language.

Rule of thumb

In an academic specialist domain, learners will need 3000 words or more to approach full comprehension.

Coverage in Different Languages

This discussion of coverage and comprehension has, thus far, drawn almost exclusively on English language corpora and studies of English language learners for information. These have produced some useful figures, which suggest that measuring the knowledge of the most frequent words in English will provide good insight into the learner's capacity to function in English. Knowledge of the most frequent 2000 lemmatised words, giving 80% coverage of normal text, can tell us whether a learner is likely to be able to function at all outside of a classroom and draw meaning from relatively normal text. Knowledge of something like 5000 word families (slightly fewer if you are fortunate enough to identify a really restricted language domain), giving 95% or so coverage, can tell us whether a learner is able to understand most normal text more or less in the way an educated native speaker might. However, Zipf's law and Palmer's comments about the usefulness of highly frequent vocabulary are not intended to be restricted to the English language only, but should be applicable to all languages. The question arises, therefore, to what degree these ideas will translate to other languages and whether the same kinds of figures for minimal and more general comprehension can be produced in, say, French or Arabic or Chinese.

It is not inevitable that every language will produce results comparable to those for English. There may be several reasons for this. One is that the most frequent words in English include pronouns and prepositions, but not every language shares this quality. Agglutinative languages, like Hungarian, Finnish and Turkish, handle many of the functions and meanings that these words convey in English, rather differently. Typically, these meanings are conveyed by the addition of suffixes to the root form of a verb or noun with the result that a single word family might include many more word forms than would be the case in English. An example from Finnish (Table 3.8) shows just how extensive the affixation system of Finnish can be and how inflections can convey meanings which require very different word forms in English and even, in the case of the politeness clitics, a whole different approach to the structures used. This should affect the volumes of vocabulary required for coverage and comprehension. It may be possible to do more with, say, 1000 words in one language than in another.

A second reason might lie in the historical development of English. Speakers of English often pride themselves on having a language with a particularly rich vocabulary and English often appears to have a variety of words available for much the same idea. For historical reasons, English differentiates, for example, between many farmyard animals and the meat that comes from them, between *pork* and *pig* and between *sheep* and *mutton*. If this really is the case, then comprehension of English might

Table 3.8 Inflections in Finnish of the noun *valo* (light)

Valo	Nominative singular
Valot	Nominative plural
Valoa	Partitive singular
Valon	Genitive singular
Valoja	Partitive plural
Valojen	Genitive plural
Valoko	Nominative singular with the question clitic
Valonhan	Genitive singular with the politeness clitic
Valoakohan	Partitive singular with the question and politeness clitics
Valojenkohan	Genitive plural with the question and politeness clitics

require a larger vocabulary than would be needed for equivalent understanding in another language.

Further, languages can differ considerably in their word formation processes. Some languages, like German, favour compounding and combine existing words to make a new word. Other languages like English can do this too, of course; we combine *brief* and *case*, for example, to create *briefcase*, to describe the particular case used for carrying business papers. But, in English this process is not used to the extent that it is in German, and this gives German its particular characteristic of very long words. By contrast, other languages favour creating or deriving words for new concepts and ideas. The effect of this word-combining process may be compounded, as not all languages are as clear as western European languages in signalling where word boundaries occur. Chinese, for example, which combines ideographs to make words, does not mark word boundaries in writing, so it may not be immediately clear where one word ends and the next begins, or whether an expression should be treated as two or three words or as one. Table 3.9 gives some examples of this process in Chinese. 旅館 *travel residence*, it seems to me, is a highly transparent expression that might function as a phrase and the elements could well be treated as separate words rather as, in English, we use a phrase for *a block of flats* and see no need to create a new word or combine the phrase into a single word. 輪流 *wheel flow*, by contrast, is much less transparent where it carries the meaning of *to take turns*, thus there is a much stronger case for treating this as a single word or lexeme.

We are not immune from this word-combining problem in English, and in the creation of Konstantakis's business language corpus, one of the processes which had to be gone through was to tidy up confusions of exactly this kind. How should the expressions, *over estimate*, *over-estimate* and *overestimate*, which can and do occur in all these forms in business text, be counted, as one word or two? Rather more importantly in English, we routinely treat the elements of phrasal verbs (*get up*, *get out*, *get by* etc.) as separate words, when many of them are non-transparent and might be treated as separate lexemes. Different decisions would, when systematised across a whole corpus, produce different word counts.

Table 3.9 Examples of ideograph compounds in Chinese

Characters	*Transliteration*	*Literal meaning*	*Translation*
旅館	lu guan	travel – residence	hotel
電腦	dian nao	electric – brain	computer
輪流	lun liu	wheel – flow	take turns

Until recently, well-constructed corpora in languages other than English were rare. But as text becomes increasingly available in digital form, it becomes possible for a wider variety of language corpora to be constructed and for word counts in different languages to be compared. There are many questions that such a process will raise and I will restrict myself to considering just two. One is whether Zipf's law really does hold good, or work equivalently, in other languages. In English, roughly 2000 words will give about 80% coverage: is it the same or substantially different in, say, French or Greek or Chinese? The second is whether coverage and comprehension will always be equivalent. Will 80% coverage give you more comprehension and communicability in, say, French than it will in English or Greek?

The answer to the first question is that, where equivalent counts for different languages exist, Zipf's law appears remarkably robust even if there are variations between languages. A feature of all languages appears to be that a small number of words are very highly frequent and provide large amounts of coverage of a text. Some examples will help to illustrate this. Figure 3.5 overlays the line for coverage from Carroll *et al.*'s (1971) corpus of English with the Hellenic National Corpus's coverage (Hatzigeorgiu *et al.*, 2001) when lemmatised to provide something like an equivalent list. At the outset, the first few words are comparatively more frequent in Greek than in English; in Greek the definite article is very highly frequent even compared to English. Thereafter, Greek vocabulary provides proportionately less coverage and the two lines cross over. The most frequent 5000 words in the Greek corpus provide 82.6% coverage, which is substantially less coverage than the most frequent 5000 words in English provides. A particular feature of Greek is the very high number of *hapax legomena*, which comprise 49.4% of the corpus in Greek, but is nearer to 30% in English and French (Mikros, personal correspondence). Nonetheless, the details of coverage,

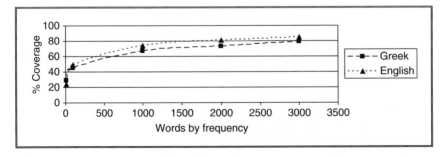

Figure 3.5 Comparing coverage between Carroll *et al.* and the Hellenic National Corpus

and the lines on the graph, are generally similar and the conclusion to be drawn is that Zipf's law works in Greek at well as English (Hatzigeorgiu *et al.*, 2001), even if it does not work identically in the two languages.

French displays similar characteristics and the figures for coverage are often even more similar to English. Again, the most frequent few words in French are rather more frequent than the most frequent in English but, unlike Greek, this trend is not lost at the less frequent levels. In the context of the kind of graphs used, until now the differences are small and overlaying the two coverage lines on the same graph, as in Figure 3.6, results in two lines that are almost indistinguishable. Nonetheless, the same number of words consistently gives slightly greater coverage in French than in English and in certain areas there are potentially important differences. Cobb and Horst (2004) point to the coverage provided of academic texts by the most frequent 2000 words in French. The figure they quote of nearly 89% (Cobb & Horst, 2004: 30) would be equivalent to the General Service Word List of 2000 words plus Coxhead's Academic Word List, some 2600 carefully selected rather than purely frequency-based words, in English. It appears that, in French, the most frequent vocabulary does the service of everyday language and the specialist academic vocabulary that English requires. Again, Zipf's law that the most frequent words will provide a disproportionately high amount of coverage in a text holds good, but the details of this coverage appear to differ between languages.

Zipf even appears to hold good in Chinese. While Zipf's law does not apply to Chinese characters, the interlingual differences suggested above may be at work here and individual characters may not always represent separate words. Once words are counted, rather than characters, then Zipf's law appears to hold (Shtrikman, 1994). There are some differences at the most frequent levels, but generally Le *et al.* (2002) report that the curves which Zipf functions in English and Chinese produce are almost

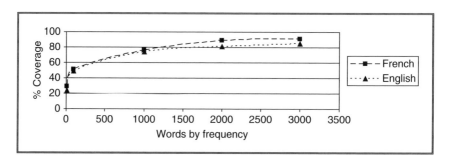

Figure 3.6 Comparing coverage between Carroll *et al.*'s (1971) English corpus and Baudot's (1992) French corpus

identical. The answer to the first question, whether Zipf's law holds good in other languages, is that with differences in detail, it does. Therefore, it should be possible to use frequency information in a variety of languages and they should function similarly in terms of their ability to focus on the useful words that are most likely to be encountered and learned. It is equally clear, however, that the curves that different languages produce are slightly different and the same number of words will produce slightly different coverage according to the language being investigated.

The answer to the second question, whether the same amount of text coverage or the same number of words will provide the same level of comprehension in all languages, is much harder to answer. There is a lack of direct research in this area on which to draw. There is some evidence from the Council of Europe project, which drew together syllabuses and vocabulary lists for a number of different languages at the Waystage and Threshold levels of the Common European Framework of Reference for languages. These, generally, produce words lists of very similar size in most European languages. The B1 *Threshold* level materials contain wordlists of about 2000 words. The A2 *Waystage* materials for French and English (e.g. Van Ek, 1990) both contain wordlists of about 1000 words. The sizes of these vocabulary lists appear to mimic the figures for coverage in the different language, as far as can be judged with the information currently available. For example, the French list contains just under 2000 words (Coste *et al.*, 1987) and the English list just over 2000 words (Van Ek & Trim, 1990). French, of course, requires slightly fewer words to achieve the 80% coverage figure, which in English has been thought so important. This suggests that figures for the percentage coverage of a text might be generalised across different languages, but that the actual numbers of words needed for equivalent comprehension might vary. I have suggested (Milton, 2006c) that the Threshold level descriptors imply that equal coverage, and roughly equal vocabulary sizes, would be required for equivalent knowledge in English and French. However, beyond this level, the implication of Cobb and Horst's study is that French and English, at least in terms of the number of words required for similar comprehension, need not be so closely aligned. It might seem logical that 95 or 98% coverage of a text might be required for full comprehension in any language, but we have no direct evidence to support this. There are no easy answers to the question of whether the same coverage or vocabulary knowledge is needed for equivalent comprehension in different language, and this needs further investigation. I have been working with colleagues in Spain, Greece and Hungary to run parallel studies in different languages with a view to filling this void and the results are considered in Chapter 8.

Conclusion

This chapter has considered whether the most frequent words in a language are also the most useful, as Palmer (1917) suggested. There seems to be considerable merit in this idea. The most frequent words in any language contribute hugely to coverage in a text, and considerable coverage is required before a reader or listener has enough information to be able to grasp meaning in most normal languages. This provides a second reason for focusing tests of vocabulary knowledge on the most frequent words in language: this information should tell us whether the words which a learner knows are useful and can contribute to communication.

In considering coverage, a number of figures have emerged and are frequently repeated. One such is the figure of 95% coverage for reasonable or full comprehension. Despite the difficulties surrounding this figure, such as what exactly is meant by comprehension, it continues to be used, probably because there is some kind of truth there, which we all understand. Learners will need to know almost all of a text before real meaning can be taken from it. This further underlines the importance of the most frequent words, as these words are so frequent it is impossible to achieve 95% coverage without them. A second figure of 80% coverage has emerged as a threshold below which comprehension and communication become almost impossible in anything other than the most contrived and limited circumstances. This suggests that learners require considerable knowledge of vocabulary before they can begin to function independently. The idea that communication can be achieved with a very small number of carefully selected words appears untrue despite its popularity.

In English, these figures suggest that tests which assess knowledge and use of the first 2000 and 5000 most frequent words may be particularly insightful for an assessment of general or academic competence. It seems likely that in languages similar to English, similarly sized tests should yield equally insightful results, but since languages do vary in the frequency of their words and the coverage they provide, comparing vocabulary across different languages is an exercise fraught with difficulty. Only by taking these measurements and by trying to apply them to our understanding of comprehension, however, will we be able to clarify how languages work and make the kind of inter-language comparisons that, in a multilingual society, would be so useful. The chapters that follow will report the measurements of vocabulary and will attempt to make sense of the results that emerge.

Chapter 4

Measuring Vocabulary Breadth: Passive Recognition Vocabulary

This chapter will examine how to measure vocabulary breadth, the number of words that a learner knows or recognises, and what happens when these tests are used to collect measurements among learners at different levels of knowledge and in different learning environments. It will consider:

- *the volumes and regularity of vocabulary growth that might be expected;*
- *the demands that examinations and syllabuses make;*
- *studies of vocabulary growth over the course of learning;*
- *time spent in class and vocabulary learning rates.*

These measurements suggest that vocabulary breadth increases regularly and at a predictable rate in well-established systems.

Alderson (2005) has pointed out that we really know very little about what is normal and what is abnormal in foreign language development. If the process of foreign language is to be better understood, then the collection of normative data is essential. Only then can we begin to understand not only what is learned and when, but also how individuals and groups will vary. Measuring vocabulary knowledge in foreign language learners should be part of this process. In the previous two chapters, I have argued that it is possible to construct a well-directed test of vocabulary knowledge by targeting a learner's knowledge of the most frequently occurring words in a language. This should allow an estimate to be formed of the words the learner is most likely to have encountered frequently, and is therefore likely to know. It should allow an estimate to be made of how useful the learner's vocabulary is for the purposes of comprehension and communication. What tests of vocabulary breadth are there, that conform to this specification and what measurements do they give us when they are applied to learners?

Tests of Vocabulary Breadth

Some of the best-researched tests of vocabulary are checklist tests of passive vocabulary recognition, designed to give an estimate of vocabulary breadth or size. Passive recognition is likely to be the most basic, catch-all definition of word knowledge; the learner recognises the form of a word and that it is a word rather than a meaningless jumble of symbols or sounds. Every other quality of knowing ought to fall within such an estimate, as you cannot translate or know details of collocation for a word you cannot even recognise as a word.

The format of checklist tests is deceptively simple. The learner is presented with a series of words and is asked to tick the ones they know or can use. Examples of this kind of test, in English, French and Greek, are provided in Appendix 1, and an example of the format is given in Figure 4.1.

There is no perfect testing method of course and this checklist method has its advantages and disadvantages. The advantages include the relative speed and ease with which these tests can be constructed provided a suitably constructed frequency list is available. It is possible to test a large number of words, compared to other testing methods, relatively quickly. The results are likely to be more reliable both because a larger sample size is always likely to give better results than a smaller sample, and because the test can be relatively brief and there is less opportunity for learners to become bored and lose concentration. The test usually selects words from across the frequency bands and this format also has an enormous benefit in that it is possible to quickly and easily create multiple versions of the test, with different words selected from the frequency bands, which should perform the same way. It is not uncommon for the correlations in the high 0.9's to emerge where scores taken from tests using different selections of words are compared (e.g. Adamopoulou, 2000). David (2008a) uses three versions of this test (with different words included) in her research in order to prevent students copying each other. She concluded there was no significant difference in the results obtained from the three versions (ANOVA results: $F(2, 480) = 0.332$, $p = 0.717$).

The disadvantage is the degree to which learners are able to guess, when they do not really recognise a word or are not sure. Earlier,

Please look at these words. Some of these words are real French words and some are invented but are made to look like real words. Please tick the words that you know or can use. Here is an example.

☑chien

Thank you for your help.

☐de   ☐distance   ☐abattre   ☐absurde   ☐achevé   ☐manchir

Figure 4.1 Example of a checklist test (French version from Meara and Milton, 2003)

I described this type of test as deceptively simple because, in these tests, learners are often faced with a tricky decision. If they think they recognise a word but are not sure, how is this to be scored? A straight *Yes* may result in words that are not known at all being included in the size estimate, resulting in over-estimation, but omission may cause under-estimation, as words which are known, at least partially, are omitted. Some of these tests include a *Not Sure* category to help separate out words like this. More usually, false words are often included in such tests to allow compensation for this kind of uncertainty, and for outright guesswork. False words are words constructed to read and sound like real words, but which do not really exist. In Figure 4.1, *manchir* is such a false word. These are words which learners cannot have encountered and which they do not know and which they should not tick. The proportion of *Yes* responses, or ticks, to these false words allows an estimate to be made of the degree of over-estimation which a learner is making and scores can be adjusted on the basis of this.

The idea is very attractive and it might be thought that a system that allows you to make some kind of compensation for guesswork or over-estimation would be a good thing. However, it appears that learners can respond very differently when faced with a checklist test. There are even national characteristics that tend to emerge. Shillaw (1999) reports, for example, that the Japanese learners he studied were so conservative in their estimates of their own knowledge that these false words were very rarely checked. Al-Hazemi (1993) and Vassiliu (1994) report that learners in Saudi Arabia and Greece can use rather larger amounts of guesswork in this type of test, perhaps because they are trained in examination technique, but that the tests appeared to work reliably nonetheless. Eyckmans *et al.* (2007), in a study of Belgian learners, reports huge amounts of over-estimation; up to 60% of false words were, on average, identified as real. Part of the problem identified is to do with response bias, which is the tendency for people, faced with Yes/No questions of this type, to answer *Yes* regardless of the question. But this cannot explain the tendency of this group to say *Yes* to almost everything and one wonders just how seriously the learners took the test. It provides a warning, however, that not all tests may work equally well with all learners, and if the learners are unwilling or unable to interact with the test in the way we expect, then the data they provide may be worthless.

Two of these tests are deliberately constructed to give an estimate of vocabulary size, within strict frequency limits, and would seem very suitable for measurements that seek to assess vocabulary growth over time. One is the Eurocentre's Vocabulary Size Test (Meara & Jones, 1990), which is auto-adaptive, tests about 150 words, and forms an estimate of a learner's knowledge of the most frequent 10,000 words. X-Lex (Meara & Milton, 2003) tests 120 words, 20 randomly selected words from each of the first five 1000 word frequency bands and a further 20 pseudo-words. The number of *Yes* responses to these pseudo-words allows the score on the real words to be adjusted for guessing and over-estimation of knowledge. A learner's vocabulary knowledge is calculated by counting the number of *Yes* responses to real words and by multiplying this by 50 to give a raw score out of 5000. The number of *Yes* responses to pseudo-words is then calculated and multiplied by 250. This figure is deducted from the raw score to give an adjusted score, also out of 5000, which thus includes a compensation for guesswork. There is no time limit to the test, which generally takes only 5 or 10 minutes to complete.

A second, very widely used, type of test method in estimating vocabulary knowledge involves requiring learners to demonstrate that they know translations or explanations of foreign language words. Tests can be passive, and provide learners with translations or explanations to choose from, or rather more productive in requiring the learner to produce a foreign language word in response to a native language stimulus. In the literature, these two tests are known as *recognition* and *recall* tests.

Nation's widely used Levels Test (Nation, 1990, revised Schmitt *et al.*, 2001) is an example of this type of recognition test where learners are provided with test words in the foreign language and a selection of explanations which must be matched up. An example is given in Figure 4.2.

This format allows rather more than passive recognition for word form to be tested and this form of test should allow an estimate of knowledge of words and their meanings to be formed. It is quite a complex test, however, where success relies not just on learner's knowledge of the test words (on the left hand side), but also on knowledge of the words in the explanations (on the right hand side), and it is not completely clear which items are being tested. Further, each

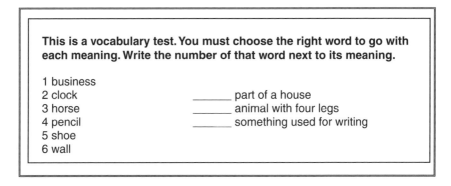

Figure 4.2 Level's Test example taken from Nation (2001: 416)

question contains multiple test items, and the learner's knowledge of some of the items is likely to have an impact on the ability to work out the answers to other items where these are not known. We know that learners often try to maximise their scores by making educated guesses in these circumstances, it is called *economy of practice*, but it is much less easy to work out the effects of guesswork in a test of this kind and there is no mechanism in the test for making this kind of calculation. Kamimoto (2005) recently reported speak aloud protocols conducted with learners taking this test. The feedback he received suggests that a considerable amount of guesswork and calculation goes on in answering this kind of question and that the learner's choice of guessing strategy can produce considerable differences in scores. The Levels Test might have much more variation according to guesswork than most users ever imagine. However, there is no explicit way in the test for taking account of this phenomenon or compensating for it.

The impact of standardised testing methods of this kind in measuring vocabulary breadth is potentially very considerable. It becomes possible to compare learning among different groups of learners in schools or in different countries in a way that could not be done before. It may even be possible to compare learning in different languages, as word counts, using the same kinds of counting method, can be done. This brings its own problems and difficulties, not least because languages can inflect, derive and combine words so very differently. It is not certain that knowing 1000 words in German, for example, will provide as much potential language competence as knowing the same number of words in English. Estimates of vocabulary knowledge in these different languages may tell us very different things about overall language knowledge and performance. Nonetheless, it becomes possible to attempt these investigations and to consider, in the light of the data that emerges, just how informative this kind of analysis is. In this chapter, the data produced by tests of passive, receptive vocabulary recognition will be considered. Measuring other types of vocabulary breadth is attempted in Chapter 5.

Predictions of Growth in Vocabulary Breadth

It appears that it is possible to test vocabulary knowledge meaningfully, to test learners from beginners up to fairly high levels of knowledge, and to make good estimates of their vocabulary knowledge within the most frequent bands; so what would we expect to see in a longitudinal study of a language learner, or in a cross-sectional study of learners of different levels? Certainly, we would expect to see vocabulary growth. You cannot be good in a foreign language without a sizable vocabulary. It may be possible for the reverse to be true, to know lots of words in a foreign language but be unable to use them. But, for a learner to be able to function fluently and idiomatically in the wide variety of language registers and environments which most native speakers handle with ease, then a very large vocabulary is required. The numbers are considerable. If they are to read and write well, then really able foreign language learners will presumably have to master thousands of words. This implies that, in a good course of instruction, we might expect to see regular input of carefully selected vocabulary. And we would hope, presumably, for fairly regular vocabulary growth on the part of the learners. A course that concentrated on nothing but vocabulary learning, or omitted it in entirely, would be a strange course indeed and probably unsuccessful. With a large task such as vocabulary learning, it would make much more sense to divide the task into smaller and more manageable elements and to tackle these regularly throughout the course of instruction. This is the assumption of many writers. Scholfied (1991), for example, draws up graphs showing idealised input from a foreign language textbook, which presupposes that equal vocabulary loading per unit or hour of learning might be an intelligent norm.

There is an idea, too, that vocabulary uptake might vary according to the level of the learners, or the needs of learners might change, and that input might be adapted somewhat to take account of this. Gairns and Redman (1986: 66), for example, suggest that learning 8 to 12 new productive words per hour would be a reasonable aspiration for learners, but they assume that the further language learning progresses, the more efficiently learners will be able to learn. The upper figure they suggest is suitable for more advanced learners and the lower figure for elementary levels. It is not hard to think of a justification for this, although Gairns and Redman do not suggest any themselves. The more advanced learners might be able to use their existing knowledge of lexis and morphology to commit to memory new derivations or combinations. Lower-level learners would not have this knowledge or ability. This is speculation, however, and it is not clear that this is what learners really do.

There is a potential counter-argument to this, which suggests that some front-loading of the most frequent words in a course would be desirable. Nation (2001: 16) recognises the importance of these very frequent words to communication and to meaning and, therefore, advises that every effort is taken to teach these words at the outset of learning. Potentially, learners might experience a spurt of vocabulary learning at the very outset, as they are force fed these words. The explicit concentration on vocabulary would decline later in the course of learning. It is not difficult to think up a justification for the vocabulary front-loading idea also and advance the idea of a heavy concentration on vocabulary at the earliest stages. As the previous chapter has demonstrated, knowledge of the most frequent vocabulary can allow learners to achieve a certain measure of independence in language comprehension and use. The benefit to motivation of getting learners as quickly as possible to this level of independence ought to be considerable. Thereafter, learners might take responsibility, through extensive reading and listening, for the further expansion of their vocabulary knowledge. It could also be suggested that if learners were not making progress in building this basic vocabulary knowledge, then it should be cause for concern. Low-level learners who do not acquire additional vocabulary will probably not advance, as a vocabulary of several thousand words appears to be a condition of full comprehension of any normal text. Conceivably, however, very advanced learners, who already have large vocabularies, might develop depth and fluency of use at the expense of breadth, in order to make gains and become more proficient.

Vocabulary Knowledge Expectations in Examination and Other Curricula

Some information on the vocabulary loading of courses is provided in the curricula supplied by ministries of education and by examining bodies. Some of these are surprisingly detailed. For example, the Hungarian National Core Curriculum (Krizsán, 2003) gives precise figures on how much active and passive English vocabulary students should gain by the end of different grades in the primary and secondary schools. A summary is provided in Table 4.1.

This suggests that vocabulary learning will not necessarily be a regular process. It appears learners are expected to gain 350 words in their first year, but add a further 150 only in their second year of study. Classroom contact in the foreign language stays the same, however. In the 8th grade, uptake is expected to be ten times larger than in 4th grade, some 500 words are expected to be added, and this is only partly explained by additional classroom hours. By the time learners take the *Maturity* level exams (B1 level), a vocabulary target of approximately

Table 4.1 Active and passive vocabulary growth targets in the Hungarian National Core Curriculum

	3rd grade	*4th grade*	*5th grade*	*6th grade*	*7th grade*	*8th grade*
Active vocabulary	200	350	500	600	800	1200
Passive vocabulary	150	150	200	250	300	400
Active and passive vocabulary	350	500	700	850	1100	1600

Source: Krizsán (2003)

3000 words is expected (Orosz, 2009). Overall, this anticipates vocabulary learning of about 260 to 270 new words per year.

Not all education ministries are this explicit in their curriculum targets. As Häcker (2008) notes, the British National Curriculum attainment levels omit all mention of vocabulary up until level 8, and then describe attainment only in the most general of terms. Formal examining boards, however, often set useful figures as guidance for learners, for teachers and for the writers of the test materials they use. Cambridge First Certificate in English (FCE) assumes knowledge in the region of about 4500 words for learners to take and pass this examination (Hindmarsh, 1980), which is pitched at CEFR B2, and assumes that learners will have had a minimum of 600 contact hours of tuition to achieve this level of knowledge (University of Cambridge Local Examination Syndicate, 2001: 14). In the UK, the French foreign language examining boards produce minimum core vocabulary lists for the age 16 GCSE exams, CEFR B1, containing about 1000 to 1500 items (Milton & Meara, 1998). This implies that learners are typically expected to know more than this, but it is unclear how much more. In these cases, words clearly refers to lemmas or word families, as plurals and other inflections and derivations are excluded from the lists, as are items such as nationalities and some cognates. Whatever the limitations of this kind of list and vocabulary size target, it must be useful to have targets against which teachers can schedule their language teaching and learners can measure their progress.

It seems to me that these are important considerations in the construction of a well-designed syllabus, but there appears to be a dearth of data which can suggest how vocabulary develops over time and learning, and which might provide background to syllabus content and loading. Historical studies of vocabulary knowledge tend to be snap shots of learners at one level. Burns (1951) and Robson (1934), for example, concentrate on the first year of French learning in UK schools. They do not give a picture of how the lexicon develops in breadth, or any other feature of knowledge, over the course of learning and throughout an educational system. These researchers faced very real difficulties, in the absence of reliable corpora, in constructing tests at different levels of knowledge and, almost certainly, time constraints prevented them extending their study beyond a single cohort for one year. But, by using frequency-based testing techniques, it is now possible to carry out cross-sectional studies and examine what happens in the course of learning. It is possible to examine learning and to discover whether some of the assumptions I have just explained, such as regular growth or vocabulary front-loading, really do occur in real language learning. It is also possible to see whether the kind of targets that examinations and other curricula set are, in fact, met.

Studies of Growth in Vocabulary Breadth

Frequency-based tests of vocabulary have now been around for a sufficient length of time for a number of studies in different countries to have been undertaken. In this chapter, I have chosen to concentrate on studies in countries where we have some vocabulary targets and against which the results of these tests can be compared. In Greece and Hungary, we have the FCE and Hungarian National Core Curriculum figures and the impression is given of a robust foreign language learning environment. In the UK, we also have targets, but regular doubts are expressed in the press and even by the Qualifications and Curriculum Authority (QCA, 2002a, 2002b) as to the standards and levels achieved by learners. What can vocabulary measurements in these environments tell us?

In private English as a foreign language (EFL) schools in Greece (called frontisteria), progress seems very like the ideal of learning I have just described. Figure 4.3 charts the mean vocabulary size of seven classes over seven annual levels, from beginner to students preparing to take the FCE at CEFR level B2. Every learner in this school was tested at the end of the year's teaching in June using Meara and Milton's X-Lex (2003) test, providing an estimate of the number of words known out of the most frequent 5000 lemmatised words in English. The 227 learners in this study received 100 hours of classroom instruction per year over the first five years (Junior to level D) and 125 hours of input in years 6 and 7 (class E and the FCE class). Generally, classes progress through the school and the series of levels on an annual cycle without a process of selection. However, the FCE class is slightly different from the others in that only those thought capable of taking the FCE and passing will be let in.

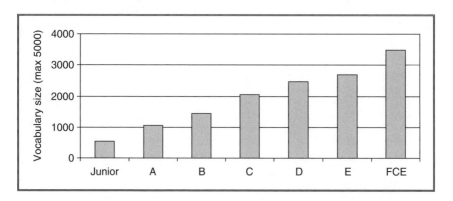

Figure 4.3 Lexical growth in learners of EFL in Greece (Milton, 2006a)

There are a number of features of vocabulary learning in this school that, I suspect, are typical of the good frontisteria I have visited in Greece. These features include highly regular vocabulary growth, and quite substantial growth. About 500 words from the most frequent 5000 are learned every year over the cycle of seven years until they reach the FCE level with knowledge of approximately 3500 words out of the most frequent 5000. This figure fits well with Cambridge's own estimates of the likely vocabulary size needed to pass this examination. Hindmarsh's (1980) lists include approximately 4500 items with a concentration, not surprisingly, at the most frequent levels, but also a range of thematically related low-frequency vocabulary which will not have been included in the 5000 word test. The impression for the learners as a group is very regular. There is no evidence of the kind of front-loading of vocabulary that Nation suggested. In truth, this data is drawn from what is probably a very good school indeed. It is a popular school with excellent results in external examinations and high parental involvement in the progress of the learners who generally start learning at 7 or 8 years of age. The owners and teachers use quite sophisticated techniques to match course books and learner level with vocabulary knowledge particularly in mind (Vassiliu, 1994, 2001).

These are mean scores and, of course, there is considerable variation. Individual variation is a subject to be tackled later in this volume in Chapter 11, but an idea of the scale of the variation that occurs can be seen in Figure 4.4, which shows the spread of scores around the mean for the figures provided in Figure 4.3.

While most learners clearly make good and regular progress in their vocabulary development, it is also clear that many students do not. There is considerable overlap between the classes. Some students make what appears to be spectacular progress. The best students, these results suggest, can acquire over 1000 new lexical items in the first year and,

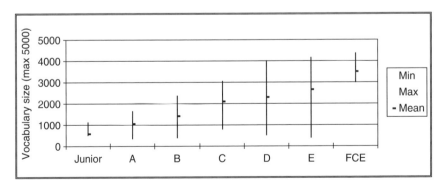

Figure 4.4 Spread of lexical size scores among learners of EFL in Greece

subsequent figures imply, continue to make considerable progress thereafter. These learners, at the end of this course of study, seem to have very real knowledge of the vast majority of frequent words in English and are presumably well placed to read with understanding and communicate well through English. Not all students are as good, of course, and the lowest scoring students have estimated vocabularies in the region of 400 to 500 words across all the levels up to the FCE group. The least able students have been omitted from the FCE class where the lowest scoring student knows an estimated 3000 words. This probably reflects a general truth that, even in the best schools, some learners will find the demands of academic language learning more than they can easily cope with and will make little or no progress. It is less clear that the figure of 400 to 500 really does accurately represent the minimum knowledge of learners in this group. There are always sampling problems where learners have very little knowledge of the material being tested and the test format encourages learners to give themselves the benefit of the doubt. The false alarm rate (the number of pseudo-words identified as real) in this sample is relatively small, however, which suggests the test is working well. The teachers at this school felt that this might be a realistic estimate, as even the worst performing student would have some English vocabulary gained from TV programmes, films, songs and advertisements in Greece where the use of English is commonplace.

Vocabulary growth in the Hungarian state school system appears to display similar features to the Greek school, with regular and considerable growth from class to class as learners progress through the school system. In this study by the University of Szeged (Orosz, 2009), 726 learners in 2 Hungarian schools were tested at the end of the academic year. The gap between the two schools, when students progress from one to the other, is between grades 8 and 9. Data was collected from beginners, starting English in grade 3, up to school leavers taking the *Maturity* examination in grade 12 when the learners should be at CEFR B1 level. Learning hours are not entirely regular across the course of study, with learners in grades 3, 4, 9 and 10 receiving 55 hours of instruction, grades 5, 6, 7, 8 and 11 receiving 83 hours of instruction, and learning in their final year receiving 100 hours as they build up to the final examinations. Orosz's results, mean, maximum and minimum scores, are shown in Figure 4.5.

The overall impression, as with the Greek data, is that vocabulary learning among classes of learners is, generally, a very regular business. This is quite different from the curriculum that anticipated far from regular progress. The only kink in the pattern of growth occurs between grades 8 and 9 when students complete their education in one school and progress to a new school at a higher level. Generally, learners, on average, appear to add 300 to 400 vocabulary items to their English

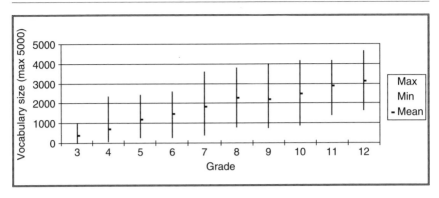

Figure 4.5 Lexical growth in learners of EFL in Hungary

lexicons each year at a rate and volume of progress that appears to be about 50% greater than the national curriculum requirement. Learners take their B2 *Maturity* examination with approximately 3500 words; almost identical to Greek learners of English at the same B2 level. As with the Greek data, however, there is considerable individual variation. The lowest scoring students at the outset of learning appear to acquire very little vocabulary, just a few hundred words in three or four years of study. This is in huge contrast with the best performing students who, as in the Greek data, appear able to acquire up to 1000 words a year at the outset of learning. As with the Greek results, there is no obvious sign of the front-loading of vocabulary in the early classes suggested by Nation, nor of a faster up-take in the more advanced classes, as suggested by Gairns and Redman.

Rule of thumb
Successful language teaching environments are characterised by regular vocabulary uptake in classes of learners. Individuals may vary.

Not all classes of foreign language learners display the kind of reassuring regularity in their progress that the Greek and Hungarian systems have shown. Learners of French as a foreign language in UK schools, for example, show a very different pattern of progress (Milton, 2006b). Figure 4.6 charts the mean vocabulary size of 449 learners at a secondary school in the UK and entering university. The data is a cross-sectional picture of learning, with learners at each of the seven years of study from beginners at age 11 up to the national examinations, which are taken at age 16, GCSE (CEFR B1) and 'Advanced' level (CEFR B2) at age 18. The learners were tested at the end of the year's teaching. They have received somewhat less foreign language input than the Greek

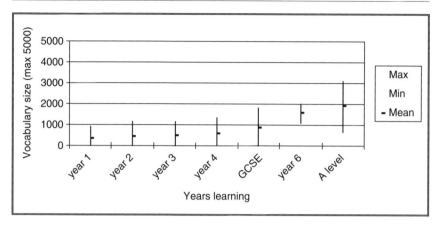

Figure 4.6 Lexical growth in learners of French as a foreign language in the UK (Milton, 2006b)

learners in Figure 4.3 and the Hungarians in Figure 4.5, with approximately 80 hours of tuition each year in the first, fourth and fifth years, about 60 hours per year in years 2 and 3, and 100 hours or more for learners who retain French in years 6 and 7. As with the Greek learners, there is a selection process in operation at the higher levels of study, with some students dropping the subject after year 4, and only the most able learners progressing to years 6 and 7, the Advanced level. These learners were tested using a French version of Meara and Milton's (2003) X-Lex, constructed using frequency data from Baudot's (1992) corpus and using the same criteria for the selection of words as for the English test.

The features of vocabulary learning in schools in the UK include growth that is irregular and where, over several years at least, little noticeable progress in tested vocabulary knowledge is made. Learners appear to make a good start in language development, knowing on average about 300 words at the end of the first year, but thereafter, knowledge appears to plateau. Less than half this number of words, about 150 words, appears to be added on average in the next two years of study. While this dip in progress coincides with a decline in the hours of input, there is no obvious reason for so marked a decline in progress. Learners at this level have only a few hundred words in their foreign language and cannot be communicative. It might be expected that vocabulary growth would be a priority of the syllabus at this stage. So, if the learners overwhelmingly are not learning vocabulary in their foreign language classes, then presumably new vocabulary is not contained in the materials they encounter in class. Häcker (2008) observes in the UK curriculum a negative washback effect where teachers restrict input, including vocabulary, to those limited topics that occur in examinations.

This supports the idea that students in the UK do not receive the range or volumes of vocabulary that learners elsewhere are exposed to. This observation requires some further investigation. Whatever the reason, it is only from the fifth year of learning, when some learners are allowed to drop the subject, that the learning of vocabulary appears to pick up again. Learners take their B1 GCSE examinations with, on average, 850 words of French and the B2 Advanced level with just under 2000 words. These figures are replicated, including the plateau in progress after year 1, in a similar study conducted elsewhere in the UK (David, 2008a). These results are considerably smaller than the minimum core vocabulary figures which the UK state examinations at these levels specify. Even allowing for the presence in the core vocabulary lists of infrequent words outside the content of the test used in this study, the figure appears small and learners with this level of knowledge of the most frequent vocabulary would struggle to communicate. Placed alongside the results from learners at B2 level in Greece and Hungary, these figures also appear very small. The learners in the UK are learning a different language, but it is not clear that this explains the difference. An attempt to unpick the details of this type of international comparison is made in Chapter 8.

As with the Greek learners, there is very considerable individual variation. In the first year of study, some learners appear to have acquired close to 1000 words of French. The same kind of figure which the highest scoring learners in Greece managed, but in only half the contact hours. But, consistently, the lowest scoring learners appear to know no French words at all. Only when the very best learners are selected for Advanced level study does the tail of low scoring learners disappear. Probably, these figures reflect the fact that some learners do, indeed, take little or nothing from the experience of learning French at school. These learners are not surrounded by French outside of class, through films, songs and advertisements, and it is much harder for these learners to access the foreign language. French as a foreign language is not valued as an educational or professional asset by many, even most, UK pupils and their parents. It seems entirely possible for learners to recognise nothing by sight even after several years in class. But, more curious than this is the plateau among the highest scoring learners, which occurs in the second, third and, to a lesser degree, fourth years of study. These are learners who apparently could make huge vocabulary gains in their first year, but who appear to stop learning an essential aspect of their foreign language after the first year, and for several years. Only when the weakest students drop out, do these learners appear to resume their progress at approximately 500 per year on average, which seems much more satisfactory. Again, this observation would merit closer investigation.

> **Rule of thumb**
> Less successful teaching environments are characterised by irregular vocabulary growth and unexplained plateaus where no vocabulary growth appears to occur.

What can be made of these figures? What general conclusions can be drawn? In the systems I characterised as rather good, Greece and Hungary, learners end up with large vocabularies. The figures suggest regular progress, and quite sizable annual progress. Curricular targets, set by ministries or examining bodies, are met or exceeded. Admittedly there is variation, but overall, good regular progress which is what it was hoped would be seen, is observable. In the UK system, which I suggested had been criticised, progress is not regular. Vocabulary learning in some periods of instruction may be very small and plateaus in knowledge may emerge. The vocabulary targets set by examining bodies appear not to be met. Of course, in both Greece and Hungary there are tremendously supportive environments for learning EFL. Parents and learners both want English language success, and knowledge of English opens up channels of educational and professional advancement. In the UK, the system is regularly called into question and the standards are often said to be declining. Further, in the UK no such supportive environment for foreign language learning exists, languages are not valued. Gaining regular and communicative access to French outside the classroom can be difficult.

These results bear out that impression, and even begin to quantify the scale of vocabulary learning and progress that takes place in schools. However, these studies are relatively small scale and confined to one or two schools only. Also, whatever overall progress may be in these schools, there is tremendous variation, with some learners making staggeringly good progress, and others little or none. Nonetheless, these figures provide the kind of normative data that allow standards to be set, progress monitored and comparisons, with other schools or with other systems, to be made.

There is no sign in any of these studies of the front-loading of lexical learning that Nation suggested might be appropriate for the most frequent vocabulary. This appears to be a good idea, but one that has not yet made it into the classroom. Nor is there any sign of learning increasing with level of ability, as suggested by Gairns and Redman. Progress in vocabulary learning in Greece and Hungary appears remarkably even. Conceivably, there may be ceiling effects with 5000 word tests among learners at the top of the system and these may disguise the scale of learning in the better classes.

Time Spent in Class and Rates of Learning

Comparisons between educational systems, and even comparisons of progress from one year to the next year within the same system, are often difficult because the time spent in class, and therefore the opportunity to learn, varies. Without some kind of adjustment or correction for the time spent in class and the volume of input, then comparisons can become invidious. Learners in the UK often appear in a particularly bad light and it is easy to mischaracterise the learners. An example of this would be to compare the annual progress in vocabulary knowledge among French learners in the UK with the other learners in this chapter. The progress among the UK learners is much smaller than among EFL learners in Greece, and the ultimate level of attainment is smaller. But the amount of time available for learning in the UK system is also much smaller. The Greek learners receive 100–125 contact hours per year, while the UK, for much of their education, receive half that input. Again, Milton and Meara (1998) review a number of papers that report annual rates of vocabulary growth in Europe and Japan. Typically, these learners might expect to learn 500–600 words in each year of formal study. By comparison, the equivalent learners in the UK were left languishing at the foot of the table that was produced (Milton & Meara, 1998: 74), as they learned only about 200 words. But the UK learners had spent far less time in class than either the Europeans or the Japanese with which they were compared. The UK learners may not be the bad learners that these comparisons suggest, but the educational system they learn in may have denied them the time and opportunity to learn, which other countries provide.

One solution to the difficulty in comparison, which widely varying classroom time creates, is to look at vocabulary uptake per contact hour. It is possible to infer uptake per hour or uptake per class from the examination and ministry curriculum figures, which were described earlier. In Table 4.2, I have taken the information we have from Hungary, Greece and UK syllabuses and school systems to calculate the kind of learning per hour that is, apparently, expected. The Hungarian system gives annual targets, while for the other systems, we have only end targets associated with examinations to work on.

The Hungarian curriculum figures suggest annual words per hour uptake and these can vary from less than one word per hour in grade 4, to over six words per hour in grades 3 and 8. The Hungarian learners have been far more regular in their vocabulary learning. In Greece, the University of Cambridge Local Examinations Syndicate (UCLES) is unusually specific in stating that some 600 contact hours would be needed by able learners preparing to take the FCE examination, and this would imply a vocabulary uptake of some 7.5 words per contact

Table 4.2 Anticipated vocabulary uptake per hour in Hungary, Greek frontisteria and the UK

	3rd grade	4th grade	5th grade	6th grade	7th grade	8th grade	B1 level exams	B2 level exam
Hungary	6.3	0.9	3.6	1.8	3	6	4.5	
Greece								5–6
UK							2.8–4.3	

hour, including infrequent words outside the X-Lex test range, and probably five to six words per contact hour as measured by X-Lex. The UK GCSE target of some 1000–1500 words as a minimum core vocabulary suggests a more modest uptake of between 2.8 and 4.3 words per contact hour.

These are useful, if very general averages, and can provide a yardstick against which any course or learner could be compared. How do these figures compare to the actual figures that the learners really display? Milton and Meara (1998) went on to review papers where vocabulary learning is calculated and also the number of hours tuition is specified, which allowed a calculation for vocabulary uptake per hour to be made. These results were compared with the vocabulary uptake rates in their own study of learners in the UK, Germany and Greece. They concluded that in normal classroom learning, taken over a course of study and where the learners are not selected for ability, vocabulary uptake for a class of learners appears remarkably regular at about three or four words per contact hour. A summary of their results is shown in Table 4.3. I have added the results from the learners described in this chapter, at their B1 examination level, to the original table.

Viewed in this light, the progress of learners generally appears more consistent and the UK learners, in particular, compare slightly better with learners elsewhere. The Hungarian learners appear to be learning vocabulary consistently over six years at a rate approaching the maximum their curriculum suggested. The Greek learners, who have had rather more than the 600 contact hours that is suggested as the minimum for FCE preparation, appear to have acquired vocabulary consistently at a rate approaching the five and six words per contact hour the syllabus suggested. The UK learners have learned French vocabulary on average at a rate lower than the examination target suggested and, even after adjusting for differences in contact time, at a lower rate than other learners investigated in this chapter. It is not clear what role the selection of students has in determining these figures. The Greek learners

Table 4.3 Vocabulary learned per contact teaching hour

Learners	Foreign language	Vocabulary uptake per hour	Source
Hungarian	English	5.4	This chapter
Greek	English	4.7	This chapter
Greek	English	4.4	Milton and Meara (1998)
German	English	4	Milton and Meara (1998)
UK	French	3.8–4.3	Milton and Meara (1998)
Greek	English	2.8	Vassiliu (1994)
UK	French	2.4	This chapter
India	English	1.7–3.3	Barnard (1961)
Indonesia	English	1.7–3.3	Quinn (1968)

Source: Adapted from Milton and Meara (1998: 75)

at FCE level are a selection of the most able and included only those who stood a reasonable chance of passing the examination. The learners who were not expected to pass, and who presumably would have learned vocabulary at a slower rate, were excluded from the class and from the sample. This may account for the comparatively high vocabulary rate of uptake. But the UK group have also undergone some form of selection too, as learners are allowed to drop the study of French the year before the GCSE (B1 level) examinations and the group tested were, presumably, also the most able and quickest learners.

Despite these considerations, the outcome of this analysis confirms what Milton and Meara wrote in 1998, that vocabulary uptake per classroom hour appears remarkably consistent between classes and systems. And where big differences in the overall level of knowledge and achievement emerge, between learners and examinations, it appears to be the product of the very different amounts of time made available for formal study. The figure they suggest of about four words learned per contact hours seems like an extremely useful yardstick for teachers and learners. There will be variation, of course, and good learners will learn faster while others will learn more slowly. Nonetheless, it does appear to be a mark against which they can gauge whether learning appears to be normal. This suggests that with time and good classroom practice, it appears possible to grow sizable vocabularies, enough for competence even if not native-like performance in a foreign language.

Rule of thumb

Learners, as a very general average, appear to gain about four words per hour from regular classroom contact.

But even this approach cannot iron out all the anomalies in the UK data. The plateaus, where very little vocabulary growth appeared to occur, may coincide with reductions in contact hours, but progress still appears inconsistent. UK learners can make the kind of progress other learners display, but do not do this with the same regularity. A comparison of the Greek and UK data taken from the previous section, converted to uptake per classroom hour, demonstrates this and is shown in Figure 4.7.

Although the Greek learners of English complete their seven years of study with double the foreign language vocabulary that their UK counterparts obtain, for four of the seven years, progress is very similar when measured as uptake per hour. In the remaining three years, the second, third and fourth years, the UK learners appear to make little or no vocabulary progress, less than 50 new words in the third year, less than one word per hour.

Can vocabulary sizes like this be compared meaningfully across two languages? Languages do differ and it may be possible to do more with fewer words in one language than another. Cobb and Horst's (2004) paper on whether an Academic Word List was necessary or feasible in French suggests that French and English do differ slightly. The comparison of coverage by French and English frequency lists in Chapter 3 confirms that it is possible to obtain greater coverage with

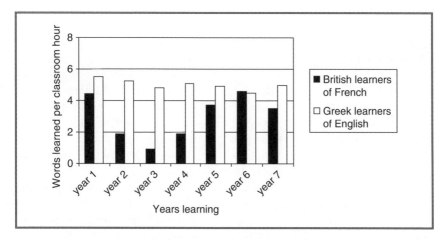

Figure 4.7 Comparison of words learned per classroom hour over each year of study in the UK and in a private school in Greece

fewer words in French than it is in English. But, by and large, French and English are very similar, especially at the most frequent levels, so there is no major reason why these two sets of figures, based only on the most frequent vocabulary in both languages, should not be similar. The fact that for four of the seven years, learners can learn at the same rate of vocabulary acquisition tends to support this idea. This may not be the case in other languages, and the question of how to compare vocabulary levels and learning in different languages is addressed in Chapter 8.

Conclusion

The tests of passive receptive vocabulary breadth described in this chapter have allowed credible estimates of learners' vocabulary knowledge and progress to be made. In the examples taken from Greece and Hungary, the results suggest that English vocabulary is learned consistently across the course of instruction and in relatively predictable amounts. These learners taken as a group consistently learn something like four words per contact hour, or slightly better, over hundreds of hours in class. The tests used have been tests of recognition of the written form of the words and this suggests good progress towards the volume of vocabulary, several thousand words at least, required for good communication, including writing and reading. Of course, the samples are still small, they are snap shots of a handful of schools in only three countries, but, nonetheless, there is no sign of the kind of vocabulary loading at the outset of learning which Nation implies might be useful, nor of the increasing speed of vocabulary learning which Gairns and Redman suggested might occur.

The testing systems have allowed results from learners of other languages, of French in the UK, to be compared directly with the English learners. It was suggested that the UK foreign language learning system had been under some criticism and this method of analysis suggests what some of the problems are. Vocabulary uptake appears slower than elsewhere, slow even by the standard of the comparatively modest targets set for learners, and there are unexplained plateaus in learning where little or no progress is visible. The concerns of the media and the Qualifications and Curriculum Authority described in Milton (2006b) are borne out.

The observations of vocabulary growth and progress made in this chapter also bear out Alderson's observation of how important it is to establish normative data in these areas of learning. Only by collecting data of this kind can it be established how much vocabulary knowledge is normal at any stage of learning, and what progress is possible in the course of study. Data of this kind allows judgements to be made of other systems and learners: whether progress appears normal or is better or worse. They help establish, too, what are appropriate vocabulary levels for learners in education and what vocabulary knowledge is needed for general attainment or for success in milestone examinations such as UCLES FCE, Hungarian *Maturity* and UK GCSE and 'A' level. There is a consistent trend in all these sets of data, however, for very great individual variation among learners and even if guidelines for groups of learners can be usefully produced, we still have to address how and why some learners will learn large volumes of vocabulary and how and why others do not, and whether this kind of variation is telling us only about vocabulary knowledge or is providing deeper insights into the more general understanding and communicability of learners.

If tests of passive word recognition, using the written form of the word, work well and provide useful data, then how do other tests of vocabulary breadth work? Measurements of phonological vocabulary size and first language/second language translation of words are considered in the next chapter.

Chapter 5

Measuring Other Aspects of Vocabulary Breadth

This chapter will examine the other aspects of vocabulary breadth found in Nation's taxonomy and which tests of vocabulary size delivered through writing do not measure. This chapter will look at:

- *measuring phonological vocabulary knowledge;*
- *measuring knowledge of morphology and the way words inflect;*
- *derive new forms.*

These measures produce different results from measurements of ortho-graphic vocabulary breadth. In the case of knowledge of word parts, they do not produce a size estimate as other aspects of vocabulary breadth do, rather investigations produce a scale or sequence of acquisition. Nonetheless, all these measures, at least in populations of learners, interact predictably and in relation, probably, to the effect of frequency.

This chapter, like Chapter 4, considers how to measure a foreign language learner's vocabulary breadth. Nation's table of what is involved in knowing a word (Nation, 2001: 27), described in Chapter 1, shows that the tests and measurements described thus far, approach only one of the 18 aspects of knowledge that are given. The passive receptive measuring systems described in Chapter 4 have measured vocabulary breadth only in terms of what a word looks like. These measures have proved credible, they give believable results, and the results they produce appear, in cross-sectional studies, to suggest much about how consistent vocabulary uptake can be over the course of learning, and the levels of vocabulary knowledge that learners typically achieve in various educational settings. Nevertheless, these tests, potentially, only give a partial insight into a learner's vocabulary breadth, and for a more complete picture of this aspect we would also want to know, among other things, about learners' knowledge of what words sound like and their ability to use and understand inflections and affixes. In this chapter, therefore, I intend to describe the mechanisms we have for measuring these aspects of knowledge, and some of the results that they provide.

Measuring Phonological Vocabulary Breadth

Measuring word knowledge in terms of how a word sounds, comes right at the top of Nation's list and yet, strangely, it is an aspect of knowledge that has attracted very little systematic interest from researchers. This might be the result of an unspoken assumption that if a word is known, then it is likely to be known in both written and aural forms. In traditional, school-based foreign language classes, this assumption may be broadly true, as the goals of these classes are likely to include the ability to function in both the spoken and written register, and teaching is likely to address both aspects of word knowledge. But, this is not the only way of learning a foreign language. It is possible to learn a language by sound only and never learn to read or write in it. Some teaching methodologies actually promote this approach, but more common, at least from the evidence of my linguistics classes, are people who have lived overseas and acquired functional competence through everyday interactions like shopping. Apparently, they can become very competent in speech but, because they have never done it, struggle to read the simplest passage in their foreign language. It is possible to know how words sound, therefore, without recognising what they look like in writing. The reverse may not be true. Learners, when faced with written words in a foreign language, have a strong tendency to sub-vocalise and when faced with unfamiliar words may actually 'sound them out'. Except, perhaps for profoundly deaf learners, it seems possible that a sound representation of a word is much more central to the existence of a word in the mental lexicon for most learners than the written form. A second reason why phonological vocabulary knowledge may be less well researched than orthographic knowledge may well be a practical one. It is generally much easier to administer a written form of a test to large numbers of students, than an aural one. Only with recent developments, such as higher specification computers with good sound cards, and relatively easy programming languages, has it become practical to test aural knowledge as readily as orthographic knowledge.

Whatever the reason, phonological tests of vocabulary breadth that are constructed with the same rigour and on the same principles as orthographic tests, are a recent phenomenon. A dictation form of Nation's Levels Test (Fountain & Nation, 2000) can be found in Nation (2001: 429), but studies of how performance on this test ties in with other aspects of vocabulary knowledge are lacking. AuralLex (Milton & Hopkins, 2005) is designed as a phonological equivalent test to the orthographic X-Lex (Meara & Milton, 2003) and is also designed to estimate the phonological size of learners in a way that can be directly compared to the measures of orthographic vocabulary knowledge that X-Lex produces. Both forms test knowledge of each of the first five 1000 lemmatised word frequency bands in English, and estimates overall knowledge of this vocabulary. The frequency bands are drawn from work by Hindmarsh (1980) and Nation (1984). They are both Yes/No tests, which present learners with 120 words, one by one, but in AuralLex the learners hear but do not see the words. In AuralLex, the screen gives

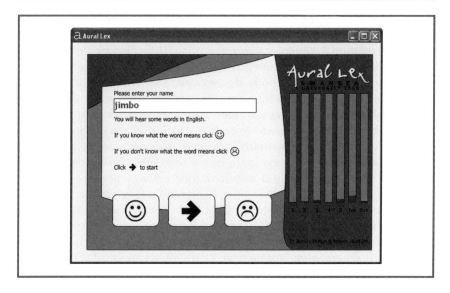

Figure 5.1 Screen shot of AuralLex

the learner a button to press in order to hear the test word as often as is needed to form a judgement. In both tests, learners have to indicate whether they know each word. There are 20 words from each 1000 word frequency band and a further 20 pseudo-words that are designed to sound like words in English but are not real words. The number of Yes responses to these pseudo-words allows the score on the real words to be adjusted for guessing and overestimation of knowledge. The tests give an overall score of words known, by sound rather than in writing, out of 5000. Figure 5.1 demonstrates the presentation of AuralLex.

Measurements of Phonological Vocabulary Knowledge

Again, it is worth considering what might be expected in the development of this aspect of vocabulary knowledge before reviewing the kind of measurements that a phonological test produces. As with the written form of word knowledge, it would be reasonable to expect growth over time and the course of learning. Several thousand words will need to be recognised if a learner is to become a fluent user of the language and, for most learners, these words will probably need to be recognised by sound as well as in writing. In good classroom learning situations, therefore, patterns of regular growth might be expected similar to those seen in orthographic vocabulary recognition. However, there are also reasons for thinking that some differences might be found. While the written form of a word rarely changes, example such as *not* changing to *n't* in certain circumstances are comparatively rare, changes in the pronunciation of words are much more common. This poses a challenge as to which form of a word should be presented for recognition in a test. With a word such as *and*, is it appropriate to present the citation form /ænd/ or one of its weak forms /ənd/ or /ən/? The spoken test format also raises questions as to the accent to be used in modelling the test words. Differences in spelling occur, of course, between American and British English but, again, the number of words concerned seems small when compared with the ubiquity of difference that a change in accent brings. Users of aural tests report an unfamiliar accent to be especially disconcerting. This kind of variation may, potentially, desta-bilise the test when only one form of the word is presented. AuralLex uses citation word forms throughout, but for highly frequent, one-syllable function words, this form may have been heard far less frequently than the weak forms. It also uses, in its current form, UK received pronunciation (RP), which would probably be appropriate across Europe, but inappropriate where American or other pronunciation forms are used.

Differences may also occur because of frequency effects. The im-portance of word frequency in learning to recognise a foreign language word has already been noted. But, there are also differences between word frequencies in spoken and written register. Two effects might be at play here. One is that the most frequent words are much more frequent in speech than in writing, so there may be a tendency to acquire these spoken word forms more easily at the outset of learning than would be the case for their written equivalents. I think this suggests that recognition of spoken vocabulary is likely to grow faster than recognition of written vocabulary in the early stages of learning. A second effect is likely to be at the other extreme of frequency. Infrequent words tend to be less frequent in speech than in writing and good coverage can be achieved with fewer words in speech than in writing. This ought to imply that learners will encounter in writing, and therefore have the chance to learn, words which they may never encounter in speech. Even if learners use grapheme-phoneme decoding rules to 'sound out' unfamiliar words, there is no guarantee the form they produce will be correct and recognisable when encountered in speech. They should, in principle, be able to grow orthographic vocabulary knowledge that is greater than their phonological vocabulary knowledge at the more advanced levels of knowledge. This might also mean that several very useful written vocabulary size tests may work less well if transferred directly to an aural form. Both Nation's (1990) Levels Test and Meara and Jones' (1990) Eurocentres Vocabulary Size Test (EVST) have a 10,000 word range, for example. This concentration on infrequent vocabulary, however, might be much less useful in speaking and listening contexts where fewer vocabulary resources are required for comprehension and communication. These tests may fail to assess in sufficient depth the frequent lexical levels that are important for speech. The concentration in AuralLex (Milton & Hopkins, 2005) on the most frequent 5000 words of English only, may actually be an asset in this context.

Figure 5.2 demonstrates the kind of results that a test of phonological vocabulary produces when administered to learners in a cross-sectional study. In this case, AuralLex was used to test 11 randomly selected learners from eight successive ability levels taken from a school in Greece. The scores presented are the mean scores for the 11 learners at each level. The learners ranged from beginners aged six or seven, who were completing their first year of English at level 1 (Figure 5.2), to learners aged about 14 taking the Cambridge First Certificate in English (FCE) at level 7 and, above them, older learners preparing for the Cambridge Certificate of Proficiency in English (CPE) at level 8.

The results that emerge should be comparable with the cross-sectional studies of orthographic vocabulary knowledge described in Chapter 4, and in this case the learners were also tested with X-Lex; these results have also been included in Figure 5.2. The pattern of, apparently, regular vocabulary growth from year to year and from level to level, already noted in orthographic vocabulary development, is replicated in aural vocabulary knowledge. However, one obvious difference is that the scores suggest that at every level, phonological vocabulary knowledge is less than orthographic vocabulary knowledge. This might reflect a truth, that learners tend to build bigger recognition vocabularies of words in written form than the words they hear, but it might also be the effect of some of the extra difficulties associated with the aural form of the test. Words that are known in weak form, for example, are not recognised in the aural test because of the citation form of the presentation. The frequency effect discussed above may be emerging in this data, however,

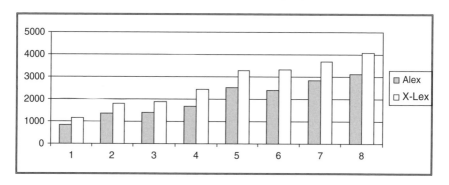

Figure 5.2 Growth in phonological vocabulary in a Greek school

because as proficiency and vocabulary size increases, so too does the difference between the two scores. It seems that higher-level learners may know disproportionately more words in their written form only. It is probably not possible to tell from this data whether the most frequent words are learned by sound earlier than in written form. This would require an analysis score at each level of frequency. Two studies by Milton and Hopkins (2006) and Milton and Riordan (2006) examine phonological and orthographic vocabulary scores in rather greater detail and suggest how they link to one another as learning progresses.

Milton and Hopkins (2006) tested 126 Greek English as a foreign language (EFL) learners, and Arabic-speaking learners of English predominantly from Saudi Arabia. Both groups were faced with the challenge of learning not just a new language to speak, but a new writing system to represent it in. The learners, again, came from a variety of levels and were tested using both AuralLex and X-Lex. Their AuralLex results suggest that the type of individual variation in vocabulary knowledge seen in Chapter 4 is also a prominent feature of results gained from measuring phonological vocabulary knowledge. Scatter-grams are used to plot individual scores on the tests against each other to reveal the extent of this variation. A scattergram of the scores obtained by Greek learners in Figure 5.2 is shown in Figure 5.3.

It will be noticed that the overwhelming majority of these scores fall well below the diagonal confirming the individual's tendency for their

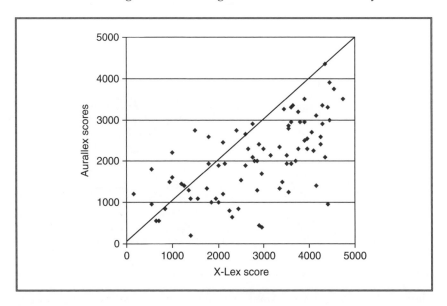

Figure 5.3 Scattergram of Greek learners' X-Lex and AuralLex scores

orthographic vocabulary size to exceed phonological vocabulary size. At the lowest levels of knowledge, at or below the 1000 word X-Lex mark, it appears this trend is reversed. All but three of the learners' data points fall above the diagonal, suggesting that among these learners it is common for phonological knowledge to exceed orthographic knowledge, something which is masked by the presence of more knowledgeable learners even in the first year of learning in the Greek classes (Figure 5.2). This trend is even more noticeable among the Arabic-speaking learners they investigated, whose results are shown in Figure 5.4. Among these learners, below the 2000 word X-Lex mark, every dataset falls above the diagonal. At the outset of learning and at the very lowest levels, therefore, it seems that words are learned phonologically before they are learned orthographically. For some members of the Arabic-speaking group, this phonological bias extends to quite high levels of vocabulary knowledge, several thousand words whether measured phonologically or orthographically.

Beyond the lowest levels, however, and as vocabulary size increases, orthographic vocabulary increases at a faster rate than phonological knowledge. It is in post-beginner, intermediate and advanced learners that orthographic vocabulary size tends to exceed phonological vocabulary size. A feature of advanced learners, in particular, is that their orthographic recognition of English words almost always exceeds their aural recognition, often by a surprisingly large margin. Overwhelmingly,

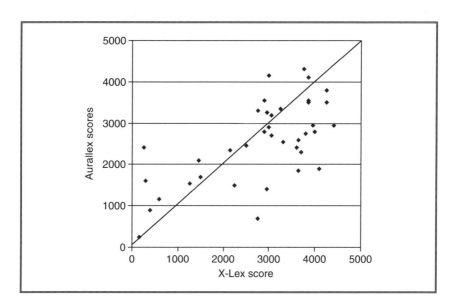

Figure 5.4 Scattergram of Arabic-speaking learners' X-Lex and AuralLex scores

the scores are below the diagonal although there is still considerable individual variation. Milton and Hopkins demonstrate this trend by redrawing their graph showing the progress of the two types of vocabulary, but this time dividing their learners into groups: those who score less than 1000 on X-Lex, those who know between 1000 and 2000, and so on, then calculate the mean AuralLex score for each of these groups. The result is shown in Figure 5.5.

Milton and Hopkins separate the results from the two different groups of learners, and in both groups of learners the tendency for orthographic vocabulary to grow faster than phonological vocabulary, after the earliest stages of learning, is evident. The most able learners, those with the largest vocabularies, appear to recognise a large proportion of these words in written form only. This data supports the assumption that frequency effects may influence the way the two different types of vocabulary are learned. Frequent vocabulary is proportionately more frequent in speech than in writing, giving the development of the phonological side of the lexicon an advantage at the outset of learning. Beyond this stage, less frequent vocabulary is much more accessible in written form, giving the orthographic side of the lexicon an advantage at the higher levels of knowledge. It appears that the Arabic and Greek-speaking groups behave rather differently, however, with the Arabic-speaking learners being rather slower to develop the

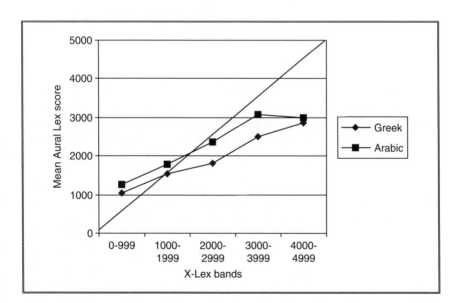

Figure 5.5 The inter-relationship of phonological and orthographic vocabulary knowledge (Milton & Hopkins, 2006: 143)

orthographic side of their vocabularies and much less likely to develop a very large vocabulary whichever way it is tested. It would appear that there is more to vocabulary learning than just frequency effects and that individual and learning differences can influence this relationship. It is not immediately obvious how this might work and an investigation of this is the subject of Milton and Riordan (2006) comparing written and aural vocabulary size.

Rule of thumb
The more advanced a learner becomes, the more words they will know by sight rather than by sound.

Language Effects in Phonological Vocabulary Learning

Milton and Riordan (2006) speculate whether the relatively slow growth of orthographic vocabulary in Milton and Hopkins' Arabic speakers could be attributed to the effect of Arabic script decoding strategies. Arabic word formation and script differs significantly from either English or Greek in that each word is based on three consonant sounds and symbols. While this may not be so significant in hearing these words, in writing it provides the speakers of Arabic with a quick route to decoding. Readers hone in on the consonant symbols to the exclusion of other information in the written text. This makes them very different from equivalent readers in English who will use whole word recognition and will concentrate on the beginnings and ends of words in particular, because of the morphemic weight that these areas carry. It is suggested that where decoding strategies are transferred from Arabic to English this will make reading comparatively inefficient. It appears that users of this script, and Arabic speakers in particular, are reluctant to lose these strategies. This should inhibit the ability of these learners to access the less frequent words that are more frequent in writing than speech and will inhibit the development of a large lexicon and an orthographic vocabulary.

To investigate whether these script decoding strategies are particularly entrenched and hard to lose, and are having a material effect on vocabulary learning, Milton and Riordan test both Arabic and Farsee speakers learning English in the United Arab Emirates (UAE), using X-Lex and AuralLex. They reason that if the comparatively slow development of orthographic vocabulary in the Arabic group is the result of a script effect, then Farsee speakers, who use the same script, should develop similarly. If, however, the Farsee speakers develop their vocabularies more like the Greeks than the Arabic speakers, then the cause of the difference probably lies elsewhere.

In Milton and Riordan's study, the Farsee and Arabic learners were very similar in the way the two types of vocabulary knowledge developed with increasing proficiency, but were not entirely similar in the way that was expected. As with the learners in Milton and Hopkins' study, there was a tendency for learners to favour phonological knowledge over ortho-graphic vocabulary at the lowest level of vocabulary knowledge, and for orthographic vocabulary to grow disproportionately thereafter. If any-thing, the learners in this study were even more prone to favour phonological vocabulary early in learning. In Figure 5.6, the Arabic-speaking learners in this study have been divided into groups, as in Figure 5.5, and the scores are overlaid on the scores from Milton and Hopkins.

Contrary to expectations, however, both sets of learners in the Milton and Riordan study performed like the Greek learners in the Milton and Hopkins study and, overall, the learners' orthographic vocabulary exceeded their phonological knowledge. The results from both studies are summarised in Figure 5.7.

Milton and Riordan tentatively conclude that the problems acquiring knowledge and proficiency in using phonological vocabulary, which some Arabic-speaking learners display, is probably not a direct result of their script. Users of Arabic script appear able to acquire knowledge of written vocabulary equivalent to other learners in some cases. Users of Arabic script appear able to acquire knowledge of written vocabulary equivalent to other learners in some cases and where learners fail to acquire these

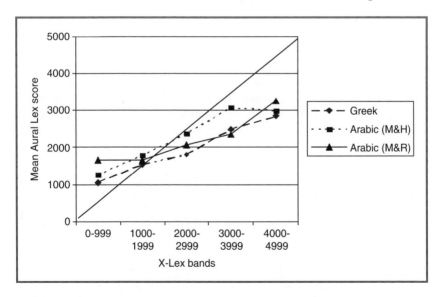

Figure 5.6 The inter-relationship of phonological and orthographic vocabulary knowledge

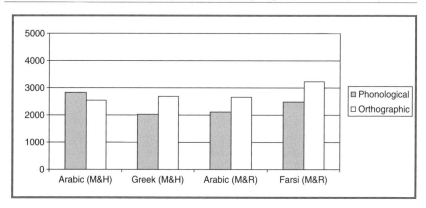

Figure 5.7 Comparison of mean orthographic and phonological vocabulary sizes among learners in Milton and Hopkins (2006) and Milton and Riordan (2006)

large orthographic vocabularies there are probably causes other than script effect. Milton and Riordan suggest that the effect of delaying the introduction of the written form of words and teaching only the aural form at the outset of learning, might be investigated. It is suspected that this occurred for the Arabic-speaking group in Milton and Hopkins' study. This delay may have had long-term consequences. These learners will be less able readers and will receive less exposure to written material than learners who master written forms early. The knock-on effect of reading less and less quickly may contribute to the inability to take up new vocabulary. Less reading means that such learners would encounter and learn fewer infrequent words, which tend to proliferate in writing, and this would prevent orthographic vocabulary growing beyond phonological levels. For certain types of learner, being held back in the development of knowledge of written vocabulary may not be a problem. Learners who are not interested in using their foreign language for academic purposes will not be inconvenienced by its absence. But, for learners who have academic ambitions that involve studying through the medium of a foreign language, or who are expected to develop a large second language (L2) lexicon, the lack of this vocabulary, and the lack of the ability to develop it easily, will be a serious handicap.

Rule of thumb
It is probably very difficult, if not impossible, to grow a large foreign language vocabulary purely from oral input.

In recent years, it has become almost axiomatic that a single measure of vocabulary cannot capture the variety and complexity of a learners' knowledge in this area of a foreign language. Even two measures that appear as similar as written and aural vocabulary size measures appear to produce significant differences. One conclusion that emerges from making this kind of comparison is just how sensitive learners can appear to be in response to the language they are exposed to in class. Teachers may often feel that learners learn despite what they do rather than because of them, but in these studies it is suspected that the emphasis that some teachers placed on the development of aural language at the expense of written language is visible. All groups of learners investigated thus far appear to favour phonological vocabulary knowledge at the outset of learning, but this raises further questions. It is not yet clear whether this is the result of teaching procedures that favour introducing words orally in initial classes or whether this a feature of the way learners instinctively categorise and store new foreign language words in response to frequency. A further question emerges from the variety of student scores. There are some very surprising contrasts even within a single class who appear to have had very similar or identical foreign language exposure and input. Some learners seem to have large written knowledge of words, but very little phonological knowledge, which ought to make them good at reading but poor in aural comprehension, while others have large aural knowledge of words and poor written recognition of words, which ought to make them good in speech but poor readers. As yet, we have little idea whether these characterisations turn out to be true and whether learners with such an imbalance of vocabulary knowledge suffer long-term effects. The learners who have poor orthographic vocabulary knowledge, for example, should struggle in formal, academic, foreign language examinations that appear to rely so heavily on this ability.

Measuring the Acquisition of Word Parts

Table 1.2 in Chapter 1 illustrates Nation's table, showing what it means to know a word. The final element of knowledge of Form, in addition to recognising what a word looks like and what it sounds like, is the ability to recognise and use the various word parts that can make up a word. Learning vocabulary does not simply involve learning the root forms of words, but also the affixes we attach to add or change meaning, or to make words grammatical. It involves knowing not just *jump*, *table*, *red* or *man*, for example, but also *jumping*, *tables*, *redish* and *manly*, and that endings like -*s* can routinely make a word plural. In Chapter 1, I referred to Bauer and Nation's (1993) lists of affixes, which are divided into nine bands. These are summarised in Table 5.1.

Some of these are very frequent and are easily recognised, like the regular -*s* suffix for most plurals. But others are rather rare, as in the -*en* suffix, which is also a plural as in *oxen*. There are only three occurrences

Table 5.1 Summary of Bauer and Nation's list of affixes

Level	Affix
1	n/a different form is a different word
2	Regularly inflections: plural, 3rd person singular present tense, past tense, past participle, -ing, comparative, superlative, possessive
3	-able, -er, -ish, -less, -ly, -ness, -th, -y, non-, un- (all with restricted uses)
4	-al, -ation, -ess, -ful, -ism, -ist, -ity, -ize, -ment, -ous, in- (all with restricted uses)
5	-age, -al, -ally, -an, -ance, -ant, -ary, -atory, -dom, -eer, -en, -ence, -ent, -ery, -ese, -eque, -ette, -hood, -i, -ian, -ite, -let, -ling, -ly, -most, -ory, anti-, ante-, arch-, bi-, circum-, counter-, en-, ex-, fore-, hyper-, inter-, mid-, mis-, neo-, post-, pro-, semi-, sub-, un-
6	-able, -ee, -ic, -ify, -ion, -ist, -ition, -ive, -th, -y, pre-, re-
7	Classical roots and affixes

of this plural ending in modern English. Some of these affixes appear to be duplicated in this list. This reflects the way some affixes with very different uses and meanings may present the same form in sound and writing. Thus, the -er suffix might be added to an adjective to form a comparative adjective (*small, smaller*), which is in level 2 or, with a quite different sense, be added to a word and usually a verb to indicate an agent (*whisper, whisperer*), which is in level 4. The number of these affixes is also quite large. It would be unreasonable to think that mastery of all these affixes would be acquired at once, especially as some will be so infrequently encountered. Their uses often appear slightly unpredictable to the learner. Why, for example, can you make an opposite using the prefix *un-* with some words, for example *unknown*, but not with others if the learner wants to be native-like in correctness. *Uncomplete* would be understandable to most English speakers, but would be thought wrong and *incomplete* would be expected.

This area of vocabulary knowledge is scarcely to be found in studies of vocabulary acquisition and there are no standard tests in the vocabulary tester's toolbox to measure it. Despite the fact that morphological knowledge of this kind is clearly signalled in Nation's table of word knowledge, there is an assumption that knowledge of word parts lies more naturally with syntax and grammar. A recent paper by David *et al.* 2009, for example, is entitled 'Lexical development in instructed learners of French: Is there a relationship with morphosyntactic development?' implying both that lexical and morphological knowledge are separate and that morphological and syntactic knowledge are linked. The work that has been done in this field has mostly been carried out by researchers interested in grammatical development rather than lexical learning. Further, in testing vocabulary breadth to date there is also an assumption that some inflectional and derivational affixes are known. The tests and measurements described thus far in this volume work in lemmas, suggesting that regular and frequent inflections are acquired sufficiently early in the learning process that they need not be a concern for vocabulary researchers.

What do we know about the acquisition of word parts and how does this relate to other aspects of vocabulary knowledge and learning? The studies that exist most frequently address the question of whether there is an order in the acquisition of morphemes and other syntactic features, and what this order is. This is of direct relevance to the business of vocabulary measurement because if regular and frequent inflections are learned early, it can help provide support for the assumption that lemmas are a good basis for making frequency counts and measuring language breadth. If, however, learners really do not recognise some of these frequent forms, then tests that use them are likely to confuse learners and give confusing results as a consequence.

Methods for Measuring the Acquisition of Affixes

There is no standard method of collecting and analysing data about the learning of affixes, and researchers tend to create tests for the particular groups of learners they have available or have a professional interest in. Akande (2003), for example, uses two common techniques to investigate this area of knowledge. One is an elicitation technique where learners are asked to write essays that are examined for the affixes being investigated. Errors in the use of test structures, such as plural markers in nouns, are calculated as a proportion of total usage as they occur in relative free language. A second is the creation of more controlled, objective-style, exercises that precipitate the use of the inflections being investigated, and in controlled quantities. The number of errors as a proportion of total test items can, again, be calculated. An example of Akande's test, effectively a multiple-choice exercise, is given in Figure 5.8.

Still other researchers use carefully structured games and other activities to elicit the use of the structures that are under investigation. Glahn *et al.* (2001: 396), for example, provided informants with a sheet on which were small, scattered, colour illustrations (e.g. cups for different sizes and colours), in order to test whether they could correctly form predicative adjectives. The informants were asked to give the colour of an item on the sheet and form a sentence in doing so (e.g. [Question] Hvad *farve er de små kopper?* – [Expected answer] *De er brune.* 'What

> *Instruction:* Fill the gap in each of the sentences below by choosing the appropriate word in the bracket ...
>
> The man always _____ his wife every day. (is beating, beat, beats)
> The two _____ came. (chief, chiefs, chieves)
> John thinks he's _____ than us. (wise, wisest, wiser)

Figure 5.8 Multiple-choice inflectional morpheme test (Akande, 2003: 11)

colour are the small cups?' 'They are brown'). The test contained 15 items that mixed number and gender. The comparatively large number of pictures on the sheet was intended to force the informant to hold information in memory while searching for the correct picture to provide an answer, thus forcing them to focus on the identification of items and colours rather than the morphological form of the adjective.

Studies like this, which examine the language output or the language knowledge of learners, allow the adoption of various morphemic and structural affixes to be recorded and implicational tables to be drawn up. Table 5.2 is adapted from Pienemann (1998) and shows how aspects of grammatical knowledge can be sequenced to suggest an order of acquisition among adult learners of English as a Second Language (ESL).

In Table 5.2, the stages refer to the stages in which grammatical features such as word order and structures, including highly frequent derivational and inflectional morphemes, are acquired. In principle, this sounds simple, but deciding on emergence criteria (describing exactly where the boundary between acquisition and non-acquisition is drawn) and then applying them consistently is not always easy. Again, not everyone applies the same criteria. Akande (2003) characterises the performance of his informants on some of his test morphemes as poor where these are produced correctly on more than 95% of occasions. Most researchers would apply much less stringent criteria.

I have chosen to illustrate these implicational tables using some of Pienemann's work because his processability theory, of which they form part, has some important implications for measuring vocabulary knowledge. Pienemann's (1998) processability theory is predicated on the idea that certain types of procedural skills are needed for processing language, and that these will give rise to a sequence of development. At the outset of the sequence is an understanding or appreciation of the lemma: the connection of meaning, a form of a word and an appreciation of some of the grammatical possibilities of the word. The sequence is summarised in Table 5.3.

In level 1, therefore, learners acquire words, but these are equipped with no grammatical information. In level 2, however, the learner is able

Table 5.2 Implicational table

		Informants							
Stage	*Structure*	*van*	*IS*	*my*	*ks*	*tam*	*bb*	*ij*	*phuc*
6	Cancel inversion	−	−	−	−	−	−	−	−
5	Aux 2nd/do 2nd	−	−	−	−	−	−	−	+
	3 sg-s	−	−	−	−	−	−	+	+
4	Y/N inversion	−	−	−	−	−	+	/	+
	Copula inversion	−	−	−	−	+	+	+	/
3	Neg + V	−	−	−	+	+	+	+	+
	Do front	−	−	+	+	+	+	+	+
	Topi	−		+	+	+	+	+	+
	ADV	−		+	+	+	+	+	+
2	SVO	−	+	+	+	+	+	+	+
	Plural	−	+	+	+	+	+	+	+
1	Single words	+	/	/	/	/	/	/	/

Source: Adapted from Pienemann (1998)
Note. +: acquired; −: not acquired; /: no context

Table 5.3 Implicational hierarchy of processing pre-requisites and structural target language outcomes predicted by processability theory

Level	*Processing pre-requisites*	*Structural outcome*
5	Clause boundary	Main and subordinate clause
4	S-procedure	Inter-phrasal information exchange
3	Phrasal procedure	Phrasal information exchange
2	Category procedure	Lexical morphemes
1	Word/lemma	'Words'

Source: From Pienemann and Håkansson (1999)

to categorise these words and apply some grammatical information, in the case of English as an example, the use of the -s to indicate plurality. In level 3, the learner relates words within a phrase so that grammatical information can be exchanged between them. This might involve using agreement between a noun and an adjective or determiner, things that are not prominent features of English but which are important in other languages where, for example, a feminine noun requiring an article would have to have a feminine article. In level 4, grammatical information can be exchanged across phrases allowing, for example, subject-verb or subject-predicate agreement. In English, this would include the acquisition of the -s suffix in the third person singular form of a verb (*I buy* but *he buys*). In level 5, main and subordinate clause structures can be handled differently.

Two points emerge even at this stage in considering this aspect of vocabulary learning. One is that there appears to be a distinction between two different groups of affixes in L2 acquisition. Firstly, there are those that are the product of the regular inflections and derivations and form lemmas, which are learned early. And second, there are other affixes that may contribute to a broader definition of a word family, and are learned later. Secondly, and this is implied by the first point, the order of acquisition of words parts is likely to be related to frequency. The inflected and derived forms that comprise the lemma are the most frequent and fall within levels 2 and 3 of Bauer and Nation's frequency count of affixes. Other affixes are less frequent and almost all fall in the less frequent of Bauer and Nation's levels; levels 4, 5 and 6. It will probably be useful to consider these two groups separately.

Acquisition of the Most Frequent Affixes Forming the Lemma

Fortunately for lemma-based tests of vocabulary breadth, there is empirical evidence that learners really do tend to work in lemmas and that the idea that they will move quickly to a knowledge of, for example, regular plurals and past tenses, is sound. Studies of the validity of processability theory often bear out the order of acquisition it suggests. Kawaguchi's (2000) study of the acquisition of Japanese verbal morphology, for example, concludes that verbal morphology is acquired in a fixed order that is predictable through the hierarchy of processing. However, not all studies are able to bear out the sequence implied in processability theory precisely. Glahn *et al.* (2001: 390), for example, in a study of acquisition in three Scandinavian languages concludes that while the theory appeared to hold good for its syntactic levels, other levels, such as the acquisition of number versus gender, revealed a mismatch with the theory.

Other studies can be even more precise about the order of acquisition of such features and, as is often the case, English has been particularly well researched over nearly 40 years. Table 5.4 summarises Brown's (1973) order of acquisition of English morphemes and is often used as the basis for these investigations.

Table 5.4 Brown's (1973) order of acquisition in English morphemes

Rank	Morpheme
1	Present progressing -ing
2/3	in, on
4	Plural −s
5	Past irregular
6	Possessive 's
7	Uncontractible copula (is, am, are)
8	Articles (a, the)
9	Past regular −ed
10	Third person singular −s
11	Third person irregular
12	Uncontractible auxiliary (is, am, are)
13	Contractible copula
14	Contractible auxiliary

This is very precise in the sequence it suggests but, again, it placed the regular and frequent inflections, such as the plural -*s* and regular part tenses, at the outset of learning. Less frequent affixes, such as *hyper-* and *neo-*, are omitted from this list and are, by implication, learned later. Brown was investigating the acquisition of first language (L1) morphemes, but a feature of these studies is the way investigators are seeking a natural order and one where L1 and L2 acquisition are likely to follow broadly the same sequences. Kwon (2005) summarises nine studies of both L1 and L2 acquisition and concludes that while the sequences that emerge are not identical, there are strong similarities, and the differences can be explained through differences in the cognitive development of the learners.

These studies have concentrated on some of the most frequent affixes and other morphemes. The researchers themselves are often very aware of the significance of this, although the conclusion that frequency is the principal determinant of the order of acquisition is not easy to draw. While Brown's study of L1 acquisition examined the frequency of morpheme use in parental speech, he concluded that there was no evidence to suggest this determined the order of acquisition. In L2 learning, the picture seems to be different. Larsen-Freeman (1976) found strong correlations where, as the basis of frequency, she used frequencies in obligatory contexts. She firmly concludes (Larsen-Freeman, 1976: 132) that frequency is the principal determinant in the order of acquisition. Dulay and Burt suggest an argument against this in that the most frequent morphemes are even more frequent in language than the most frequent lexis, yet they are acquired late when compared to lexis, but, as Kwon (2005) points out, this is not to compare like with like. There is a categorical difference between the two and the comparison may be irrelevant. Other L2 acquisition studies, for example, Kesslar and Idar (1979) and Gass and Mackey (2002), which also consider frequency, assume it has an influence even if they are unable to quantify it. Part of the difficulty in investigating the impact of frequency has been the absence of good frequency counts, but the presence, at least with affixes, of Bauer and Nation's list may mean that this is an area that can now be examined more systematically than before.

Rule of thumb
The most frequent and regular affixes are probably going to be learned earliest in a well-structured course of instruction.

Even if frequency does play an important role in the acquisition of word parts, as seems likely, this does not rule out a role for other factors that might also affect their learnability. Kwon (2005) advances a case for two additional factors. One is semantic complexity and, in particular, a hierarchy of semantic complexity where morphemes with multiple meanings are acquired later than those with fewer meanings. The second is language transfer, where forms and structures in the learner's L1 are likely to impact the learner's performance in the second or foreign language. The degree to which either of these factors may interact with frequency is also unknown.

Assuming there is a relatively predictable order by which word affixes are acquired, then this would beg the question whether there is a relationship between this order and other aspects of vocabulary acquisition such as vocabulary size. Are there certain volumes of vocabulary that are required before some affixes can be systematically used in language, for example? And it would be useful to know at what level of vocabulary knowledge sufficient affixes are mastered for us to say that lemmas have emerged and that the breadth tests based on lemmas will work reliably. This is an area that is under investigation, for example, Pienemann is trying to link this kind of lexical knowledge more explicitly into his processability theory, but results have yet to emerge. Nonetheless, in the current state of knowledge, the evidence we have supports the use of lemmatised lists in calculating vocabulary size, and helps explain why they can work so reliably.

Measuring the Acquisition of Less Frequent Affixes

The investigation of acquisition among less frequent affixes appears to be much less well understood and much less systematically researched than the regular and frequent word inflections. There is evidence among L1 learners that they develop their knowledge and use of affixes incrementally and, comparatively speaking, quite late in their language development. Thus, for example, Tyler and Nagy (1989) note that by the fourth grade, children can recognise familiar stems in derivatives, but by the eighth grade they appear to have increased their knowledge of the syntactic properties of derivational suffixes. Nagy *et al.* (1993) suggest that the process of learning to use suffixation correctly may continue to develop into high school. It would seem that among these L1 learners the process of mastering word affixes continues even after a very sizable vocabulary is established: native-speaking high school students might be assumed to have vocabulary sizes larger than all but the most able and fluent non-native speakers. The acquisition of word affixes in L2 learners is much less well understood and the authors of the few studies we have, reflect that we are still searching for a good and consistent way to access this knowledge of learners and measure it reliably.

Schmitt and Meara (1997) test both productive and receptive affix knowledge in L2 learners using 20 prompt words. On the receptive task, learners are asked to select allowable suffixes from a list of 14 provided: -*ed*, -*er*, -*s*, -*able*, -*en*, -*ly*, -*ion*, -*ment*, -*age*, -*ance/ence*, -*al*, -*ee*, -*ive* and -*ure*. The test thus includes very frequent and regular inflected suffixes as well as less frequent derivational suffixes. In the productive task, the learners are asked to produce all allowable suffixes from the prompt words. Over the course of an academic year, the learners increased their ability to recognise and produce allowable suffixes by 5% to 47% on the productive task, and by 4% to 67% on the receptive task. These increases are considered modest by the authors who conclude that the learners as a group had a weak awareness of derivational suffixes and failed to show complete mastery even of the inflectional suffixes. Schmitt and Meara were able to demonstrate a statistically significant correlation between vocabulary size and suffix knowledge of 0.41. They surmise that greater suffix knowledge helped produce greater vocabulary knowledge. This idea might equally well be turned on its head however, and it could be suggested that increased vocabulary is a pre-requisite of recognising and being able to produce these affixes. Some of the affixes are quite unusual and a sizable vocabulary might be needed before sufficient words using a particular suffix were known and the significance of the suffix appreciated.

Mochizuki (1998) attempts to develop an improved method of data collection. He comments that Schmitt and Meara's study investigates only 14 affixes, that their methodology uses only verbs as prompts and that the results might be produced by knowledge of the derived and inflected forms of the test's verbs rather than knowledge of the properties of the suffixes themselves. In the revised methodology, he offers his subject three examples of a test prefix and four choices of the prefix's meaning from which they must choose the best. As a test of suffix knowledge, the learners are offered three words demonstrating the use of the suffix from which the subjects must choose the word class of the words. Examples are given in Figure 5.9.

Mochizuki and Aizawa (2000) attempt to build on this study by using pseudo-words rather than real words in the test method. They investigate the link between vocabulary size and affix knowledge and derive an order of affix acquisition among 29 affixes – 13 prefixes and 16 suffixes. The affixes were drawn from levels 3 to 6 of Bauer and Nation's hierarchy of affixes, summarised in Table 5.1. Level 2 affixes, which are inflections and perform functions other than indicating word class, were excluded as qualitatively different from the items to be included in the test. The test affixes were also selected because they occurred in more than two words in Nation's (1996) wordlists. The subjects also took a vocabulary size test, which knowledge of the most frequent 7000 words in English was estimated. Their results suggested a stronger relationship between vocabulary size and affix knowledge than was the case in Schmitt and Meara's study. Significant correlations of 0.58 with prefix knowledge, 0.54 with suffix knowledge and 0.65 with these scores combined were noted. From this, Mochizuki and Aizawa are able to conclude that affix knowledge increases in proportion to vocabulary size, although whether there is a causal relationship between the two is not suggested. This is an interesting conclusion as it begins to provide an

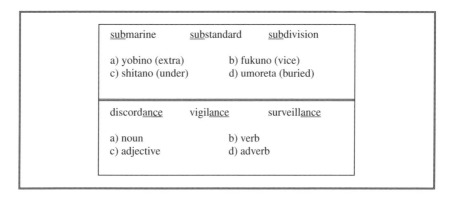

Figure 5.9 Affix test format in Mochizuki (1998)

answer to a question that is raised in Chapter 3: whether it is possible to teach a very highly reduced vocabulary to learners that need to read academic texts in a restricted academic subject area. Specialist academic texts can make quite extensive use of affixation. The link between vocabulary size and affix knowledge suggests that learners may need quite a large general vocabulary to be able to handle the complex word structures involved, even if the text itself uses a far more restricted vocabulary. How large that vocabulary might have to be is not investigated specifically by Mochizuki and Aizawa, but is suggested by their data.

Rule of thumb

Affix learning and vocabulary size appear to be linked. A large vocabulary seems to be needed before complex word structures are mastered.

Mochizuki and Aizawa's results allow the knowledge of individual affixes to be examined and suggest how bit a learner's vocabulary has to be before such affixes begin to be mastered. Table 5.5 is taken from their results and provides this information for the affixes they examined.

What emerges from this data is that the subjects in this study appear to have gained very large vocabularies without mastering all these affixes. Scores of over 5000 words on a test of the 7000 most frequent words in English usually suggest very great levels of performance, probably at the top, C2, level of the Common European Framework of Reference for Languages (CEFR). Yet, learners with this knowledge would still be unable to recognise the function of affixes such as *inter-*, *in-* and *-ish*, consistently: the kind of knowledge that educated native-speakers would certainly possess. The regular inflections in Bauer and Nation level 2 appear to be mastered relatively early in L2 language development, therefore, the less frequent derivational affixes at level 3 and beyond clearly emerge much later.

If this appears to be an argument totally in support of the effect of frequency on the order of affix learning, I have added the position in Bauer and Nation's list of the affixes tested as a means of seeing whether the frequency has any obvious effect beyond level 2 on the order of acquisition this data suggests. If it does, then it is hard to see it in this data. While the suffix *-y* does appear to be a very late developer and is little understood by the majority of subjects, the prefix *pre-*, which is also at level 6, appears to be one of the earliest prefixes to emerge. There is no obvious pattern in the other affixes' levels, although the selection of items scarcely lends itself to this kind of analysis. Mochizuki and Aizawa speculate why the order they observe may have emerged and frequency

Table 5.5 Mochizuki and Aizawa's classification of affixes into groups

Group	Prefixes	% Correct responses	Vocabulary size	Bauer and Nation list
1	re-, un-, pre-	80%+	3000+	5, 3, 6
2	non-, ex-	80%+	4000+	3, 5
3	anti-	80%+	5000+	5
4	semi-, en-, post-	60%+	4000+	5, 5, 5
5	inter-, counter-, in-	40%+	5000+	5, 5, 5
6	ante-	Little improvement irrespective of vocabulary size		5
	Suffixes			
1	-ation, -ful, -ment-	80%+	3000+	4, 4, 4
2	-ist, -er, ize, -al, -ly-	80%+	4000+	4, 3, 4, 4, 3
3	-ous, -ness, -ism, -able	80%+	5000+	4, 3, 4, 3
4	-less, -ity	60%+	4000+	3, 4
5	-ish, -y	Little improvement irrespective of vocabulary size		3, 6

Source: Mochizuki and Aizawa (2000: 298–299)

is one of the factors they consider. One additional factor is the effect of loan words in Japanese, which may make the order they observe particular to Japanese learners. A second is the effect of instruction. It is common to teach at least some of these affixes explicitly and the effect of this is not just to enhance the learning of target structures, but also to provide a salience for these structures in the language that learners are exposed to, so they have frequency to these learners far greater than Bauer and Nation would have observed. A final factor is the difficulty of the affixes in terms of their meanings and functions. While some affixes are quite limited in their meaning and use, others are polysemous and multi-functional, which should, in principle, make them harder to master.

Conclusion

It is a by-word in testing vocabulary at the moment that a single test of vocabulary knowledge is unlikely to give a complete picture of the state of a learner's vocabulary resources and his or her potential to use them. Measurements of vocabulary knowledge beyond passive, receptive breadth of knowledge of written form can tell a rather different story from just the standard tests that are mostly used by researchers.

Measuring the knowledge that learners possess of the phonological form of words seems to cast light on the way different parts of the lexicon develop and has revealed just how limited word knowledge is. Highly able learners, it seems, are able to function well with a recognition of written word form and only a hazy notion of what a word might sound like. But, this is not to suggest that the development of the phonological side of the lexicon takes place entirely separate from the orthographic side. In both, the effect of word frequency is apparent. The two sides of the lexicon, at least on the basis of the very limited information available, also appear to develop systematically in relation to each other with learners showing a preference for the way words sound at the earliest stages of learning, but growing ever bigger knowledge of the written form of words as they improve. This may even be a pre-requisite of getting better and becoming a highly able language user in the sense that formal examinations of foreign languages test these things. This form of measurement potentially allows insight into the learning processes to be made. It allows better assessment of partial knowledge and for researchers to recognise that good learners can have limited knowledge of some aspects of form.

Measuring the acquisition of word parts suggests a similarity between L1 and L2 learning, at least in the order in which the most frequent and regular word inflections are acquired. This has an important implication for the measurement of L2 vocabulary knowledge, as it provides reassurance that the use of the lemma as the unit of word counting is a satisfactory method, at least for learners beyond the most basic level of knowledge. We have very few attempts to measure the knowledge of affixes beyond the most frequent inflections and, as with testing phonological vocabulary knowledge, conclusions can only be tentative as to how this knowledge ties in to the development of a whole lexicon. It appears from the limited data available, which is restricted to EFL, that less frequent affixes are learned comparatively late in the learning process and appear to emerge systematically once large vocabularies have been established. Potentially, this conclusion rather undermines the idea that you can teach a lexically reduced technical language to handle specialist registers where the volume of vocabulary taught to the learner would be very small; say 1000 or 2000 words only. It is not clear from the studies to date, but the development of this area of knowledge may be contingent on growing a big enough vocabulary to be able to encounter these comparatively rare word parts sufficiently to appreciate their significance and functions. In a more hopeful light, however, the order of acquisition that emerges from the data we have, suggests this aspect of knowledge may be sensitive to a number of factors including what goes on in the class and the goals of teaching, as well as the inherent complexity of some of the affixes that are available for learning. Potentially then, knowledge of word parts might be successfully taught even to learners with small vocabularies. This is clearly an area, like knowledge of phonological form, where there is ample opportunity for further studies to provide us with fresh insights where we have little hard evidence to date.

One final conclusion relates to the way both measures considered in this chapter correlate with breadth. These correlations suggests that vocabulary breadth, the knowledge of word form and how many of these word forms are known, is a relatively unified dimension of knowledge. This is not to deny the importance of multiple measures in assessing vocabulary knowledge, but it does suggest that standard tests of vocabulary breadth will give a good general indication of knowledge in this whole dimension.

Chapter 6

Measuring Productive Vocabulary Knowledge

Measuring the productive vocabulary that learners possess poses methodological problems for the investigator in how best to capture this quality. The problem is not so much how to devise a test, but how to choose from the many approaches that researchers have used. A single, definitive method of measuring this quality of knowledge has yet to emerge. This chapter will examine various approaches to quantifying this kind of knowledge via:

- *translation and elicitation methods;*
- *statistical analysis of free production in speech or writing;*
- *association test;*
- *measures of automaticity.*

What emerges is that productive vocabulary knowledge is generally less than receptive, estimates usually suggest that it is generally of the order of 50–80% of receptive knowledge. The scale of this knowledge seems to be sensitive to teaching and the learners' foreign language experience; if learners learn and practice vocabulary use productively then a higher proportion of their vocabulary will be both receptive and productive. And there may be an effect on vocabulary size; it is harder to use infrequent words, only encountered occasionally, in production.

There is a general assumption that a learner's passive or receptive vocabulary knowledge will be different from his or her active or productive vocabulary knowledge. The number of words a learner can recognise in the context of speech or writing is likely to be different from the number of words the same learner can call to mind and use. As far back as 1921, Palmer (1921) was discussing exactly this division of knowledge and Dolch (1927) takes up the point in discussing the validity of vocabulary tests that concentrate solely on passive word recognition. As Waring (1997) points out, it is not immediately obvious why a learner's knowledge should vary in this way, but there are factors outside a learner's knowledge that might be at play. In making assessments of passive knowledge, it seems reasonable to assume that the listener or reader of a text can often call on a variety of contextual and other information to reach meaning. However, in production, and speaking especially, when the learner is under pressure of time for communication, these cues will be missing and the learner will have to rely on the fewer words they have accessible in memory. This is not something that is restricted to foreign language learners. Even native speakers will know the phenomenon where you know that you know a word, but you cannot call it to mind at the precise moment you need it. And when someone else supplies the word, you know it is the one you wanted. In the opening chapter of this book, I drew attention to Nation's summary of what it means to know a word, and he separates every category of his chart into receptive and productive knowledge to codify this disparity in knowledge and skill. To language teachers and learners, this seems like an obvious and very clear distinction. But, in developing ways to measure this kind of knowledge, it has proved rather harder to produce a convincing characterisation of this quality of knowledge, still less operationalise it so it can be successfully measured. Even the binary distinction of receptive and productive knowledge has been questioned and has been characterised as a continuum of knowledge (Meara, 1990).

Thus far, I have looked exclusively at the passive and receptive side of knowledge and at ways of measuring the recognition vocabulary knowledge of learners. The frequency model of vocabulary learning, which is used as the basis for measuring instruments in this area, has suggested that tests that focus on sampling the most frequent bands can provide believable and reliable estimates of learners' knowledge, at least within the framework that they operate. When used with real learners, the measurements these tests produce appear to make sense in a whole variety of contexts. They show differences where you would expect to see differences, for example, between learners of obviously different levels, and they show growth where you would expect to see growth, for example, over the course of a scheme of foreign language training. However, these tests rely on testing a carefully selected sample of words from a frequency list and it not so straightforward to use this kind of sampling in measuring productive knowledge. Speech and writing do not usually produce words that are conveniently arranged in equal numbers across a range of frequency bands, but rather, in production we draw on vocabulary from a whole range of frequency bands. The words chosen by the learner will vary according to the nature of the message being conveyed and exactly how the learner chooses to convey it, but will always draw heavily on the most frequent bands. This may provide very little information about the range of knowledge in the less frequent bands, not how readily this knowledge can be accessed. So, how do you get a sample of productive vocabulary from which it is possible to draw useful conclusions about the full extent of learners' knowledge and accessible vocabulary resources?

A variety of techniques can be used, collecting different kinds of knowledge in different kinds of ways. This suggests to me that the construct of productive knowledge is not very well defined, in addition to being difficult to access. Generally, it is assumed that productive vocabulary knowledge includes the range of vocabulary that the learner has access to, but there is also a speed criterion involved, this vocabulary has to be readily accessible for use. A word that you need in a conversation has to be accessible almost immediately or the moment is past, and communication may break down. Recall may be rather longer in writing where, generally, the learner has much more time to call a word to mind and can even go back and correct or change a word if need be. Few researchers consider this speed criterion in productive vocabulary measurement, which takes measurement into something like the fluency dimension described in Chapter 1. The following sections will describe at least some of the methods used to measure productive knowledge and consider the results they produce. Mostly, these tests try to characterise in some useful way the breadth or range of vocabulary that a learner has available for use. But, at the end of the chapter, I will try to describe some of the measures that are made of fluency and automaticity in the use of words; measures of how quickly learners can access their knowledge of words.

Measuring Productive Vocabulary Using Translation and Elicitation

Translation and forced answer measures, such as gap-fill exercises, have the great virtue that the test designer can control, at least to some degree, the language that the subject will produce. It is possible, therefore, to take a controlled sample of the words a learner can produce from which to estimate the breadth of overall knowledge. Some of these methods have a very long history. The use of translation as a measure of productive knowledge extends far back into the last century. There are some real advantages to this form of measurement. Translation tests are relatively quick and easy to construct, for example, a list of words in the first language (L1) can be given to the learner who has to provide a foreign language equivalent. If the foreign language words in the test are selected from the same source as words for receptive testing, you have scores that are directly comparable (as in Burns, 1951). It is also quick and easy to mark since, where words have a direct L1 equivalent, there is little room for subjectivity or judgement in recognising the correct answer, and this should make the test reliable. The use of translation as a teaching or testing tool is not always liked, however, and communicative approaches to language teaching, in particular, favour an approach that uses the foreign language exclusively. In these cases, vocabulary test writers have to find a way of eliciting the words they are interested in from the language learners.

C-test, or gap-fill tests are one way of doing this. Laufer and Nation (1995) construct a productive version of Nation's (1990) receptive vocabulary placement test and the structure of both tests draws test words from across a range of frequency bands. As with equivalently constructed translation tests, this has the advantage that receptive and productive vocabulary knowledge scores can be directly compared. The testing procedure presents the learner with a series of sentences, each with a missing word, which must be completed. Waring (1997) gives the examples in Figure 6.1.

The test words are primed with the first two letters to precipitate exactly the word for testing rather than an alternative, which might make sense to the learner but provides less information to the tester. As with the receptive version of the placement test, there is the potential for difficulty in testing, in that even though a single word is produced, knowledge of a wider range of words is required for success. Confusion or ignorance about the other words in the test may cause learners to misrepresent their knowledge. All the words are controlled for frequency level, therefore, in order to minimise this effect, but this does imply that a minimum level of knowledge is required before this form of measurement can be used and it would very likely give misleading information about elementary-level learners.

What can these tests tell us about the relationship between a learner's receptive and productive vocabulary knowledge? Eyckmans *et al.* (2007) use a translation method as a check on the receptive Yes/No vocabulary size tests she investigates, in order to see how well these tests perform. They use the differences in scores between recognition and translation tests to question whether the results of recognition tests can always be reliable and note that learners may be able to translate only 50% of the words they claim to recognise (Eyckmans *et al.*, 2007: 74). Normally, differences in receptive and productive knowledge can be at least partially explained by the differences of context. However, in single-word translation tests, the test removes words from context. Contextual factors cannot explain the difference between recognition and translation test scores. Nonetheless, it is a feature of tests of productive vocabulary

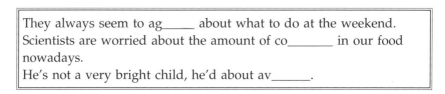

They always seem to ag_____ about what to do at the weekend.
Scientists are worried about the amount of co_____ in our food nowadays.
He's not a very bright child, he'd about av_____.

Figure 6.1 Productive version of Nation's Vocabulary Levels Test (Waring, 1997: 99)

knowledge that the figures that emerge are smaller than the figures for receptive knowledge.

Rule of thumb

Measurements of productive vocabulary knowledge are always smaller than measurements of receptive knowledge in equivalently constructed tests.

If the effect of context cannot explain these differences, does this mean that vocabulary measurements are inherently unreliable or are there other factors at play? As Nation's table (Table 1.2) implies, one answer is that receptive and productive tests, including translation tests, will measure different kinds of knowledge. Passive receptive Yes/No tests require the learners to access only their second language (L2) orthographic or phonological receptive lexicons (possibly both if they subvocalise before arriving at a decision as to whether a written word exists). Learners only have to try to recognise a word in some form. By contrast, a productive test requires the learner to access the L2 productive lexicon and possibly also the L1 lexicon, via semantic, collocational, orthographic or phonological routes, or some combination of these. Learners may have to start with their L1 word and then search for the L2 equivalent that carries the right shade of meaning. They will have to make choices as to the correct form and not just spelling or pronunciation, and also whether it needs to be inflected. Additionally, the learner has to check whether the word selected will fit with the other words being used, for example, has the right combination of words been chosen in a collocation. Production seems to be a much more complex task than the receptive recognition of single words in isolation. Fitzpatrick (2007) attempts to model up the ways word knowledge is activated in different kinds of tests and her analysis suggests that a translation test is also likely to be different from other tests of production which, in turn, may differ from each other. Fitzpatrick's models of activation for translation and two kinds of productive test are shown in Figure 6.2.

It will be appreciated that with so many different factors at play in the productive tests, more things could go wrong and there are more things that might interfere with a learner accessing their knowledge of a word. It seems likely that this is what depresses scores in production when compared with the far simpler processing involved in recognising a word. This factor may also cause differences in measurement between tests that appear to test exactly the same construct. Even though the three productive tests Fitzpatrick considers appear to measure the same construct, it is likely that they may produce very different results from each other as well as from receptive tests. Fitzpatrick notes that

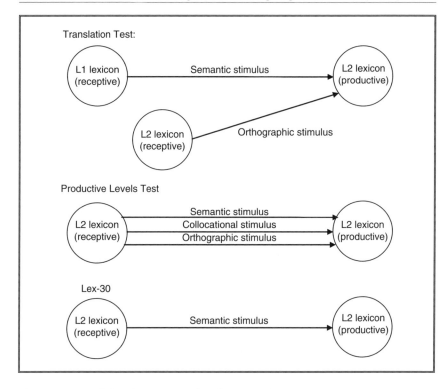

Figure 6.2 Models of activation for three productive tests

comparisons of the results of such tests generally produce only modest correlations. No single test in this area is yet capable of capturing this element of knowledge authoritatively and comprehensively. In the absence of a definitive measure of productive knowledge, Nation notes (2007: 39) that multiple measures are probably desirable if a better picture of a learner's knowledge is to be gained. This is not entirely a recent idea, for example, Burns (1951) attempts to measure both productive and receptive vocabulary knowledge of the learners he examines, yet it is still rarely done.

Notwithstanding these problems, the measurements produced by translation and elicitation tests behave as might be expected. As a learner becomes more proficient then, generally speaking, more words are known productively. The frequency effect that is so prominent a feature of receptive vocabulary knowledge is also a feature of productive data. Figure 6.3 presents data from Waring (1997) that clearly shows these two features. Waring tests productive knowledge of the 1000, 2000, 3000 and 5000 English as a Foreign Language (EFL) word bands among three groups of intermediate-level learners in Japan. His high group, his most

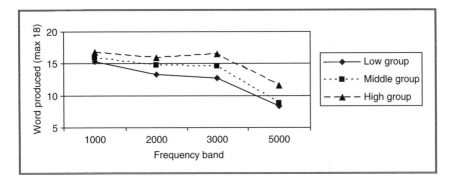

Figure 6.3 Productive vocabulary knowledge and language level (adapted from Waring, 1997: 102)

able group of learners, can produce more vocabulary at every frequency level than his middle group who, in turn, produce more vocabulary than his least able group, illustrating the growth of productive vocabulary with level. In presenting his data as a frequency profile in the manner of Meara (1992), the slope of the plot downwards from left to right illustrates the effect of frequency (Figure 6.3).

While both forms of vocabulary knowledge appear to behave relatively predictably, and similarly, in some ways, what is far less predictable is the way they relate to each other. In the experiment reported in Figure 6.3, Waring also ran a receptive version of the productive test and noted, like Eyckmans *et al.*, that these scores were, on average, higher than the productive scores. He notes too, however, that this relationship between productive and receptive vocabulary is so strong that every learner in his data set showed this effect. This also suggests that the testing tools are robust and reliable. Beyond this relationship, however, there appears to be great variation in the ratio between words known productively and those known receptively. The scale of difference noted by Eyckmans *et al.* (2007), where productive knowledge is only about half the size of receptive knowledge, is not unusual. Stoddard (1929), for example, taught 328 learners 50 French and English word pairs and found that, on testing, scores on the recall test were almost exactly double those on the English-French translation test. Yet, in other studies, productive knowledge can be a smaller proportion of receptive knowledge. Erigna (1974) reports that after five years of French at school, learners have a productive vocabulary only about 40% of the size of their receptive vocabulary; 1000–1500 words compared to 2500–3500 words. Still other investigators find the two are much closer in size. Burns (1951) studied first year learners of French in UK grammar schools and observed that productive vocabulary appeared to be nearly 80% of their receptive vocabulary. The mean estimated productive vocabulary was 555 words among these learners, and the mean passive receptive vocabulary was 718 words at the end of their first academic year. A study by Moesberger-Verhagen (1980, cited in Waring, 1997) found that while 42% of the 3200 words in the *Le Français Fondemental* corpus could be recognised receptively, only 29% could be produced (about 70% of the receptive vocabulary size). Melka Teichroew (1982: 19) deduces from this result that the difference between receptive and productive vocabulary knowledge is 'of little significance'. But it is of significance, of course, if the object of language learning is to become communicative in a foreign language and to be able to speak and write fluently. For this, you would need access to as many words as possible and as rapidly as possible.

These experiments suggest a factor that may contribute to this variation. Stoddard points to the effect of learning on the scores produced. Half of his learners learned French-English pairs (receptive learning), while the other half learned English-French pairs (productive learning). Those who had learned productively obtained higher scores on the productive test than those who had learned receptively. While this may seem like common sense, it is important that the assumptions we make about the effect of teaching are checked empirically. In this case, it is reassuring to know that if the goal of language teaching is to encourage the productive use of vocabulary, then this can be achieved through the use of appropriate teaching methods, and the effect can be measured.

Rule of thumb

You can improve productive vocabulary knowledge by teaching vocabulary productively.

Waring (1997) draws attention to the effect of frequency and the effect of language level on the proportions of receptive and productive vocabulary a learner knows. Among his 76 Japanese learners of English, it appears that frequent words were much more likely to be known both receptively and productively than less frequent words, which tended, overwhelmingly, to be known only receptively. Frequent words will have been encountered more often, in more contexts and probably used more often productively, than infrequent words. One result of this tendency might be that as learners grow larger vocabularies in a foreign language, a greater proportion of the words they know will be known only receptively. Learners will eventually run out of frequent words to learn and will, therefore, run out of words that are easy to learn both receptively and productively. They will have to extend their knowledge with words that they meet only infrequently in limited contexts and will have less opportunity to use. These are much more likely to be known only receptively. The differences in the proportions of productive to receptive words that learners know may be driven by their language level as well as the details of their learning experience.

Measuring translation knowledge of foreign language words, or eliciting these words, appear to be techniques that can yield insightful results. But, the drawback of these techniques is that they are not very productive. It can be argued, for example, that the translation of single words is a rather artificial task at some remove from the reality of communicative language use. Some writers, and I am one of them (Milton & Hopkins, 2006), have placed estimates of vocabulary knowledge gained through translation with receptive tests of vocabulary size rather than productive tests, as they rely on linking form with meaning rather than measuring the production of vocabulary items in context and for communication. The estimates of productive vocabulary knowledge gained this way may not be much more informative than other receptive tests in telling us how learners can use the vocabulary they know in communicative contexts.

Measuring Lexical Diversity in Free Language Production

Researchers, teachers and learners themselves are likely to be interested also in the words they can use productively in writing and in spontaneous speech. Language is meant to be communicative, therefore, we would like to measure vocabulary knowledge in some kind of fitness for purpose context; what vocabulary resources does a learner deploy when writing academic-style essays at university or to pass an examination, for example? There have been lots of attempts to measure this quality in a way that makes sense of the expected relationship between the words a learner knows and the words they use. They are usually put together under the umbrella term of *lexical richness* measures, and there is still little agreement on which techniques might best be used and when, and what the results of these techniques can possibly tell us about vocabulary knowledge. Daller and Xue (2007) summarise these efforts.

Perhaps the earliest is the use of Type Token Ratio (TTR) (Johnson, 1944), which attempts to measure the 'variety of active vocabulary deployed by a speaker or writer' (Malvern & Richards, 2002: 87) and is a measure of *lexical diversity*. This ratio demonstrates the number of words in a text, tokens, in relation to the number of different words, types. As Daller *et al.* (2007: 13) point out, these concepts are not always made clear by definitions and are best understood through examples. Thus, in the sentence, *The cat sat on the mat*, there are six tokens, six different words, but only five types because *the* is repeated twice. This gives a TTR of 5:6 or 0.833. The implication behind this kind of figure is that the better a learner is in the foreign language, the better able he or she is to call on a variety of words in use, and the higher the TTR will be as a result. While this measure is widely used, and is still used with texts of equal length, it has been criticised as unreliable (e.g. Broeder *et al.*, 1993; Vermeer, 2000) and has the particular limitation that it is sensitive to length. Guiraud's (1954) Index, Malvern and Richards's (1997) D and Daller *et al.*'s (2003) Advanced Guiraud Index are all attempts to overcome this shortcoming while still measuring lexical diversity. There is a considerable and growing literature that involves the use of these measures. Five of the 13 articles in Daller *et al.*'s volume on *Modelling and Assessing Vocabulary Knowledge* consider and demonstrate the use of these measures. The parameter D is available as a standard CLAN program of the CHILDES project (MacWhinney, 2000a, 2000b), which means that, potentially, a measure for lexical diversity can be used by anyone who is interested.

What can lexical diversity measures tell us about the vocabulary that learners know and can produce? One thing it may do is to give some indication about the size of a learner's productive lexical resources. Lexical diversity scores tell us about the variety of vocabulary which a language user produces in a text. It might be expected, therefore, that a very able foreign language learner, with a large vocabulary that can be activated and used, would produce a greater variety of words in a language activity like writing an essay, than a user who has only a small vocabulary and little ability to activate these words. Broadly, this is what the results from learners appear to show. Table 6.1 summarises the results obtained from learners of French in Tidball and Treffers-Daller (2007).

The learners in this study were undergraduate students of French at a UK university. Level 1 students were in their first year of university, and level 3 students were in their final year of university and had completed the previous year either one semester or one academic year's study in France. Scores for an equivalent native-speaker group are included as a control. All the participants in this study were asked to look at two

Table 6.1 Development of lexical diversity in learners of French

	D	*Guiraud*	*Advanced Guiraud*
Level 1	18.78	4.30	0.33
Level 3	26.46	5.25	0.65
Native speakers	34.87	6.27	1.37

Source: Tidball and Treffers-Daller (2007: 146)

picture stories and, with no pressure of time, tell these stories. The lexical diversity scores for the text they produced suggest, as might be hoped, that the learners were better at the end of their course, and after a prolonged stay in France, than they were at the outset. That is to say, they were able to produce a wider variety of vocabulary in their speech when they became more knowledgeable and more fluent. This kind of result offers the hope that measures of this kind can assess the size of vocabulary that a learner has available for use. But, there are other, rather different uses for this kind of analysis.

Rule of thumb

As learners improve in level and fluency, they are likely to increase the variety of words they use in production.

A second thing a lexical variety measure can tell us is about the quality of the vocabulary in a specific text. Chapter 9 addresses the role of vocabulary size in formal examinations in more detail, but one of the issues associated with formal assessment is the subjectivity of the marking process. Examiners are required to make a judgement as to the grade to be awarded an essay or a learner's speech in an oral interview, on the basis of factors such as the vocabulary that is used. There is considerable room for doubt and uncertainty over the grades that emerge at the end of this process, which is inherently less reliable than objective assessment. Therefore, the idea that these judgements could be supported by an objective measure is very attractive. In this usage, the lexical variety measures will tell us about the quality of vocabulary that conforms to the kind of criteria which examiners have to consider in awarding the appropriate grade to a piece of writing or speech.

Daller and Phelan (2007) investigate this possibility. They compare examiner ratings of the lexis in 31 formal academic essays with the scores obtained from a number of lexical diversity and lexical sophistication measures. Inter-rater reliability, as measured by Cronbach's alpha, was acceptable for overall grading, but there was rather more disparity between the grades when separate aspects of performance were rated. Cronbach's alpha scores in the 0.6 range for coherence and cohesion, and arguments and ideas, suggest a wide variety among the markers in the awarding of marks and emphasise the subjectivity of the process. Vocabulary-related sub-scores were more reliable with scores in the 0.8 range, but variety in marking of this order would generally be thought unacceptable (Rietveld & van Hout, 1993). The correlations between the examiner general ratings and lexical richness measures are shown in Table 6.2.

Table 6.2 Correlations between the examiner general ratings and lexical richness measures

	D	Advanced types	PLex	Advanced Guiraud	Guiraud	TTR
Correlations	0.235	0.549**	0.494*	0.471**	0.577**	− 0.030

Source: Daller and Phelan (2007: 242)
$n = 31$ for all measures except PLex ($n = 20$)
$* = p < 0.05; ** = p < 0.01$

The correlations that emerge appear fairly modest in size and correlations with D and TTR are not statistically significant. But the others are probably quite good, bearing in mind that vocabulary is just one factor in several that should inform the overall grade judgement for academic essays. These correlations suggest that it may be a particularly significant factor in forming these judgements. The effect of vocabulary may be even more important given the instability of the examiner ratings that will have destabilised the analysis and lowered the correlations. Nonetheless, Daller and Phelan's conclusion is that it is the lexical sophistication measures which probably contribute more to the examiner's overall rating judgements than lexical diversity measures, and that examiners may tend to focus on rare words in reaching those judgements. Lexical sophistication measures are considered in the next section.

One feature that does emerge from this data is that the measures, D and TTR, which are specifically designed to measure lexical diversity, did not correlate significantly well with examiner ratings of essays, even though other lexical diversity measures did. This should not be seen to discount the potential usefulness of lexical richness measures in certain situations and Richards *et al.* (2008) have succeeded in correlating D, for example, with examination grades in French intermediate-level examinations within the UK system.

Nonetheless, the question remains of how well and how reliable these measures are performing if they do not produce similar results? Doubt about the value of lexical diversity measures in assessing productive vocabulary knowledge seems to be a feature of the literature that makes use of these techniques. Van Hout and Vermeer (2007: 99) draw on data from Broeder *et al.* (1987) to illustrate this and the results they gain are shown in Table 6.3.

This data was drawn from a study of lexical richness in 20 adult L2 speakers from a variety of language backgrounds and whose L2 production in two different genres, film retelling and free conversation, were recorded three times at nine-monthly intervals. One problem is that

Table 6.3 Lexical diversity measures in different genres

	Film retelling			*Free conversation*		
	Time 1	*Time 2*	*Time 3*	*Time 1*	*Time 2*	*Time 3*
Tokens	607.65	790.65	888.65	917.15	917.35	1118.95
Types	141.65	182.25	208.20	176.90	177.05	205.80
Guiraud	5.89	6.42	6.90	6.61	6.71	7.19
TTR	0.27	0.24	0.24	0.32	0.35	0.28

Source: Van Hout and Vermeer (2007: 99)

the scores on the lexical diversity measures tended to remain about equal (Guiraud) or even to decrease (TTR) over the time of testing, even though the researchers, presumably, feel that there are appreciable differences that should be measurable. It seems in some circumstances that these measures can behave unpredictably and may sometimes be insensitive to changes, even quite large changes in knowledge and ability. These measures vary slightly in how they make their calculations and it is often suspected that the reason for instability in the results they produce is that one index or another is not examining or measuring the quality of lexical variety in precisely the right way. However, the figures for the two different genres in Table 6.3 indicate some of the reason for this instability.

Van Hout and Vermeer point out that the kind of language activity used to elicit the language being assessed has a significant effect on the outcomes. In this case, the lexical richness scores are higher on the free conversation than they are on the film retelling. Differences in scores appear to be not just the product of the abilities of the speakers, but also of the requirement of the language activity. This sensitivity to genre is not something that can be easily controlled. Genuinely free conversation, for example, may cover a whole range of often unpredictable topics. To this must be added a further problem in that the language users themselves may choose to vary their output. Writers and speakers accommodate to each other, so if one speaker is not very proficient then the other may moderate their vocabulary selection (or attempt to) to match the lower (Turner *et al.*, 2004).

The significance of this is that it becomes hard to meaningfully compare scores from these measures unless the activities used to precipitate speech or writing can be rigidly controlled. The tasks must be standardised if these techniques are to be useful beyond the realms of pure research. This may not be easy to achieve, but it will be understood from this why, in assessed interviews, examining bodies like the University of Cambridge Local Examinations Syndicate (UCLES) now largely script the interlocutor's speech and the random pairing of learners is avoided. Where learners use an identical task to elicit language production (as in Richards *et al.*, 2008) then the potential for using vocabulary richness measures for validating language grades is clear. Nonetheless, a further shortcoming of these techniques is the absence of a consistent mechanism for interpreting the scores. Does a score of around 6 on Guiraud's Index for a particular film-retelling activity indicate huge productive vocabulary resources or average resources or poor ones? There is no definitive answer to this question and, to be really useful in assessing overall productive vocabulary knowledge, we would need a set of normalised scores to go with the standardised tasks. The conclusion to be drawn is that lexical diversity measures tell us about one of the lexical qualities of a text, but that text may or may not tell us something about the lexical knowledge of the person who produced it.

Rule of thumb

If you want to observe the changes in the variety of words that learners produce as they improve, then you have to control the tasks used to elicit production. Different tasks will affect the variety of words used.

Using lexical diversity measures to assess the level of vocabulary performance on specific examination-related tasks appears more hopeful. There is only a single task, so the effect of task type is avoided, and the use of scores is not concerned with assessing overall productive vocabulary knowledge, but only the level and appropriateness of the vocabulary produced for that task. Daller and Phelan's results in investigating this are equivocal, as two of the four lexical diversity measures did not correlate with examiner judgements, but the single lexical sophistication measure they investigated did correlate, suggesting that examiners are sensitive and reward the use of infrequent vocabulary. Daller and Phelan are probably a little hasty in appearing to dismiss the usefulness of lexical diversity measures in this context, as other studies (Lorenzo-Dus & Meara, 2005) suggest that examiners are sensitive to the variety of vocabulary used by examinees, although the same research also suggests that the quality of lexical variety is something that examiners find unusually hard to judge consistently. Lorenzo-Dus (2007) further confirms the observation that examiners tend to award high marks to examinees using infrequent vocabulary, supporting Daller and Phelan's thought that lexical sophistication may be a useful measure of lexical production. What, then, can an assessment of lexical sophistication tell us about the way a learner's vocabulary and language develops.

Measuring Lexical Sophistication in Free Language Production

One reason why measuring lexical diversity in learners may not, by itself, be very informative is that the techniques tell us very little about the words being used. A learner's choice of words, whether they rely on highly frequent vocabulary or choose infrequent words, or whether they use structure and function words in appropriate proportions, ought to provide useful information about the learner's lexical resources. A learner who can produce *The feline reposed on the antique Persian rug*, would seem to possess a very different order of productive lexical ability than the learner who writes *The cat sat on the mat*, even if the message appears substantially the same.

A calculation of the proportion of infrequent words in a text is a measurement of *lexical sophistication*. There is no absolute rule as to the point at which a word stops being frequent and becomes infrequent. Meara and Bell's PLex (2001) places any word outside the most frequent 1000 in this category. Profiling methods such as Laufer and Nation's (1995) Lexical Frequency Profile (LFP) or Heatley *et al.*'s (2002) RANGE and FREQUENCY programs allow the user to choose a cut-off level. However, LFP and the RANGE32 software compare a text against the General Service Word List (West, 1953), so effectively the 2000 most frequent words provides a baseline of frequent and anything outside that is infrequent. The popularity of RANGE suggests that there is something like a consensus emerging at 1000 or 2000 words as a dividing line between frequent and infrequent. In the example, *the cat sat on the mat*, there is only one word, *mat*, that falls outside the 2000 word band. A ratio of 1:6 gives a score for lexical sophistication of 0.167.

A calculation of the numbers or proportions of infrequent vocabulary that a learner uses in a text, takes us back to the frequency model of vocabulary learning. Laufer and Nation (1995: 316) state it explicitly: the better a learner is, the more likely they are to use more infrequent vocabulary in production. Learners will tend to learn frequent vocabulary earliest and low-level learners can, therefore, only use small volumes of infrequent words in production. Higher-level learners will have progressed to learning higher proportions of infrequent vocabulary and will, as a consequence, use this resource in speech or writing. A measurement of lexical sophistication, the proportion of low frequency words in a text, should, in theory, give an indication of the amounts of productive vocabulary a learner has in his or her lexicon.

The programs that measure lexical sophistication in language production are now relatively easy to use once the language produced has been turned into digital text. This need not be a negligible step because it raises questions about how to transcribe mis-spellings or illegible handwriting in written production, and incomprehensible words in speech. However, once this is done, the programs will analyse the text and produce a statistical summary. In the case of Heatley *et al.*'s (2002) RANGE, this will produce a profile like those discussed in Chapter 2. Building on the experience of precursors such as Meara's Tintin profiles (1993) and Laufer and Nation's (1995) LFP, two types of report can be produced. One categorises the words in a text into four levels. Level 1 and level 2 correspond to the first and second 1000 words of West's (1953) General Service Word List. Level 3 are words in Coxhead's Academic Word List (Coxhead, 2002). Level 4 is everything else not in these lists. The second type of report produces a larger list and categorises the words in a text according to the first fourteen 1000 word divisions of a lemmatised version of the British National Corpus. Level 5 contains a list of proper nouns and names.

Table 6.4 and 6.5 illustrate the reports that are produced. For a text, I have used the opening paragraph of Dickens' *A Tale of Two Cities*:

> IT WAS the best of times, it was the worst of times, it was the age of wisdom, it was the age of foolishness, it was the epoch of belief, it was the epoch of incredulity, it was the season of Light, it was the season of Darkness, it was the spring of hope, it was the winter of despair, we had everything before us, we had nothing before us, we were all going direct to Heaven, we were all going direct the other way – in short, the period was so far like the present period, that some of its noisiest authorities insisted on its being received, for good or for evil, in the superlative degree of comparison only.

If the 119 words this passage contains appears a small sample for analysis, remember that most foreign language learners will only ever be asked for small quantities of language in examination conditions. The longest essay in UCLES's International English Language Testing System (IELTS) writing paper is 250 words. The writing examination for UK GCSE foreign languages asks for forms such as postcards and diary

Table 6.4 RANGE output using GSWL and AWL

Wordlist	Tokens/%	Types/%	Families
1	101/84.87	42/72.41	38
2	8/6.72	7/12.07	7
3	3/2.52	3/5.17	3
Not in the lists	7/5.88	6/10.34	–
Total	119	58	48

Table 6.5 RANGE output using BNC lists

Wordlist	Tokens/%	Types/%	Families
1	101/84.87	42/72.41	38
2	8/6.72	7/12.07	7
3	3/2.52	3/5.17	3
4	1/0.84	1/1.72	1
5	0/0.00	0/0.00	0
6	0/0.00	0/0.00	0
7	0/0.00	0/0.00	0
8	0/0.00	0/0.00	0
9	0/0.00	0/0.00	0
10	0/0.00	0/0.00	0
11	0/0.00	0/0.00	0
12	1/0.84	1/1.72	1
13	0/0.00	0/0.00	0
14	3/2.52	2/3.45	2
15	0/0.00	0/0.00	0
16	0/0.00	0/0.00	0
Not in the lists	2/1.68	2/3.45	–
Total	119	58	52

entries, a few tens of words only. It is on the basis of this that examiners have to judge the learners lexical resources among other things.

These results tell us that Dickens appears to write using a large proportion of very frequent words. Table 6.4 indicates that only ten tokens from the 119 token paragraph fall outside West's General Service Wordlist, which represents approximately the most frequent 2000 words in English. Of these 10 words, three are included in Coxhead's Academic Word List. Table 6.5 confirms this impression. Only 10 words fall outside the most frequent 2000 words in English and only six words outside the most frequent 3000.

These analyses provide a large amount of information and many figures, and there are times when this is very useful. Laufer and Nation (1995) suggest that this sort of analysis can produce results from text which may be insightful in that they can reflect differences in productive vocabulary ability and are unaffected by task. A summary of the results Laufer and Nation obtained in trialling LFP is shown in Table 6.6. Results from three groups of different ability are compared and each subject produced two essays on a variety of topics. Group 1 is the group with the lowest proficiency. They use the percentage of words that fall outside levels 1 and 2 (2000 words therefore) as the basis for analysis.

These results suggest that as proficiency in a foreign language increases then, in essay writing, the proportion of frequent words (in the first 1000 or 2000) used decreases and the proportion of infrequent words (everything else) increases. The results appear stable even when essays on two different topics are compared, as the scores on composition one and composition two appear very similar in each case. However, since the individuals in each group wrote on a variety of different subjects for both compositions, it is not yet clear from this data that this measure is not subject- or register-specific in the results it produces. The general principle appears sound, however, that groups of learners are likely to produce relatively predictable results in controlled language production.

Table 6.6 Results summary of Laufer and Nation's LFP study

	1st 1000		2nd 1000		UWL		Not in lists	
	Comp 1	Comp 2	Comp 1	Comp 2	Comp 1	Comp 2	Comp 1	Comp 2
Group 1	86.5	87.5	7.1	7.0	3.2	4.1	3.3	2.8
SD	3.8	5.3	2.0	2.3	1.8	2.5	2.3	1.8
Group 2	79.7	79.4	6.7	6.8	8.1	7.8	5.6	6.6
SD	5.3	4.5	1.7	2.2	2.3	2.3	3.5	3.3
Group 3	77.0	74.0	6.6	5.6	8.1	10.1	7.5	8.7
SD	6.1	5.9	2.6	2.5	3.2	2.9	2.9	3.5
F-test	19.35	33.1	0.29	1.89	24.46	27.40	10.46	22.74
p Value	0.0001	0.0001	0.75	0.16	0.0001	0.0001	0.0001	0.0001

Source: Laufer and Nation (1995: 316)

> **Rule of thumb**
> As learners improve in level and fluency, they are likely to increase the proportion of infrequent words they use in production.

One further question that hangs over the use of this technique of analysis is what effect length has on these results. Laufer and Nation cut all essays to 300 words, or left them at under 300 words if the essay was short. It is not clear to me why this was done, as this analysis ought not to be sensitive to length in the manner that, say, TTR is, where longer and longer texts will produce smaller scores. Excessive length should not be a major problem, however, the analysis may be affected if very few words are produced and inferences drawn from a text as short as Dickens's paragraph may be unreliable. Laufer and Nation (1995: 314) report that texts of less than 200 words in length do not produce stable results. This has important implications for the usability of the technique especially in formal situations, as in examinations, where the results produced by this technique may have to be treated with caution. The writing tasks in the IELTS test for example, ask for two essays of about 150 words and 250 words; under or only just above this minimum level for reliability. There is a very good reason why short texts below 200 words are problematic. Meara and Bell (2001: 8) point out that the proportion of words, outside the 2000 word range, in a learner's written text rarely exceeds 10%. In short texts of the type that learners tend to produce, far less than 200 words, the number of words being considered is often close to zero. It does not take much, maybe only a word or two, to destabilise this. The principle of lexical sophistication is that the number or proportion of infrequent words ought to tell us something about a learner's productive lexicon, and what is often wanted is something more simple than a complete profile of scores: a single figure that will tell you what this measure is and which will work consistently with short texts. PLex (Meara & Bell, 2001) attempts to provide this.

The PLex program divides a text into 10-word chunks and calculates the number of infrequent words (words outside the 1000 words ranges and words that are not proper nouns or numbers) in each chunk. It is a system that is calculated to put more of a learner's production into the infrequent band allowing for greater discrimination between levels to occur. The distribution of these scores is graphed up and an example, using the Dickens paragraph again, can be seen in the screenshot in Figure 6.4. Three of these 10-word chunks have no infrequent words, four chunks have one infrequent word, two chunks have two infrequent words, and there are two remaining chunks with three and four infrequent words each. It is a feature of normal text (continuous writing rather than lists or bullet points) that it contains few infrequent words

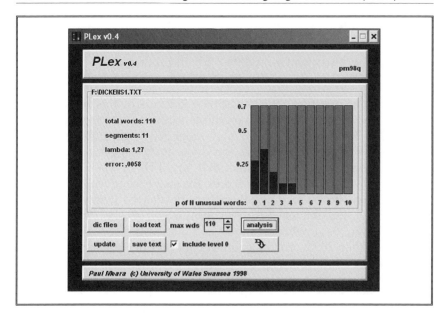

Figure 6.4 PLex data drawn from the opening paragraph of Dickens' *A Tales of Two Cities*

and the result, as in Figure 6.4, is that the distribution is strongly skewed to the left. Distributions that are skewed in this way are *Poisson distributions* and the program calculates a figure, lambda, for the curve each *Poisson distribution* produces. In Figure 6.4, the lambda figure for the extract from Dickens is 1.27.

PLex allows a second calculation of lambda to be made where level 0 words can be excluded from the text. This 150 or so very highly frequent and largely structural vocabulary may destabilise the calculation where the focus of interest is on the proportion of infrequent largely lexical vocabulary. Figure 6.5 presents data for the same passage excluding level 0. Not surprisingly, since the text is in effect shorter, the lambda figure that emerges is higher than before and is 2.35.

The trials that Meara and Bell make using PLex broadly replicate the pattern of finding reported in Laufer and Nation's trial of LFP. Using this technique, groups of learners produce very similar scores in two essays written within a week of each other suggesting the technique produces reliable data. PLex data was also able to discriminate reliably between learners at different levels of proficiency, where the more able learners produced a greater proportion of infrequent words and obtained higher lambda scores. One thing Meara and Bell are able to do with this data is to use their separate plots for 10-word chunks to

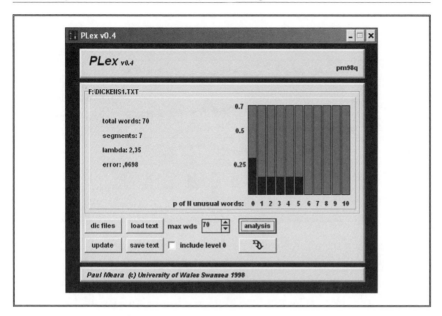

Figure 6.5 PLex data drawn from the opening paragraph of Dickens' *A Tales of Two Cities* excluding level 0 words

plot the way the lambda score changes with length, which should help to suggest how many words are needed before stable results are produced. Figure 6.6 summarises this plot for essays drawn from three learners.

Meara and Bell conclude that essays of about 150 words and beyond produce stable scores and it is clear from the pattern of results in Figure 6.6 that thereafter the lambda score appears little affected by length. The ability of PLex to work with shorter texts and be demonstrably insensitive to length thereafter, are advantages and the single score provides a useful summary of the infrequency of a learner's vocabulary production in a single score. However, I am not sure if this is significantly different from the LFP. It will, very likely, suffer the same problems as lexical diversity in its sensitivity to genre and the personal decisions of the writers or speakers. As discussed in Chapter 3, a learner engaged in a casual conversation might produce lots of high frequency items and a low lambda score. But the same person writing a car repair manual, would be obliged to produce language full of low frequency items producing a high lambda score. Even writing a shopping list might confuse this form of analysis. Lists, by their nature, omit most structure and function words and are likely to produce very different scores from continuous prose. Again, written texts are likely to be more heavily

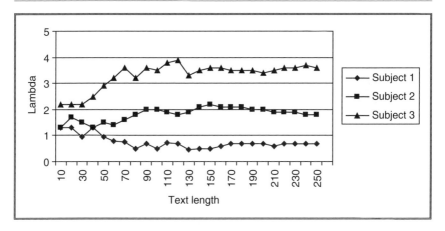

Figure 6.6 Data from three students showing the effect of text length on the lambda score

loaded with less frequent vocabulary than spoken texts. Lexical sophistication measures of free language output may not be as informative about the knowledge or ability of the learner as has been hoped. A single piece of writing or speech may not reflect a learner's knowledge or ability with any great accuracy because of their likely sensitivity to register and genre. It seems that, as Daller and Phelan (2007) suggested, these measures are potentially useful in assessing the lexical qualities of specific texts within a single genre.

Rule of thumb

If you want to observe the changes in the proportion of infrequent words that learners produce as they improve, then you have to control the tasks used to elicit production. Different tasks will affect the variety of words used. And learners have to produce at least a couple of hundred words.

There have already been applications that have attempted exactly this task using lexical sophistication measures. Milton (2004) points to the increasing need for examining bodies to demonstrate that the examinations they set are consistent in the nature and difficulty of the tasks they set and that the results they produce are stable from year to year. In the case of foreign language reading comprehension tasks, this should, presumably, include using texts of similar difficulty in examinations for the same level (Cambridge First Certificate in English [FCE] examinations from one year to the next, for example), and differing difficulty for

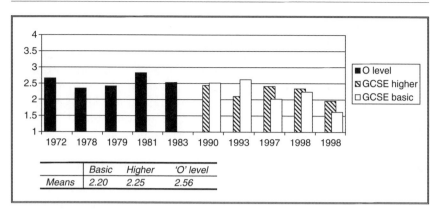

Figure 6.7 PLex scores in French 'O' level and GCSE examinations (Milton, 2004: 10)

examinations at different levels (Cambridge FCE and Proficiency examinations, for example). A survey of the comprehension texts used in French 'O' level and GCSE, analysed using a French version of PLex, produced the results shown in Figure 6.7.

The PLex scores summarised here suggest, but only suggest, that in the GCSE examinations the texts used in the GCSE higher level examination contain, overall, more infrequent vocabulary, and are presumably harder than the texts used in the GCSE basic examinations. This helps confirm the intentions of the writers and the examination boards who seek to make a distinction in difficulty between these two examinations. The scores also suggest, however, that the lexical sophistication of texts used in the old 'O' level examinations are, overall, higher than in either of the GCSE examinations, which suggest that the difficulty of the texts used for reading comprehension is diminishing over time and the age-16 examination may be becoming easier to pass. If the overall data is suggestive, the individual questions are even more revealing. The 'O' level reading comprehension examinations contained two types of question formats: texts for translation and texts with open-ended question requiring global understanding of the passage. GCSE contains no translation passages, short passages with open-ended questions, and many more objective-style questions where global understanding of a text is not required and only individual words and expressions need be recognised. It will be appreciated that with the latter style of questioning it may be possible to gain credit knowing only a few crucial words in a text but with very little overall understanding, something that is impossible with a translation exercise where all the lexis in a text must be known. A comparison of the passages with similar open-ended question formats suggest that GCSE may be even easier than is often thought. The PLex scores for these passages in the Midland examining board 1997 and 1998 papers used in the above analysis are 1.52 and 1.23, respectively, which suggests carefully manipulated texts calculated to produce very light lexical loading where global comprehension is required. These results are scarcely definitive, of course, but where it is important to provide evidence that texts are comparable levels of lexical sophistication and difficulty, then this type of analysis should help add objective weight to otherwise purely subjective judgement.

Other Ways of Assessing Vocabulary Production

Making an assessment of the number of different words and the number of infrequent words a learner uses in production has provided much interesting data, but little insight into the nature of the L2 acquisition process. It has proved difficult with these measures to characterise the growth of a productive lexicon in a way that we can all recognise and apply to learners' speech and writing. Therefore, attention is turning to other ways of handling the words used in free production and one of these looks interesting and even hopeful.

Marsden and David (2008), in a study of the language produced in spoken tasks by learners of French and Spanish as foreign languages, analyse the proportions of different word classes that are used; that is, the proportion of the text that are nouns, verbs and adjectives. The results they produced are summarised in Table 6.7.

It is an interesting observation that in both languages, the proportions of these word classes changes with learning and with increasing proficiency. Learners in year 9, who have three years of study and are elementary level, are comparatively 'nouny', to use Marsden and David's expression. With training and with increased language level the learners in year 13, who are probably more intermediate in level, have become more 'verby'. The year 13 learners have decreased the proportion of nouns they use and increased the proportions of verbs and also adjectives. There is some evidence that this is not an isolated observation (David, 2008b). While this looks hopeful and may be a way

Table 6.7 Mean proportions of different word class types out of total types

	Noun types/total types		Verb types/total types		Adj. types (excl. colour)/total types	
	Sp	Fr	Sp	Fr	Sp	Fr
Year 9 (20)	39% (10)	28% (5)	14% (5)	12% (4)	2% (2)	2% (2)
Year 13 (20)	33% (4)	25% (4)	18% (3)	15% (2)	7% (2)	6% (3)

Source: Marsden and David (2008: 193)

of recognising the knowledge and proficiency of a learner from a relatively small piece of speech, it is unclear whether these proportions, like other measures, change with task type. It also seems to me that learners who can produce only nouns in production must be very, very limited in their knowledge and this observation may be relevant only to the very earliest stages of language learning. It may be no coincidence that this observation comes from the UK foreign language teaching system where the nature of language input to students has been criticised (Häcker, 2008).

Measuring Vocabulary Knowledge with Word Association Tasks

If controlled and elicitation tasks can be criticised because they may not measure a learner's ability to produce vocabulary in a range of communicative tasks and free production tasks are criticised because they may not usefully reflect the totality of a learner's knowledge or ability, is there another method, a third way, which can avoid both of these pitfalls? Is there a technique that would allow the learner to be relatively free in language production, yet produce results which could be standardised and provide a measure of overall productive ability? One attempt to produce this involves the use of word association tasks.

Word association tasks have been used for many years for research in psychology and have recently received interest in foreign language learning circles because the technique possesses some potentially useful qualities. It was noted above that in using free production in writing or speech, any measure used is hampered by the presence of a large quantity of highly frequent vocabulary, which is necessary for well structured and grammatical language. It takes a lot of language production before learners produce enough low frequency words for meaningful results to be gained, and learners are often poor at producing large quantities of language. Word association tasks work in a very different way and people carrying out such tasks are not hindered by the requirement to produce grammatical or well-structured language. In a typical word association task, a testee is given a stimulus word, such as *white*, and is asked to produce a word in response, the first word that comes to mind. In the case of the stimulus *white*, very likely the response would be *black*. In principle, it should be possible to use this technique to elicit larger numbers of low frequency words, in a shorter space of time, than would be possible with writing or speaking tasks.

Lex30 (Meara & Fitzpatrick, 2000) attempts to operationalise this idea and turn the word association idea into a lexical, free production task. A version of the test is given in Appendix 2. An illustrative portion of the paper and pencil version of this test is shown in Figure 6.8, taken

Name:	*anonymous*		Date:	*ddmmyy*

Look at the words below. Next to each word, write down any other words that it makes you think of. Write down as many as you can (more than three, if possible). It doesn't matter of the connections between the word and your words are not obvious; simply write down words as you think of them.

1   **attack**...........*war, castle, guns, armour*
2   **board**..........*plane, wood, airport, boarding pass*
3   **close**........... *lock, avenue, finish, end*
4   **cloth**...........*material, table, design*
5   **dig**............. *bury, spade, garden, soil, earth, digger*

Figure 6.8. Example of Lex30 test format

from Fitzpatrick (2007). It gives a sample not just of the kind of stimulus words that are used, but also the kind of responses that the stimuli produce.

Thirty stimulus words are given to the learner who is asked to produce four association responses. All the stimulus words are frequent and fall within Nation's first 1000 wordlist (Nation, 1984) to minimise the effect of receptive vocabulary size. The stimulus words were selected so they would not typically elicit a single, dominant primary response, and would not elicit purely high frequency responses. Thus, a stimulus like *white* would be avoided because this would be likely to produce a narrow range of frequent vocabulary. Any response outside Nation's first 1000 wordlist was considered to be infrequent. There are no right answers to this prompt in the test and the responses can be varied.

Despite this idiosyncrasy and variety, Meara and Fitzpatrick suggest some patterns emerge from the responses. One is that while the first response provided by learners is often a frequent word, the subsequent responses are much more likely to be infrequent and, therefore, more informative. If learners have large amounts of infrequent vocabulary at their disposal, then it is in these responses that they are likely to show it. A second observation is that the technique does seem successful in precipitating the use of a greater proportion of infrequent words than a free writing or speaking exercise could produce in the same time. From their 46 informants, who ranged from high-elementary to advanced level and from a variety of L1 backgrounds, nearly one third of all responses fell into the infrequent classification. The more able learners produce more infrequent responses than the less able ones. A third pattern was the relatively strong relationship between the receptive knowledge and the productive knowledge that this technique produced. The correlation of 0.841 between Lex30 scores and scores on a Yes/No test of the most frequent 10,000 words in English (Meara & Jones, 1990) was statistically significant and remarkably strong. Even where learners departed from the regression line produced by this analysis, and appeared to have either disproportionately strong or weak receptive vocabularies in relation to the productive vocabularies, reasons could be provided by the learners themselves at interview. One learner with a weak productive vocabulary explained that while she did a lot of reading of scientific journals, she rarely spoke English.

This approach to the measurement of the scale of a learner's productive lexicon seems quite useful at least as a research tool. These tests are comparatively easy to construct and comparable forms can be readily created. They can generate rather more infrequent words than a piece of continuous speech or writing can in the same space of time. It is a method that gives access to the range of a learners' productive lexicon in a way traditional methods find difficult. Free writing or speech potentially constrains the output by requiring the learner to make choices about the needs and level of the person to whom the language is addressed, and the style of the language and the register required. Lex30, however, by using a wide range of cue words, only narrowly constrains the output, which may better reflect the range of the learner's knowledge than a written or spoken language task. The association format may also tap into lexical depth as well as breadth, as learners may produce words that collocate with the cue rather than just words that associate by meaning. But the format is also essentially an elicitation task and it is possible to argue that even this method does not allow productive knowledge in genuinely communicative use to be measured.

As a testing method designed to measure productive knowledge, the method also has one potentially fatal flaw and that is that it only works when learners willingly engage with the purpose of the exercise and do not try to maximise their scores rather than reflect their knowledge. Once learners realise that the object is to produce infrequent words, any such words can be produced regardless of any real association, thus it becomes easy to create a high score almost regardless of their real ability. Learners could certainly be coached to do this.

Measuring Fluency and Automatisation in Vocabulary Use

The background to measuring automatisation lies mainly in psychology. One of the questions that is tackled in psychology is how do people manage to take complex tasks, like driving a car, and move from the learning phase where the action takes lots of time and deliberate effort, to skilled performance where the actions become relatively effort free. Using a language is considered to be a very complex task and therefore falls within this area of research. Vocabulary learning is not normally the focus of this research, but rather the way language rules are mastered and become automatic to the point where language learners can apply a rule without having to explicitly think about the rule before doing so. In vocabulary, the questions being addressed are normally how rapidly can a word be recognised or its meaning accessed.

As with so much in language measurement, there is no established and fixed methodology for measuring this, and measuring implements are often designed bespoke for each experiment. Typical tasks would include timed lexical decision tasks, making the kind of word/non-word decisions that we see in the breadth tests in Chapters 3 and 4. Tests might also include timed tasks where subjects are asked to assign an aspect of meaning to a stimulus word, saying, for example, whether the stimulus word represents a living or a non-living object, or identifying a word in a string of otherwise random letters. If these types of tests appear to be more tests of receptive ability rather than productive tasks, I have placed them here because researchers seem to regard this type of skill as an integral part of productive fluency. If access to words and word meanings is slow or difficult, then productive language is compromised, hesitations are introduced and communication breaks down. This type of measurement potentially offers a different route to gaining a measurement of productive ability in a foreign language.

Ideally, what should happen is that learners will start slowly on these tasks and become progressively faster as they become more knowledgeable and more skilled in using their foreign language vocabulary. This, in turn, should have a beneficial effect on the accuracy and fluency with which learners produce language. In two papers, Segalowitz and Freed (2004) and Segalowitz *et al.* (2004) address exactly this issue and test whether these changes can be seen and measured in a study of learners of Spanish as a foreign language both at home and on study abroad programmes. In these studies, learners attempted a semantic classification task, as a measure of lexical access, where words were presented on a computer screen and the learners had to indicate whether the word referred to a living or non-living object (e.g. the boy = living; a boat = non-living). The words selected were drawn from a list of high frequency English words translated into Spanish. Learners also took a variety of other tests of oral fluency including their productive vocabulary use. In both papers, learners were tested prior to a period of learning, either at home or abroad, and were then tested after study.

In both studies, learners increased their speed of lexical access and these increases can be correlated with aspects of productive oral performance. For example, in Segalowitz and Freed, lexical access speed correlated with the proportion of filler-free speech ($r = 0.375$, $n = 40$, $p < 0.05$), suggesting that as lexical access improves, learners become less reliant on fillers and require fewer hesitations. It has been argued (Hilton, 2008) that these hesitations, as learners search their memories for the words they need to express meaning, are the major stumbling block to communication in a foreign language. And it is vocabulary shortcomings, rather than lack of grammatical control, that create these hesitations. While these tests of automaticity appear to be testing recognition rather than productive skills, they appear to be testing a quality of knowledge that has a direct bearing on learners' productive vocabulary.

In many ways these studies provide more interesting data than the other productive measures discussed here. These automaticity measures provide something most productive tests do not clearly do, which is to link learning back to some of the theoretical models of learning we have. Seaglowitz (2003) is able to draw analogies with Anderson's (1983) adaptive control of thought theory and suggest that even in vocabulary the kind of development from declarative to procedural knowledge, from knowing a word to being able to use it automatically, is in evidence. Even more interesting is the observation that gains in fluency and oral proficiency are significantly related to the lexical access and efficiency speeds that learners possessed before they undertook study. This suggests that fluency gains may depend on cognitive readiness to benefit from learning; there may be a threshold of ability in recognising words and aspects of their meaning, which is required before learners can begin to make improvements in productive fluency. This, in turn, leads Segalowitz *et al.* (2004) to suggest that there may be a feedback effect at play where the better a learner is able to communicate, the more they do and the better they get. The effects of learning have consequences that affect the course of learning itself.

These papers also specifically identify a feature of vocabulary acquisition that most studies omit to examine in detail, which is the volume of individual variation in the scores that learners produce regardless of level. Uniquely among the papers in this chapter, Segalowitz and Freed have a way of recognising this variation and compensating for it in their calculations. Individual variation is a subject that will be considered in Chapter 11.

Conclusion

I am conscious that this chapter has turned into something like a list of possibilities and techniques for collecting productive vocabulary data and trying to make sense of the results. I think this reflects a truth, which is that there is no commonly accepted, standardised method for measuring L2 productive vocabulary knowledge, which has allowed the development of normalised data against which a learner's progress and acquisition could be compared. It is noteworthy that while these tests attempt to measure the size and scale of the productive lexicon, most do not produce the sort of figures that give you a sense of size or scale in the way that the receptive vocabulary breadth tests can. They do not produce measurements that tell you that a learner knows 5000 words, or whatever. Perhaps as a result of this, no-one has produced the kind of large-scale cross-sectional data that we see for the development of breadth of vocabulary knowledge in Chapter 4. There are no measurements that suggest what the productive vocabulary of a learner might be after so many hours of tuition, or when taking a certain level of examination, and against which learners might compare themselves.

The most commonly used techniques, essay writing and oral interviews, produce data that may only partially reflect learners' knowledge and will always be hard to interpret. The techniques for handling the vocabulary in free production are clearly not yet as robust as the receptive tests described in Chapter 4. The future of these techniques probably has to lie in standardised tasks, which will allow learners' scores to be compared where the wide variety of tasks currently used do not permit this. Productive tasks that are created *ad hoc* are satisfactory for research, but much harder to handle in formal testing situations. The efforts made by proponents of these techniques to find a definitive way of analysing the qualities of the text have rather distracted attention from using the data to understand the nature of the vocabulary learning process.

For measuring L2 vocabulary acquisition, it seems that the rather simpler, and more traditional productive tasks, such as translations or elicitation exercises, are probably more informative. These allow us to recognise some of the processes and patterns that emerge in acquisition. One is that receptive and productive lexicons are generally thought to be inter-related; the growth of one goes hand in hand with the growth of the other. Most learners, it seems, will need to develop a large receptive vocabulary in order to develop the productive knowledge that can lead to effective communication in writing and in speech. A second pattern that emerges is that the growth of a productive lexicon probably lags behind that of a receptive lexicon and there may be a variety of reasons for this. The relationship between the words you know and those you will produce can be quite complicated and, therefore, a third pattern that emerges is the relationship between training or experience and the growth of a productive lexicon. Learners who practice and use their vocabularies productively will tend to grow large productive lexicons. A final interesting possibility is that there may be thresholds of knowledge at play in productive vocabulary performance and, just as Chapter 2 suggests that a minimum volume of vocabulary is essential for communicability, so a certain level of ability in recognising words and linking them to meaning may be a requirement for productive ability in a foreign language to develop.

Chapter 7
Measuring Vocabulary Depth

This chapter turns its attention away from how many words a learner knows and examines attempts to measure the depth of word knowledge. It considers:

- *Two tests of individual elements of depth (idiom and collocational knowledge).*
- *A self-assessment vocabulary knowledge scale.*
- *Two tests that attempt to characterise the whole dimension of depth of knowledge.*

While the tests of idiom and collocational knowledge appear to give some useful information about how these elements of word knowledge develop, the other tests are far more problematic. Depth is a dimension that is hard to define accurately and to develop a comprehensive metric for. It appears to develop in relation to growth in vocabulary breadth and it may be that the tests we have are really measuring vocabulary breadth.

The previous chapters have discussed the way word knowledge is not a single quality that can be easily characterised and tested. Vocabulary acquisition is not just about learning to recognise words in a foreign language and attach meaning to them. There are other things you need to be able to do with your words and many things you need to know about words. The receptive-productive division is a convenient way of characterising knowledge in at least two dimensions; dividing the learner's lexicon into words that can be recognised in some way, and words that can be both recognised and used. It is a useful and insightful way of looking at vocabulary knowledge, which has stood the test of time. But, as Nation makes clear in his description of what is involved in knowing a word (see Table 1.2), there are, potentially, more than two dimensions in this kind of knowledge. Nation's list contains 18 separate qualities, rather more than can be easily encapsulated in a single testing model. The literature, especially in the last few decades, has made several efforts to characterise the variation of knowledge, while limiting the dimensions to a workable number to make a satisfactory model. One way of addressing these aspects of word knowledge is to make a distinction between the *breadth* of a person's knowledge, the number of words they recognise and can attach a meaning to, and the *quality* of this knowledge. Read (2000: 93) suggests that within quality of word knowledge, a number of elements might be contained.

- Partial and complete knowledge – we have already seen in Chapter 5 how learners, especially very good ones, can grow large vocabularies where many words appear to be known in a limited way only. They may only recognise the written form of a word rather than both written and aural form, and may possess only an incomplete set of inflections and derivations for many of these words.
- Receptive-productive knowledge – we have already seen in Chapter 6 how learners recognise more words when they encounter them in context than they can readily produce under pressure of communication.
- Depth of knowledge– this is a network of links between words. It is about how they associate and interact with each other, and may be restricted in use according to register and context. This would include, for example, how words collocate, form idioms and can have multiple possible meanings.

Rather confusingly, it seems that a further distinction can sometimes be made and the term *depth* of knowledge is sometimes contrasted with *width* of knowledge. Here, depth refers to the relationship between the various form and meaning components of a word, and width refers to the number and degree of the relationships between a word and other entries in the lexicon. This is not a widely recognised distinction and depth is generally used with the intention of trying to characterise the way a learner organises the words in a lexicon in relation to other entries. Depth is generally used to refer to a wide variety of word characteristics, including the shades of meaning a word may carry, its connotations and collocations, the phrases and patterns of use it is likely to be found in, and the associations the word creates in the mind of the user. All of these imply that a word will be linked to other words and ideas in the lexicon and, provided these links are correct and appropriate, enable learners to use their chosen words appropriately and well. At the heart of this characterisation of vocabulary depth is an assumption that the foreign language lexicon will not have so many links, nor links that are correct and appropriate, and that it will be fundamentally different from the first language (L1) lexicon.

Support for this idea comes from studies such as Meara (1982), which suggest that the word associations produced by second language (L2) learners are qualitatively different from those produced by L1 speakers. This study suggests that non-native speakers produce high proportions of syntagmatic and so-called 'clang' responses to prompt words, while native speakers have been shown to produce primarily paradigmatic responses. There is obviously a big difference between a lexicon that organises words primarily by clang associations, how similar words sound, and one that organises words according to criteria such as collocation. The significance of this is that this quality of depth should, in theory at least, operate relatively independently of other qualities such as breadth. As Meara and Wolter (2004: 95) comment, 'we might find learners with similar vocabulary sizes, but very different degrees of organisation in their lexicons...'. It may be useful to identify learners with lots of words but poor organisation, and to distinguish them from learners with few words but a high degree of organisation, or more native-like organisation. This might explain, for example, how learners with the same volumes of vocabulary knowledge can sometimes perform so differently in academic examinations and in practical communication.

Daller *et al.* (2007b) subdivide the concept of quality and suggest this complexity of vocabulary knowledge might be characterised in three dimensions: breadth, depth and fluency. Breadth broadly being defined as the number of words a learner knows, depth and the quality of knowledge of these words, and fluency as the ease with which words can be recognised and used. This creates a theoretical three-dimensional space in which a learner's knowledge can be characterised. While this appears very neat, it is an idea that has yet to be operationalised. Tests that can convincingly place learners meaningfully within this lexical space are often absent. It is a feature of the quality of depth, in particular, that it is not an area of vocabulary measurement where we have an accepted methodology, still less a generally accepted test to make these measurements.

The difficulties in measuring qualities, such as depth, start with the definitions of this quality. We lack clear, comprehensive and unambiguous definitions to work with and this challenges the validity of any test that might fall within this area. Read (2000: 93) has suggested that vocabulary depth may not really be a single dimension at all, for example. It is hard to see what principle unifies collocational, associational knowledge, constraints on use, polysemy and the other qualities that are placed within this dimension. Without a clear construct, it is impossible to create a test that can accurately measure and quantify a quality whatever that quality is. Nonetheless, the idea persists that there are dimensions of vocabulary knowledge, separate from vocabulary breadth, which might tell us about the degree of accuracy, appropriateness or native-likeness that learners can perform with.

The purpose of this chapter is to describe some of the tests that are used to try to quantify vocabulary knowledge in the area of depth, and to consider what these tests can tell us about the process of acquisition.

Measuring Individual Elements of Vocabulary Depth

One approach to the assessment of something as broad and as varied as depth, is to take a single element of this quality, say idiom or collocational knowledge, and to test this without reference to the other elements within the construct of vocabulary depth. There are reasons, of course, for wanting to test these kinds of knowledge separately. Features such as idioms are frequently explicitly taught, and are thought to add colour and a native-like character to the speech of non-natives, while failure to use collocations appropriately may stigmatise a learner's language performance, so it may be useful to know just how much of these qualities learners have. But frequently too, researchers have made the assumption that learners' performances on one feature of this kind is likely to be representative of their knowledge and ability in the whole of vocabulary depth. The presumption is made that a test of a single quality will allow the whole dimension to be characterised. In order to test whether this appears to be a useful approach, this section will examine measurements of learners' knowledge of English idioms (McGavigan, 2009) and learners' knowledge of collocations in English (Gyllstad, 2007). These are interesting, well constructed and useful tests in their own right, but when learners take both tests and the results are compared, interesting results emerge.

McGavigan (2009) addresses the task of creating a test to measure learners' knowledge of fixed English idioms. He notes that previous attempts to assess this quality are hampered by the absence of a standard test and it is hard to interpret the significance and meaning of test results where the data for analysis is opportunistically decided upon. Arnaud and Savignon (1997), for example, examine this area of knowledge, but note that no frequency lists of lexical phrases existed and so devise a test based on items in their own collections. They assume that because the high-level non-native speakers they tested performed comparably on this test with native-speakers, then non-natives can be native-like in their use of lexical phrases. However, as the test items were not sampled from all English lexical phrases in any understandable way, we have no idea what knowledge of these items might represent in terms of overall knowledge of lexical phrases. McGavigan (2009) also notes that because idioms are believed to be so intimately connected with native-like usage and idiomaticity, then it might be hoped that a well-constructed test in this area might be able to give a useful insight into the thorny area of vocabulary depth generally.

McGavigan takes advantage of the frequency data available on fixed English idioms in the Cobuild *Dictionary of Idioms* (Collins Cobuild, 1995) to make a principled sample of idioms for testing. Twenty idioms are randomly sampled from each of the four frequency bands that the dictionary provides, and gap-fill questions are created for each test idiom. McGavigan uses an open, gap-fill format where the learners can, in principle, write almost anything, but can only score if they know the idiom and the correct answer. An example of the test format and items are given in Figure 7.1.

This test format should allow an estimate to be made of how many idioms are known from the 4400 or so in the dictionary that McGavigan's test materials were drawn from. It is not completely certain that this gives a figure for overall knowledge of idioms. Even with Cobuild's 200 million word corpus, not all English idioms may have been present, as it appears that fixed idioms are remarkably unusual in real language. To illustrate this, McGavigan draws up a table where common English idioms are placed alongside single words of equivalent frequency and this is shown in Table 7.1.

It is sometimes hard, too, to know when an idiom is an idiom, as they are often alluded to by native speakers rather than spoken or written in full; a native speaker will very likely say that somebody is *a rolling stone* rather than use the full fixed idiom *a rolling stone gathers no moss.* Nonetheless, the construction of McGavigan's test probably gives it the potential to usefully characterise and quantify learners' knowledge of idioms. His test also has the useful characteristic that educated native

---

Idioms Test

This is a test of Idioms Knowledge in native speakers of English. For the purposes of this test an idiom is a FIXED phrase which is used metaphorically to describe a situation or feeling.

Instructions.

Please complete the following test items by providing **ONE** word for each gap. Write the answer in the box provided beside each sentence. In some cases there may be variations for the gap. Add the variation in the box next to the sentence.

If more than one word is needed to complete the sentence, the answer is incorrect.

Example

	Question	*Answer*
1	Look at the weather. It's raining cats and ....!	*dogs*

Figure 7.1 McGavigan's idioms test format

Table 7.1 Comparison of frequency in English single words and idioms

Frequency	Single words	Idioms
10 per million	butt, acorn, parson	
6 per million	aver, pique, wrest	
3 per million	dint, hoar, whelp	
1 per million	beck, lode, shad	
2 per million	avatar, miasma, sconce	
1 per 2 million	reamer, traduce, mawkish	get the hang of
		a rule of thumb
		a pat on the back
1 per 5 million	fusty, mein, acclivity	set the pace
		a war of nerves
		the kiss of death
1–3 per 10 million		from the horse's mouth
		out of your head
		as hard as nails
< 1 per 10 million		take a running jump
		live like a king
		to have kittens

Source: McGavigan (2008)

speakers score 100%, or very close to it, thus providing an additional baseline for comparison. When tried out on learners, McGavigan obtained results that suggested the test is reliable (a Cronbach's alpha figure of 0.837 is produced when scores for the four frequency bands are compared). Using this test, McGavigan mapped the growth of fixed idiom knowledge in 100 learners in Greece, from intermediate levels of knowledge up to very high degrees of fluency. His results contradicted Arnaud and Savignon's conclusions. The foreign language learners improve in this aspect of the vocabulary knowledge over the course of learning, however, even the most advanced levels of learners, with experience of living and working in an English-speaking environment, knew comparatively few English idioms in contrast to the native speakers who generally scored the maximum 80 or very close, on the test. Figure 7.2 shows the way scores developed over time and learning from grade 7 up to the Cambridge Proficiency class.

McGavigan makes several other observations using his data. One is that knowledge of idioms correlated significantly with a measure of vocabulary breadth ($r = 0.638$, $p < 0.01$). His data suggests that a minimum level of vocabulary, about 3000 words, is required before idiom knowledge is able to develop, although it is unclear whether this is a product of the course books the subjects learn from, or a feature of the idioms themselves where some parts of the idiom are quite infrequent and all parts will need to be recognised before the whole idiom can be mastered. A second observation is that there appears to be a frequency effect in learning idioms. The kind of profile his results produced is shown in Figure 7.3 and is similar to Meara's vocabulary profile for single words.

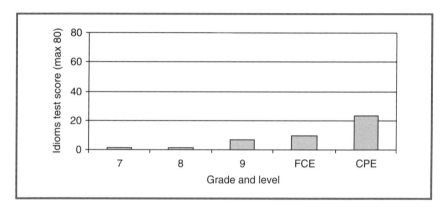

Figure 7.2 Development of L2 idiom knowledge with time and level (McGavigan, 2009)

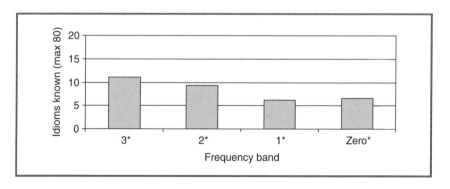

Figure 7.3 Frequency and the learning of idioms (McGavigan, 2009)

It will probably come as a surprise that what the learners acquired appears related, as with single words, to the frequency of occurrence of these idioms. Even though idioms appear very infrequently in normal speech, as captured in Cobuild's *Dictionary of Idioms*, it seems that learners knew more of the frequently occurring idioms than they knew of infrequent idioms.

A third observation to note is just how few idioms learners appeared to know. Contrary to the observation of Arnaud and Savignon, even the best performing L2 learners appear to possess only a fraction of the knowledge that native speakers possess in this area. McGavigan raises the question of how useful a gauge of foreign language knowledge idioms might actually be, when even excellent and very successful English L2 users apparently know and use so few of them and when they appear to be so rare in native usage anyway.

> **Rule of thumb**
> Learners seem to need quite a big vocabulary, 3000 words or more, before they acquire idioms in any numbers. Second language learners do not seem to approach native-like levels of knowledge in this area.

Gyllstad turns his attention to another aspect of vocabulary depth that he believes to be equally elusive to learners; words and their collocates. He is seeking to measure learners' ability to select phrases such as *make a decision* rather than *do a decision* or *set a decision*, where the latter two, despite being grammatically correct and probably comprehensible, would never be used by native speakers. Gyllstad (2007: 52) notes that existing investigations into the collocational abilities of learners, while insightful, often test very small numbers of items and often omit reliability data, so it is hard to draw firm conclusions about the extent of learners' knowledge and abilities. Nor do these studies examine the progress of collocational knowledge over the course of learning. Gyllstad attempts to create workable tests in this area that can give reliable and valid data of collocational knowledge and how it develops.

Gyllstad (2007) develops two tests, Collex and Collmatch. Collex presents learners with a larger number (50) of collocations, than is usual in collocation tests. Alongside these real collocations are 50 pseudo-collocations; combinations of words which are not collocations. The learner has to select the acceptable collocation. It is a deliberate attempt to create a passive recognition measure in this area comparable to the Yes/No tests described in Chapter 4: a measure that can test a large number of items quickly and simply. Examples of the Collex format are given in Figure 7.4.

In the Collmatch format, a series of grids are presented that invite the learner to match three verbs with six noun phrase objects. Learners are asked to tick the combinations they believe they can use in English. An example of the format is given in Table 7.2.

Test items are selected so that, overwhelmingly, the words involved in each collocational pair are taken from the British National Corpus's (BNC) most frequent 3000 word range. The co-occurrence of the words was tested using a z-score with a criterion of >3 being applied for the minimum level of acceptance. What this means is that the collocations tested are frequent combinations and involve the use of relatively frequent words only. This test does not seek to measure learners' ability to recognise and use every possible preferred combination of words in English, but only knowledge of the most frequent ones. It presumes too that learners taking this test will have a fairly sizable vocabulary, 3000 items or more, and therefore good basic competence and will be intermediate level or better.

These measures of collocational ability have certain qualities that Gyllstadt was seeking in his test. The test appears reliable with alpha scores of just above 0.8 overall. It appears from the data that the subjects are better at recognising real collocations than they are at recognising, and dismissing, false ones. The scores on the two tests correlate very well, 0.89, and Gyllstadt's interpretation of this is that it tells us these tests are presumably measuring the same underlying ability. Assuming

tell a prayer	say a prayer	☐
pay a visit	do a visit	☐
run a diary	keep a diary	☐
do a mistake	make a mistake	☐

Figure 7.4 Examples of Collex format (Gyllstad, 2007)

Table 7.2 Example of Collmatch format

	Charges	*Patience*	*Weight*	*Hints*	*Anchor*	*Blood*
Drop						
Lose						
Shed						

Source: Gyllstad (2007)

that the tests are working relatively well, therefore, the results can tell us something about the way this aspect of vocabulary knowledge develops. As with idiom knowledge, scores increase with level as might be expected. Unlike performance on idiom knowledge, however, the best performing learners obtain scores on the tests that approach the standard of performance of native speakers. The scores also increase with language level, suggesting that as students' improve their ability in English generally, their ability to recognise and use collocations also improves. Gyllstad compares results from groups of different levels of ability, learners with vocabularies in the ranges 3000, 5000 and 10,000 words, and the progress in collocation knowledge is shown in Figure 7.5.

It seems that on this test, learners do improve with general language ability and the most able learners with 10,000 word vocabularies are approaching scores of 100% on these tests, and are performing close to native speakers level. Meara and Jones (1990) characterise L2 learners of English with vocabularies of some 10,000 words as quasi-native and on these most frequent collocations it would seem that learners at this level are quite like natives. It would be interesting to know the effect on scores if this methodology for testing were extended to less frequent collocations and covered the full frequency range of collocations in the way that McGavigan's test of idioms does. But, as McGavigan has noted, with items that are so infrequent, does it really matter if L2 learners do not recognise and use these combinations? Perhaps because of the narrowness of the range of collocations Gyllstad uses, there is no frequency effect, as is noticeable in McGavigan's data.

Both the idioms test and the two collocation tests appear to function well within the limitations of the qualities they set out to measure. Both are tests that fall squarely within the domain of vocabulary depth and it would be common practice to run a test of concurrent validity by comparing the results of one test with the other. If these tests are working

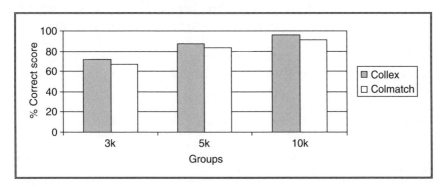

Figure 7.5 Growth in Collex and Collmatch scores (Gyllstad, 2008: 213)

well at measuring vocabulary depth, then the argument goes that the scores on one test should predict scores on the other test. McGavigan (2009) tries exactly this and gains the correlations found in Table 7.3.

These correlations are not significant, of course, and are very close to zero, suggesting there is no predictable relationship between the three sets of scores. It seems that learners can develop one of these areas of depth without the need, or the by-product, of developing other knowledge and skill in the same area. Read's observation that this may not be a single dimension that is easily defined is borne out, and this raises questions as to whether the vocabulary depth, as currently envisaged, is a useful dimension at all if the elements that are thought to make it up do not inter-relate comprehensibly. Even more perplexing is the fact that even though these separate tests of depth appear to suggest that the qualities they measure function independently, these measures almost always correlate reasonably well with vocabulary breadth. Gyllstadt's Collex and Collmatch studies produce a correlation with scores on Nation's vocabulary levels test that is very high – 0.87 to 0.90 – equivalent therefore to the correlation between the two tests of collocation he created. It has already been noted that Gyllstadt's interpretation of the high correlations between Collex and Collmatch is that they are testing the same underlying quality, so the presence of a similar correlation with breadth begs the question whether that underlying ability may actually be breadth of knowledge rather than some special quality of depth.

Vermeer (2001) points out that there has to be a connection between the breadth and depth because a large vocabulary is an essential part of building a very large number of connections between words. A learner with only a handful of words in their lexicon can only make a very limited number of links, and in order to increase the number of links, an increase in the number of words known is required. Vermeer's (2001: 222) stance is that 'the more words one knows, the finer the networks and the deeper the word knowledge'. The conclusion he draws from his investigations is that 'measuring breadth matches up very much to measuring depth' (Vermeer, 2001: 225). If there is a general conclusion to be drawn from studies such as McGavigan's and Gyllstad's, then it is that progress in learners' vocabulary depth knowledge progresses with growth in breadth.

Table 7.3 Correlations between idioms and collocation measures

	Idioms test	*Collmatch*
Collex	0.059	0.547
Collmatch	0.018	

McGavigan also draws a further conclusion from his results. He suggests that items placed within the general area of depth for convenience, may not necessarily belong there. He explains the absence of a correlation between collocational knowledge and fixed idiom knowledge by suggesting that fixed idioms are learned as single lexemes and, in effect, function as 'big words'. As such, they belong within the dimension of breadth rather than depth.

Self-assessment of Vocabulary Depth Knowledge

It appears that measuring a single quality of vocabulary depth may not be very insightful as to overall knowledge in this dimension. Learners can gain ability in one quality of depth without necessarily gaining equivalent ability in another. Ideally, if this dimension of knowledge has any substance or usefulness, we would like to be able to encapsulate the whole of knowledge in this area, so we can recognise the areas where learners know words well and in depth, and also recognise areas of depth that learners do not possess. With so many potential areas of knowledge to be included, this is no simple task. The Vocabulary Knowledge Scale (VKS) (Paribakht & Wesche, 1993a, 1993b; Wesche & Paribakht, 1996) is a word knowledge test that asks learners not simply whether they know a word or not, but rather, how well do they know the words they recognise. By implication, it seems, they are asking learners to assess their own level in vocabulary depth for each test word. It is a deliberate attempt to go beyond tests of vocabulary breadth and to assess something more than a superficial knowledge of word meaning and enable a picture to be drawn of the stages in learners' developing word knowledge.

The VKS works by presenting test-takers with a list of target words and a 5-point rating scale, shown in Figure 7.6.

Test-takers provide an initial assessment of their knowledge (1–5), and if they think they do know the test word, they have to show their assessment is accurate by translation or using the word in context. This

---

1. I don't remember having seen this word before.
2. I have seen this word before but I don't know what it means.
3. I have seen this word before and I *think* it means _____ (synonym or translation).
4. I *know* this word. It means _____(synonym or translation).
5. I can use this word in a sentence: _____. (If you do this section please complete section 4).

Figure 7.6 Wesche and Paribakht's VKS (1996)

method ought to allow some measure of both breadth and depth to be created so that they can be compared. In principle, it ought to be possible to distinguish between the number of scores of 2 or over, words that are recognised or better known and should be equivalent to vocabulary breadth, and words at levels 4 or 5, which are known in some depth. Scores for each word are compounded to try and give a quantification of the depth of knowledge.

Wesche and Paribakht attempted to demonstrate the reliability and validity of this kind of measurement in three ways on trials using 93 subjects. One was to correlate the self-reported scores for knowledge with the knowledge learners could demonstrate by producing a synonym, translation or correct use of a word in context. This revealed correlations above 0.9. A second was to deliver successive administrations of the test with a two-week interval. Results produced correlations for the 'summed' content words of 0.89, and 0.82 for the discourse connectors (Wesche & Paribakht, 1996: 32). The third method was to test concurrent validity by testing the study using the Eurocentres Vocabulary Size Test, and this produced correlation of 0.55 for 'summed' content words and 0.48 for discourse connectors ($p < 0.01$). It should be noted that the test creators make no great claims for this testing technique and merely suggest that it may, '...ultimately lead to more informative testing procedures' (Wesche & Paribakht, 1996: 34). The VKS has achieved fairly widespread use and it will crop up in a number of studies reported in Chapter 10. It has some virtue, then, in that a large quantity of data is available in this format that should, if the test is truly effective, tell us something about the way this dimension of knowledge develops in relation to vocabulary breadth and other aspects of language performance. I suspect, however, that the results of this type of test may be less insightful than might be hoped.

Wolter (2005) voices several criticisms that undermine any conclusions that scores might suggest. Wolter (2005: 29–33) points out that the test appears in use to be relatively insensitive to many aspects of depth of knowledge. It cannot test multiplicity or shades of word meaning for example. In use as well, it appears that the full range of the scale is not used and scores cluster at either end, with scores of 3 and 4 being relatively rare. As Wolter points out, it is not actually very hard to achieve a score of 5 and write a sentence containing the target word. The kind of productive use this test requires, allows learners to place words in semantically neutral contexts which give little clue to whether the writer really understands the meaning (Read, 2001: 137) or whether they appreciate any of the subtleties of a word's distribution with other words. McNeill (1996) has demonstrated that his Hong Kong students were quite capable of producing correct sentences containing target words when they have no knowledge of target word meanings at all.

Therefore, the VKS may not function in practice as a scale at all, but may, ultimately, be a binary test (*I know this word/I do not know this word*). Certainly, my own experience of trying to use this scale to measure my own foreign language vocabulary knowledge, revealed how little use can be made of the middle of the scale; either I did not recognise a word, or I did and I thought I could give a translation and use it in a sentence.

It is also revealing to note that studies using this scale often produce data from which it is hard to generalise about the development of learners' vocabulary depth. Test items are not standardised, but selected for the specific investigation. For example, Horst and Meara's (1999) case study of vocabulary gains from extensive reading, draw their test vocabulary exclusively from a single *Lucky Luke* comic, and it is not always clear what this may tell us about the development of the lexicon as a whole. It is also noteworthy that in this and other papers (e.g. Milton, 2008a), VKS is effectively used to give a measure of the growth of vocabulary breadth rather than depth. The scale tells the authors of these studies how many extra words learners can recognise, explain or translate and use as a result of an informal learning task.

Perhaps because of these problems, the studies which use VKS do not seem to show much systematic development of depth other than what has been noted already; that depth and breadth appear closely related and the more words you know, the better you know many of these words.

Association Tests of Vocabulary Depth

If self-assessment and the use of a knowledge scale can prove less insightful than might be thought, how else can knowledge of this dimension be captured quickly and accurately? Clearly, a measure has to try to capture the variety of qualities in a single test; in effect, to combine tests of various qualities to get a better overall measure of the dimension. Read (1989, 1993, 1995a, 1995b, 2001) has made several attempts at producing a Word Associates Test that is able to test several qualities of depth at once. The initial version of this test elicited knowledge via an interview. Learners were presented with a selection of words and open-ended questions designed to tests aspects of the learner's knowledge. An example of the test sheet of the word Interpret is shown in Figure 7.7.

This is an interesting idea that attempts to assess, in this example, whether the learner knows different shades of word meaning for *interpret*, whether the learner knows words that collocate and associate with *interpret*, and whether the learner is able to produce some of the less frequent derivations of *interpret*. All words were taken from the University Word List in this form of the test. Even an approach as

---

TO INTERPRET

1. Write two sentences A and B. In each sentence, use the two words given.
   A   interpret   experiment
   B   interpret   language

2. Write three words that can fit in the blank.
   to interpret a(n) _____.
                    i _____
                    ii _____
                    iii_____

3. Write the correct ending for the word in each of the following sentences:
   Someone who interprets is an interpret___.
   Something that can be interpreted is interpret___.
   Someone who interprets gives an interpret ___.

Figure 7.7 Test sheet for the word Interpret (Read, 2001: 179)

detailed as this does not manage to address every aspect of depth and yet, as Read (2001: 179) acknowledges, this approach has the practical problem in the length of time required to carry it out and the very small number of words that can be examined in this way. A revised version of the test tries to simplify the process for the learner and make it quicker so that more words can be tested, and tries to systematise the choice of words. A sample of the revised format is shown in Figure 7.8.

This form of the test drops the test of knowledge of word parts and word derivations. It includes 40 items from a higher frequency corpus than the University Word List and, by controlling the responses, allows the test administrator to control for guesswork. For each test word, the learner is expected to identify two associates in each box, four responses in all. In this example, I presume *sudden* is intended to associate with *quick* and *surprising* in the first box and *change* and *noise* in the second. Read administered this version of the test to 38 learners, in two groups, along with a vocabulary breadth test and then conducted oral interviews using a VKS format to provide further evidence of word knowledge that could be used to establish concurrent validity. The results suggested that scores on the test, as with tests of collocations and idioms, correlate remarkably well with vocabulary breadth (0.76 and 0.85), and also with scores for vocabulary depth gained from the interviews (0.92). All correlations were significant at the $p < 0.01$ level.

Read concludes (1995a: 14) that the test 'can be seen as a very efficient testing instrument and one that has the potential to focus on several different aspects of the meaning of the target word'. Wolter (2005: 37),

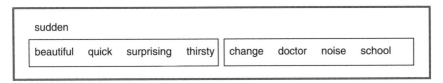

Figure 7.8 Sample items for revised version of Word Associates Test (Read, 2001: 184)

however, takes a more pessimistic view and suggests that 'it is still not possible to suggest with confidence that this test has succeeded in... assessing depth of word knowledge'. Guessing and vocabulary size are likely to play a significant role in the scores the test produces, and it cannot address all of the aspects of word knowledge that the dimension of vocabulary includes. While this test has been around for some time, it seems to be comparatively little used and has not become a standard way of trying to characterise vocabulary depth. Nonetheless, it has the germ of an idea within it that may, potentially, make a more complete and useful test. In the example in Figure 7.8, it is clear that even though two different elements of knowledge are tested, words that collocate and words that associate through meaning, this difference is disregarded for scoring and the total number of connections, of any kind, are counted. Wolter and Meara take up this idea with V_Links and devise a methodology to try to count the number of links of all kinds rather than worry about what the links are. Thus, they hope to encapsulate the whole of the depth dimension in a single measure.

The idea seems to be a workable one because when attempts are made to draw up the associations that language learners and language users make, the kind of patterns of links emerge which might be hoped for. Figure 7.9 illustrates one such network for a learner, drawn up by Schur (2007), where the numbered circles are the test words she used and the arrows between them are the links this particular learner identified.

This kind of analysis reveals a number of features of the kind we would hope and expect to see. Some words, numbers 42 and 46 for example, appear well connected, while others, 19 and 20 for example, are not. Some words in English are, indeed, very highly connected. A verb such as *get*, for example, will link frequently with pronouns (*I get, you get, she gets* etc.), will link frequently with prepositions to make phrasal verbs (*get up, get off, get on, get by* etc.), and will link with noun phrases (*get married, get divorced, get a take-away meal* etc.). By contrast, other words, such as *dint* and *kith*, are much more restricted in their use and will not collocate so widely, or may not appear to associate in the same way as *get*. In Schur's study, it seems that where the nature of the link

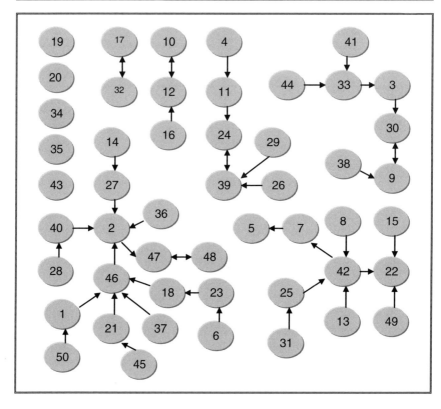

Figure 7.9 A network of a non-native speaker of English (Schur, 2007: 190)

that is expected is not specified, then learners will make a variety of connections, any of which might fall under the broad heading of knowledge of vocabulary depth. Schur interviewed her learners to confirm this. Thus, in the network above, 6 *to clean* links with 23 *to wash*, because they are near synonyms, while number 46 *to try* links to number 1 *to help* for a different reason, because they are collocated, the learner felt that to try to help someone was a frequent combination. Counting the links in a language learner's lexical network, and looking for patterns of association around words that should associate and collocate widely, looks like a workable idea.

Wolter's (2005) V_Links test is an attempt to operationalise this idea. In his test, 10 words are randomly selected from the JACET8000 wordlist (Ishikawa *et al.*, 2003), and these words are presented on a computer screen in a circle so testees can use the on-screen pointer to visually link any word in the set to any other word. The significance of selecting words and creating a test in this way may not be immediately obvious, but, in principle at least, it allows tests with different words to be created which are likely to share the same performance characteristics. Anyone who has attempted to produce a series of examinations with identical performance characteristics will know just how difficult this can be. Previous attempts using associate words taken from the *Edinburgh Associative Thesaurus* (Kiss *et al.*, 1973) produced so many links that it was difficult to score. An example illustrating Wolter's V_Links test is shown in Figure 7.10.

In this example, *true* might associate with *story* and *feeling*, and *news* might associate with *story*. It is suggested that, broadly speaking, native speakers might find more connections in a word set of this kind than non-native speakers, because their knowledge of vocabulary depth would be much greater and they would be familiar with many more potential links. It might be expected too, that as non-native speakers advance in ability and their language knowledge increases, then the number of associations they might find would also increase. Experimental evidence appears to support this. An experiment reported in Wilks and Meara (2007) used tests of this design but with learners, and native speakers, of French. It produced the results shown in Table 7.4. The native-speaking group found, on average, most links, the advanced learners (Group B) fewer links and the intermediate learners (Group A) fewest links of all.

This work is still very much in its infancy. There are a number of problems and potential pitfalls to be overcome, however, before it is

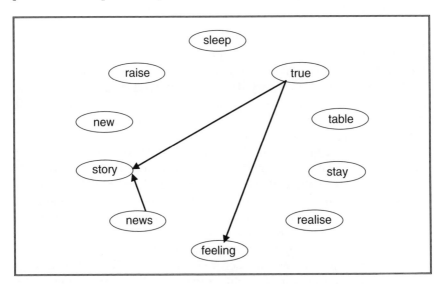

Figure 7.10 V_Links version 3.0 (Wolter, 2005: 144)

Table 7.4 Perceived word associations ('hits') for the three groups

	Mean number of hits per word set	*Standard deviation*	*n*
Learner Group A	2.16	0.94	24
Learner Group B	2.86	1.17	24
French native speakers	3.96	1.98	36

Source: Wilks and Meara (2007: 172)

possible to feel that we have a test that reliably and indisputably characterises vocabulary depth. One problem that lies in the structure of the test is that there is no way, in the form I have described it, of checking the quality of the associations involved. Once a learner realises that the idea of the test is to link as many words as possible, there is nothing to stop him or her making those links regardless of whether or not an association really exists. Researchers are trying to work through these difficulties by using highly frequent words only, to avoid confusion with vocabulary breadth measures, and by referring to native-speaker knowledge and associations, so that the learner's network can be compared to a model that should contain the qualities that the learner is aspiring to. But again, Fitzpatrick's (2006) work suggests that in any language, individuals may depart from native-speaker norms without, apparently, damaging their ability in the language concerned.

Further problems lie in what I have already suggested is a useful quality of the test structure, which is that the test format does not clearly delineate the nature of the association that the testee is to make. These problems, I think, actually challenge the nature of the construct that underlies vocabulary depth testing. In particular, it is not clear that this test is really testing vocabulary depth in a foreign language, but instead is tapping into a learner's vocabulary breadth, as so many of the connections identified in the test rely on general world knowledge and word associations, such as antonyms, which might be language general. In the example from Wolter, above, the collocation of *news* and *story* might be a common one in many languages and once a learner knows the broad meanings of these words in the foreign language, links can be carried over from the L1. Henriksen (2008) encapsulates the problem neatly in her diagram (Figure 7.11) of the three types of lexical knowledge to be found in semantic memory.

Level I contains conceptual or encyclopaedic knowledge and links can be made between items within such a group because experience teaches us that the moon comes out at night, or that moonlight creates a romantic atmosphere. Level II contains a mental inventory of lexical items or

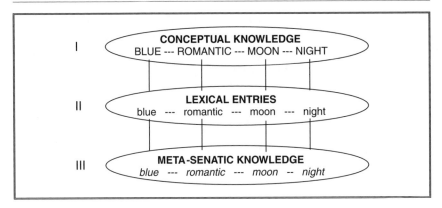

Figure 7.11 Links between and within the three levels of lexical representation (Henriksen, 2008: 29)

words in whatever form, phonemic or graphic. Level III comprises meta-linguistic knowledge of the semantic relations between lexical items, so *blue* and *moon* would be syntagmatically related, or *moon* and *sun* would be paradigmatically related. Of these three levels, only level II is thought to have primarily language-specific entries, while the other two levels are language neutral.

This idea undermines lexical depth testing at two levels. One is that it challenges the assumption that the L1 and L2 lexicons will be significantly different in structure, as it is clear that many of the depth relationships we seek to measure are in the language neutral levels. *Moon* and *night* are associated in any language and so testing whether this link exists in the L2 will not tell us anything interesting about the L2 lexicon. The second problem is that this implies that testing in this area has to concentrate its attention at level II only; the lexical entries. Lexical depth tests like V_Links are not testing whether the links exist, we know they do, but rather whether the words at either end of a link exist in the L2 inventory, and this turns the test into a test of breadth. It is not surprising, in this light, if scores on many lexical depth tests correlate so well with lexical size or breadth, as they are probably testing whether the words are known in the L2 rather than some special quality of the L2 lexicon itself. A growth in the links in V_Links may tell us, as Vermeer suggests, no more than that the lexicon has grown in size and there are more potential links that can be made.

Fitzpatrick's (2006) work on L2 learners' associations also undermines some of the ideas behind lexical depth testing by challenging whether L1 and L2 word associations are really so qualitatively distinct from each other. It will be recalled that an assumption of the L2 lexicon is that it will be more like other L2 lexicons and unlike L1 lexicons, in favouring syntagmatic and 'clang' relationships. This will change only as the L2 develops and paradigmatic associations emerge. However, Fitzpatrick's works suggest that native speakers are not uniform in their association responses in this way and display idiosyncratic responses that may be predominantly paradigmatic or predominantly syntagmatic. What learners do in developing their L2 is not to develop a uniform paradigmatic bias in their responses, but rather Fitzpatrick's work suggests that learners are recreating the associative structure of their L1. If their responses in the L2 are predominantly syntagmatic, this may not tell us how good the learner is or how well developed the L2 lexicon is, rather it may merely suggest what the L1 lexicon is like for this particular individual.

Conclusion

Attempting to measure depth of knowledge appears to have asked more questions than it has answered about the way words are acquired. I am not sure that the attempts to encapsulate depth in a single measure have contributed to our understanding of vocabulary. But this does not mean that every measure in this area is useless. The measures of idiom knowledge and collocational knowledge described in this chapter have proved, in their own ways, insightful. In both cases, it appears that these elements of lexical knowledge emerge once a substantial lexicon of single words, probably several thousand, has been established. Both measures suggest that the elements being tested here can be highly infrequent. And these two observations may not be unconnected of course, as with vocabulary breadth, it seems there may be a frequency effect present in the way these elements, complex though they often are, are acquired. What emerges, however, is that it appears quite possible to be very highly advanced and very fluent in the foreign language without a complete and native-like mastery of all these elements.

This is useful information. It can help to appropriately sequence the content of course books and to justify the choice of items for examination. Knowledge of idioms and collocation are generally thought to be high-level skills and the evidence confirms that this is the case. These results also help challenge various myths about language and the way we use it. It is commonly assumed that idioms, for example, are a very frequent and highly important part of native-like communication, and that it is important that these things are taught explicitly to learners so they can become appropriately fluent in the use of language. In fact, it appears that many of the fixed idioms that we so often teach to learners are something learners can and do manage very well without, and so too do native speakers in so much of the written language that forms the basis of the corpora we use to study language. Rather confusingly, it appears that some of the elements of depth may not be closely related to each other and that learners can acquire knowledge of idioms, for example, without becoming commensurately able in other areas that constitute vocabulary depth. This does, I believe, lead to questions about the construct of vocabulary depth and its usefulness as a dimension of knowledge that we should be measuring.

The ways we have of measuring depth as a single construct, rather than a disconnected set of elements, call the traditional idea of depth into question. There no longer appears to be good reason for thinking that the foreign language lexicon will be significantly different from the native language lexicon, while there does seem good reason for thinking that many of the kinds of organisational elements that the concept of depth seeks to capture, are language general. The task in learning a foreign language is far less a question of developing a whole new structure for a new lexicon, but rather more learning to re-label the concepts and connections that already exist in the lexicon, so that they can be used in the foreign language. Another myth is challenged in the course of recognising this. It has for some time been assumed that L2 learners will be fairly uniform in beginning their foreign language favouring clang and syntagmatic responses and will develop paradigmatic associations to match native-like performance as they improve. The evidence suggests something different, which is that learners will develop in their foreign language whatever type of association they favour in their L1 and this may not be paradigmatic. The way we have of measuring the whole construct of vocabulary depth, if it exists, has yet to be insightful in describing a developmental process that learners or teachers can recognise and take advantage of.

The conclusion probably has to be drawn that depth may have to be modified if it is to remain useful as a dimension at all, since nothing keeps the elements comprising it together terribly persuasively and it does not seem to function entirely separately from breadth. Whatever the qualities of depth and breadth are, they are linked, and qualities of depth really seem to appear only after a sizable vocabulary breadth has been attained. Read (2004: 223) is probably right in suggesting that the breadth versus depth metaphor has served its purpose, but it may be premature to dispense with the term entirely. Where L1 and L2 differ, as in the way words collocate and in some word associations and connotations, there probably remains a use for tests in these areas. This suggests that breadth is much more limited in its scope than is generally assumed and that, in our current state of understanding, vocabulary knowledge defies simple classification into a small number of easily characterised dimensions.

Chapter 8
Vocabulary Acquisition and Assessments of Language Level

Growth in vocabulary size is a prominent feature of progress in language learning over time. It should be no surprise, then, that vocabulary measures can be tied in some way to examination levels, to hierarchies of performance such as the Common European Framework of Reference for Languages (CEFR) and even to examination grades. This chapter will examine the evidence we have that in groups of learners it appears that:

- *vocabulary size and examination level, such as International English Language Testing System (IELTS) grades, link quite closely;*
- *vocabulary size links with individual sub-skills such as speaking or reading;*
- *vocabulary size can be credibly tied into the CEFR – and with allowance made for the requirements of different languages.*

The vocabulary sizes that link to language levels and grades will be described.

The previous chapters have demonstrated that various measures of vocabulary knowledge correlate with factors such as the amount of time spent learning and classroom level. This demonstrates a more general feature of organised, systematic and successful foreign language learning, which is that throughout most of the course of learning, knowledge of vocabulary will increase with general language level. Intermediate-level learners will tend to know more than those at beginner level, and advanced-level learners will tend to know more than intermediate learners. It is not uncommon for syllabus designers to build vocabulary growth formally into their descriptions (e.g. Krizsán, 2003, and quoted in Chapter 3). In one sense, this is not surprising, as one of the ways used to validate whether a vocabulary test is working properly is to see whether this knowledge increases with estimates of level (e.g. Wilks & Meara, 2007: 172). The standard vocabulary size tests, such as Nation's (1990) Vocabulary Levels Test and Meara and Milton's (2003) X-Lex, actually describe themselves as levels tests or placement tests, and their function is to allow users to quickly and easily ascribe a learner to the right class, or to assess whether a learner could cope with an activity such as academic study in the foreign language, on the basis of the volume of vocabulary that learners know and can use.

Nonetheless, users of these tests, both teachers and learners, sometimes express surprise and doubt that this single feature of language knowledge, vocabulary, can be a good general indicator of overall language competence. This seems to be a problem with vocabulary, particularly as users are often much more comfortable with placement tests based on other, equally restricted, features of language, such as grammar. In principle, language knowledge and communicative language skills are separate qualities, and it should be possible for learners to vary, at least to some degree, in their ability to use their knowledge in their quest for communication and language competence. Language level is not just about language knowledge, whether grammatical or lexical, but is about using this knowledge communicably and how well a learner can perform in a variety of circumstances. Despite this, it would be a great surprise if measures of vocabulary knowledge were to behave completely independently of more general measures of language competence, and investigation suggests that there are no surprises here, and that vocabulary ties well into these measures.

It should be expected, therefore, that measures of vocabulary knowledge would tie into suites of examinations or formal hierarchies of language level and performance, such as Cambridge First Certificate and Proficiency examinations and the CEFR. This chapter will investigate this relationship, test out the degree to which vocabulary measures tie into formal examination scores and placements in the CEFR, and place figures on the knowledge required for the various levels and some well-used examinations. I hope to demonstrate that the relationship between examination performance, level and vocabulary knowledge is probably much closer than has been generally assumed.

Vocabulary Size, Examination Grading Criteria and Language Level

There is an assumption that vocabulary knowledge ties into some language skills rather better than others and that it can contribute more to some aspects of language performance in particular. More specifically, there is an assumption that it predicts certain skills particularly well. Meara and Milton (2003: 1) report, for example, that vocabulary size scores correlate well with and predict scores in formal writing, reading comprehension and grammatical accuracy. This measure predicts oral fluency rather less well. Perhaps because formal examinations tend to rely heavily on written delivery and answers, vocabulary size tends to predict overall examination scores well.

Formal examinations, such as the Cambridge suite of examinations, can include specific reference to vocabulary knowledge in their assessment criteria. Cambridge IELTS, for example, includes written and speaking tests, where lexical resource is one of four elements that are specifically assessed by markers. Table 8.1 lists some of the lexical descriptors that Cambridge ESOL (2008) makes available.

While these descriptors are couched in the most general terms and not as measurements or quantities, it is not hard to see how some of the measures being discussed in this book would fit into such a framework. In Band 9, the references to sophisticated use of lexical features and natural use of idioms suggest not just considerable lexical size, but also great knowledge of lexical depth, so that the correct and appropriate lexis for the situation can be selected from within this wide range of knowledge. Band 7 refers specifically to the use of less common lexical items and the ability to use collocation appropriately. Band 6 mentions a 'wide… vocabulary', implying greater size is available to the speaker than in the lower bands. Bands 4 and 5 mention the ability to handle familiar topics only, implying the absence of a large vocabulary that would open up the options for talking or writing about other subjects.

These descriptors suggest that vocabulary size might be expected to grow in size through the bands and that in the upper bands, lexical depth (if it exists) might also be expected to develop. Assessors are expected to make judgements of the range and scale of vocabulary the learner possesses and uses. It appears to be surprisingly hard to assess the performance in vocabulary in writing and speaking activities, independent of other factors. Part of the reason for this might be that the vocabulary available for analysis in most language tests is very little. Writing tasks in examinations such as IELTS might ask for only 150 words from students and of these words, the overwhelming majority are likely to be highly frequent. Some 80–90% might fall within the first 2000 words leaving only 20%, about 30 words or less, relating to content on which a judgement as to sophistication, collocation and appropriateness has to be made. It must be hard for learners to be able to display their knowledge appropriately within these constraints and even harder for assessors to arrive at consistent and correct judgements. There is some evidence that when set the task of monitoring lexical performance only in spoken tasks, even experienced assessors will change their judgements when factors like accent and pausing characteristics are amended. Judgements may be made on holistic assessment of level, therefore, rather than on the specific criteria (Li, 2007). The lack of inter-rater reliability in writing assessments noted in Daller and Phelan (2007) supports the idea that specific criteria cannot be applied consistently even by experienced assessors.

Formal examinations, such as the Cambridge examinations, are often placed within the CEFR framework implying a direct link between vocabulary knowledge and CEFR levels. Despite this, the CEFR is a hierarchy whose levels are couched only in terms of performance of skills

Table 8.1 Cambridge IELTS writing band descriptors

IELTS band	Lexical resource – Writing
9	• Uses a wide range of vocabulary with very natural and sophisticated control of lexical features; rare minor errors occur only as 'slips'
8	• Uses a wide range of vocabulary fluently and flexibly to convey precise meanings • Skillfully uses uncommon lexical items, but there may be occasional inaccuracies in word choice and collocation • Produces rare errors in spelling and/or word formation
7	• Uses a sufficient range of vocabulary to allow some flexibility and precision • Uses less common lexical items with some awareness of style and collocation • May produce occasional errors in word choice, spelling and/or word formation
6	• Uses an adequate range of vocabulary for the task • Attempts to use less common vocabulary but with some inaccuracy • Makes some errors in spelling and/or word formation, but they do not impede communication
5	• Uses a limited range of vocabulary, but this is minimally adequate for the task • May make noticeable errors in spelling and/or word formation that may cause some difficulty for the reader
4	• Uses only basic vocabulary which may be used repetitively or which may be inappropriate for the task • Has limited control of word formation and/or spelling; errors may cause strain for the reader
3	• Uses only a very limited range of words and expressions with very limited control of word formation and/or spelling • Errors may severely distort the message
2	• Uses an extremely limited range of vocabulary; essentially no control of word formation and/or spelling
1	• Can only use a few isolated words

Source: Cambridge ESOL (2008)

rather than in terms of knowledge. The CEFR, in particular, has become associated with 'can do' descriptors. This has a huge benefit in terms of the flexibility of the system and allows it to be applied across a wide variety of languages and different language testing systems. Table 8.2 gives an example of some of these descriptors taken from the A1 Breakthrough level.

Whatever the advantages in the flexibility of these descriptors and the wide range of applications they can be used for, there are disadvantages too. It is not clear, for example in the A1 descriptors, what basic phrases are or what is a familiar word. What is familiar and basic in one context may be very arcane in another. As a result, it can be difficult to compare tests or course materials with any objectivity, even within a framework of this kind. It is possible for learners with very different amounts and different kinds of knowledge, including vocabulary knowledge, to be placed within the same CEFR level. It also appears possible for learners to be placed in one of two or more CEFR levels where the descriptors are sufficiently opaque to allow ambiguity. It is not always clear to what degree misplacement within the CEFR, if this is misplacement, occurs.

It seems likely from these very general descriptors, that measures of vocabulary knowledge will tie into hierarchies of levels like the CEFR in a general rather than a very precise way. It is unlikely that there will be a fixed vocabulary size, which is required to pass Cambridge Proficiency

Table 8.2 Breakthrough level descriptors

Level	*Listening*	*Reading*	*Writing*
A1	I can recognise familiar words and very basic phrases concerning myself, my family and immediate concrete surroundings when people speak slowly and clearly.	I can understand familiar names, words and very simple sentences, for example on notices and posters or in catalogues.	I can write a short, simple postcard, for example, sending holiday greetings. I can fill in forms with personal details, for example entering my name, nationality and address on a hotel registration form
B1	I can understand the main points of clear standard speech on familiar matters regularly encountered in work, school, leisure etc...	I can understand texts that consist of mainly high frequency or everyday job-related language. I can understand the description of events, feelings and wishes in personal letters.	I can write simple connected text on topics which are familiar or of personal interest. I can write personal letters describing experiences and impressions.

Source: Council of Europe (2003: 26–27)

for example. But the process of developing CEFR descriptors in particular has been a long one and the information produced to describe each of the levels has often been very comprehensive. Interestingly from the point of view of this book, the early CEFR descriptors included vocabulary lists (e.g. Coste *et al.*, 1987; van Ek & Trim, 1990). The creators had in mind, at one stage of the process of creating the hierarchy, not just specific amounts of vocabulary, but even specific vocabulary items. The lists produced are derived from notional and functional criteria and mirror each other across languages, with the result that they are very consistent in their content. They even seem to be very consistent in the size of the lists produced. *Threshold* (B1) level lists seem to contain about 2000 words. The German and English lists are largest with about 2400 and 2200 words, respectively. The French and Italian lists are slightly smaller with about 1800 words each. Only the Spanish list appears markedly different in size, containing only some 800 words. The 2000 word figure that emerges at *Threshold* level is an interesting one in light of the lexical threshold discussed in Chapter 3, as this level of word knowledge appears to be associated with 80% coverage of a text, in English at least, and the emergence of comprehension outside the most limited and controlled language environments. The *Waystage* (A2) lists contain about 1000 words. While these lists have not been withdrawn or disowned in any way, they seem to have been pushed into the background (Council of Europe, 2001) and reference to vocabulary is almost entirely absent in the latest CEFR documentation. Until very recently, it has not been clear whether these very precise numbers link to the sorts of vocabulary knowledge that might be generally expected of learners at the A2 and B1 levels of the CEFR.

Vocabulary Size and the Four Skills

But if vocabulary knowledge ties into overall language performance and if examination bodies like Cambridge explicitly tie vocabulary knowledge to their assessment criteria including both writing and speaking, why does evidence emerge to suggest that vocabulary size correlates well with some skills such as writing and much less well with other skills such as speaking? The answer may lie in the fact that the idea that vocabulary plays a significant role in determining language level is based on empirical observation rather than theory. It rests on the observation that vocabulary size measures correlate well with progressive levels of ability in hierarchies of achievement, such as IELTS scores, and with performance involving the written word in particular. Frequent users of vocabulary size measures will recognise the connection, but there is only a small amount of published academic literature to back up this claim; Meara and Buxton (1987) is usually referred to in support.

Table 8.3 Spearman correlations between vocabulary size scores and reading, listening and writing scores ($n = 88$)

	Listening	Reading	Writing
Vocabulary size	0.69**	0.83**	0.73**

Note. **Correlation is significant at the 0.01 level

Recent work has sought to investigate this in more depth. Staehr (2008), for example, examines the relationship between examination grades on listening, reading and writing papers, and the vocabulary size of the testees. The results he obtained, summarised in Table 8.3, suggest a link between vocabulary knowledge and all three elements of examination performance, and a strong link with reading in particular.

Staehr further asks the question to what degree vocabulary accounts for examination scores, and how much vocabulary is crucial for success. By dividing his examination results into two groups, below average and average and above average, and carrying out a binary logistic regression analysis, he concludes that as much as 72% of variance in the ability to score an average mark or above on the reading test can be explained by vocabulary size. Vocabulary may be less important than this in writing and listening, but the contribution of vocabulary knowledge still appears sizable. Staehr records R^2 scores that suggest up to 52% of variance in the ability to score average or above in writing, and 39% of variance in listening, can be explained through vocabulary size. He also concludes that knowledge of the most frequent 2000 words in English represents a threshold that must be crossed if learners are to gain an average score or above on these tests. It is notable that, yet again, the importance of learning these 2000 most frequent words in English has reappeared. These results reinforce the conclusion that vocabulary is vitally important in achieving high levels of performance and gaining high examination grades, but why should vocabulary appear so much more significant in reading and writing than in other skills?

Rule of thumb
Written vocabulary size and performance in reading and writing tests correlate well. A requirement of getting better at these skills is growing a larger vocabulary, especially one that can be recognised in writing.

It is possible that vocabulary knowledge may work differently in different skills and this may be connected with the differences in coverage in written and spoken corpora, which are discussed in Chapter 2. Substantially more vocabulary is needed to achieve the kind of coverage associated with good comprehension in written text than in spoken text

(Adolphs & Schmitt, 2003), and spoken communication has access to gesture and contextual information which written text usually lacks. It may be possible to be far more fluent with fewer vocabulary resources in speech, thereby gaining higher IELTS grades, than are needed in writing. Vocabulary size and breadth tests often concentrate on comparatively less frequent vocabulary, which is much less useful in oral communication. Both the Levels Test and the Eurocentres Vocabulary Size Test (EVST) have a 10,000 word range, for example, and this concentration on infrequent vocabulary might be much more useful in reading and writing, where larger vocabulary resources are required, than in speaking, where fewer lexical resources may suffice. Thus, it is conceivable that the vocabulary measurements used to date in these investigations have focused on inappropriate levels of vocabulary in the case of oral skills.

There is a second reason why research to date has only revealed a strong link between vocabulary and communicative skills involving the written word. This may be the product of the tests used in these few published studies, which tend to use tests in the written form of words rather than drawing on the learner's phonological vocabulary knowledge. Chapter 5 demonstrates that test of the written form of a word need not predict precisely the scores that result from tests of aural knowledge. In principle, therefore, it seems possible that tests of phonological vocabulary knowledge and the more common orthographic test might tell us different things about how a learner is likely to perform in oral language skills. If oral vocabulary measures are linked to speaking and listening skills, then vocabulary knowledge generally might explain more than we currently realise about performance on complete language tests.

The relevance of phonological vocabulary size is not hard to demonstrate. Milton *et al.* (forthcoming) tested both orthographic and phonological vocabulary size in 30 students of English, from various language backgrounds, attending pre-sessional courses prior to under-graduate or post-graduate study. The learners ranged in ability from intermediate to advanced. The vocabulary scores were then compared with IELTS grades, both the overall grade and the grades for the four sub-skills. They had two principal aims in mind. Firstly, they attempted to link performance in overall language skill and IELTS scores. They expected that vocabulary size measures administered through writing would correlate with the sub-skills of reading and writing that involved vocabulary in this form, and would not correlate well with scores in speaking, where knowledge of the written form of a word would not be useful. They anticipated that phonological vocabulary size would correlate with speaking ability, and that both vocabulary size scores might correlate with the listening sub-scores, given that the IELTS test requires the learner to perform in written and aural media. Secondly, they attempted to calculate the proportion of variance in overall language skill and sub-skill scores, which can be explained by the two types of vocabulary knowledge. As in Staehr's (2008) study, they are seeking to quantify just how important vocabulary knowledge is and how it might impact on vocabulary on tests scores.

Milton *et al.*'s (forthcoming) results are summarised in Table 8.4 and reveal, like Staehr's results, statistically significant correlations between the written vocabulary size test and the IELTS sub-tests, which require the learners to read in English. Orthographic vocabulary knowledge appears to be an important contributor to the ability to handle the demands of the IELTS writing test in particular, but also predicts scores in both the reading and listening tests. The written form of IELTS correlate surprisingly well with the overall IELTS grades the learners received, surprising given the presence of two aural components to the test. Statistically significant correlations also emerged between the phonological vocabulary size scores and the sub-skills involving aural communication: the listening and speaking tests. It appears that the qualities of oral fluency that, until now, have not been strongly tied to vocabulary knowledge when only written test forms were used, can now be more firmly linked with the use of aurally delivered tests.

This suggests a conclusion that, in retrospect, is not surprising, which is that orthographic-based vocabulary tests best predict elements of these tests that rely on the ability to handle written text, such as writing exercises and reading comprehension. Phonological vocabulary knowledge best predicts the ability to handle those elements of the test that involve the ability to handle spoken language, like the speaking test. A test like the listening one, which requires the learner to read and hear, draws on both, although it seems more closely dependent on phonological vocabulary knowledge than orthographic. Both vocabulary tests appear to predict the overall IELTS grade moderately well.

The correlations that are observed here are slightly smaller than those in Staehr's study, and regression analysis suggests that slightly less

Table 8.4 Spearman correlations between vocabulary size scores and IELTS scores

	A-Lex	*Read*	*Listen*	*Write*	*Speak*	*Overall*
X-Lex	0.456*	0.699**	0.479**	0.761**	0.347	0.683**
A-Lex		0.217	0.676**	0.441*	0.713**	0.546**

Source: Milton *et al.* (forthcoming)
Note. **Correlation is significant at the 0.01 level
    *Correlation is significant at the 0.05 level

variance in examination scores can be explained through vocabulary size. Nonetheless, the relationship with vocabulary is strong. Linear regression suggests that vocabulary size explains nearly 60% of variance in writing scores and nearly 50% of variance in reading scores. Listening scores are best predicted by a combination of orthographic and phonological vocabulary scores, which together explain over 50% of variance. Because reading and writing depend on the learner's ability to handle proportionately large volumes of infrequent vocabulary, the relationship between reading and writing skills and vocabulary size appears relatively simple: the more words you know, up to several thousands, the better you are likely to do. Skills that involve aural interaction may not behave this way and there may be a ceiling in vocabulary knowledge after which significant improvement in vocabulary may not be reflected in test performance. Binary logistic regression suggests that differences in scores on the phonological test of vocabulary size can explain over 60% of the learner's ability to score IELTS grade 5 or above in the speaking test (Nagelkerke $R^2 = 0.610$). The same analysis suggests that phonological vocabulary size scores can explain 45% of the variance in the learner's ability to score grade 5 or above in the IELTS listening test (Nagelkerke $R^2 = 0.450$). The two forms of the test combine to explain nearly 60% of variance on the overall IELTS grade (Nagelkerke $R^2 = 0.588$).

Rule of thumb

Phonological vocabulary size and performance in speaking and listening tests correlate moderately well. A requirement of improving at these skills is growing a larger phonological vocabulary.

Notwithstanding the other factors that will contribute to gaining high language grades, therefore, vocabulary knowledge appears to be perhaps the biggest element of knowledge and skill in the whole language performance mix. This analysis also suggests that the relationship between vocabulary size and the ability to perform in writing and reading tasks is essentially linear: the more words you know, at least up to 10,000 or more, the better you are likely to perform. Nation (2006: 59) suggests 8000 or 9000 words are necessary for reading comprehension. Performance on oral tasks such as the speaking test is also related to vocabulary, but the relationship may not be linear: there is a limit beyond which increased numbers of words may not help you improve performance. As with Staehr's results, it appears that 2000–2500 words are a minimum level of vocabulary knowledge if learners are to score a grade 5 or better on IELTS speaking and listening, but it is not obvious in this data that significantly higher vocabulary scores contribute to higher IELTS grades beyond this point. Even if the importance of an increasingly extensive vocabulary knowledge diminishes beyond a certain point in oral communication, it is still essential to have a certain level of vocabulary knowledge to achieve the higher grades in IELTS, and the figure of 6000–7000 words required for listening comprehension, suggested by Nation (2006: 59), appears entirely believable.

Rule of thumb

The ability to score an IELTS grade 5 or better probably requires learners to know 2000–2500 words (or better) out of the most frequent 5000, in both written and phonological forms.

As with so much work in vocabulary, the analysis of how vocabulary and the four skills interact has had to draw almost exclusively on the study of English as a foreign language (EFL) learners. It would be a great surprise, however, if the importance of vocabulary to examination performance and progress in other languages were to differ from the role it plays in English.

Vocabulary Size and Examination Performance

The previous section has considered the idea that vocabulary size will link to the skills, even the particular sub-skills, tested in modern communicative examinations. In writing-related skills especially and in overall grades, the greater a learner's vocabulary knowledge, the better the grade he or she is likely to achieve. This implies that particular levels of vocabulary knowledge will be associated with taking and passing particular examinations. Some of these levels are noted in Chapter 4. So, what are these levels of vocabulary knowledge and are the scores gained from vocabulary tests sufficiently sensitive to suggest the grade a person receives?

Meara and Milton (2003) explicitly link X-Lex scores (max 5000) to a variety of examination levels and examination scores, and their estimations are summarised in Table 8.5.

This confirms the suggestions made earlier in this volume that quite substantial volumes of vocabulary knowledge are needed in order to progress beyond the elementary levels of language performance, and to move from very limited capability in only limited and predictable environments to a position where the variety and unpredictability of normal language can be coped with. Knowledge of over 3500 words, or 70% of the test corpus of 5000 words, is associated with students who can take and pass the Cambridge First Certificate in English (FCE) examination. Students who take advanced level examinations would probably be expected to recognise over 4500, or 90% or more, of this corpus. These figures suggest ceiling effects and learners' overall word knowledge

Table 8.5 X-Lex scores in relation to standards, levels and EFL examinations

Comment	X-Lex score	ESU level	National language standards	Comparability with other scores		
				TOEFL	IELTS scores	UCLES examinations
Native-speaker-like performance	4750+	9 expert	Level 5	650	9	Diploma
Advanced level of performance	4500–4740	8 very good		630	8	CPE
Learners at this level would typically be able to perform well in most everyday situations, though they will not understand everything they meet, and will typically have occasional vocabulary problems.	4250–4490	7 good	Level 4	620	7	CPE
Intermediate level of performance	3750–4240	6 competent	Level 3	550–600	6	CAE
They would typically have good listening skills, and good reading skills.	3250–3740	5 independent		500–550	5	FCE

Table 8.5 (*Continued*)

Comment	X-Lex score	ESU level	National language standards	Comparability with other scores		
				450–500	4	PET
Elementary level of performance	2750–3240	4 threshold	Level 2			
Students at this level have a good basic vocabulary, but are very far from native-speaker levels. They can typically perform well in situations that are predictable, but would not be able to operate without help in more demanding circumstances.						
This level is typical of people who have followed a beginners' course. Their vocabulary is very limited, and their ability to perform effectively is undeveloped.	2000–2740	3 waystage	Level 1	400–450	3	KET
Beginner level of performance	2000–	1 and 2			2	Starters, mover and flyers
No systematic vocabulary worth talking about						

Source: Meara and Milton (2003: 5)

must be somewhat greater in the less frequent vocabulary outside the most frequent 5000 word range. EVST (Meara & Jones, 1990), a test based on a 10,000-word sample, confirms this. Learners taking the FCE might typically score 4500 or better on this, larger, test and learners taking Cambridge Proficiency are likely to score at least 6000. In my experience, students who score 8500 on EVST almost always attain a grade A in Cambridge Proficiency.

Rule of thumb

To take and pass the Cambridge FCE, learners will probably need to know about 3500 out of the most frequent 5000 words in English. To pass Cambridge Proficiency, they will probably need 4500 out of 5000 words. And to gain a grade A in Cambridge Proficiency, knowledge of about 8500 out of the most frequent 10,000 words is needed.

We also have data on other languages. In the UK, the vocabulary knowledge of learners taking age-16 GCSE examinations and age-18 'A' level examinations in French have been measured using a French version of X-Lex (Meara & Milton, 2003). The results are given in Table 8.6.

There is quite a wide variation here, but the general expectation is clear, that knowledge of about 1000 words of French will gain a learner a pass at GCSE (with something to spare) and 2000 will gain a pass at 'A' level. Further analysis in the same paper suggests that vocabulary size may be linked to French 'A' level grade and that, as might be expected with this level of knowledge, greater vocabulary knowledge is associated with higher grade. Again, these can be graphed up and the results from 69 learners who took 'A' level are shown in Figure 8.1.

An ANOVA confirms that there is a statistically significant interaction between group and vocabulary size ($F = 11.906$, $p < 0.001$). However, a Tukey analysis further suggests that the overall effect is bolstered by the scale of the difference between the vocabulary sizes of learners scoring a grade A and those gaining other grades. This confirms the observation made by Lorenzo-Dus and Meara (2005) in oral examinations, which is that it is much easier to distinguish students scoring grade A than it is to

Table 8.6 Mean vocabulary size details at GCSE and 'A' level stage

	Number	*Mean*	*Max*	*Min*	*SD*
GCSE	49	852	1800	0	440
'A' level	69	1930	3100	650	475

Source: Milton (2006b: 192)

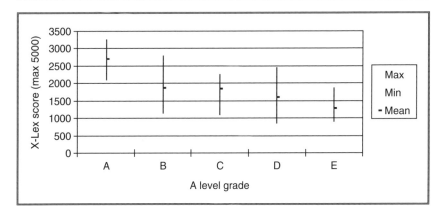

Figure 8.1 Vocabulary size and 'A' level grade (Milton, 2006b: 194)

distinguish between students who ultimately gain grades B and C. The lowest scoring grade A student's vocabulary is well above the mean scores for the other grades in this data. Notwithstanding this, there is still considerable overlap of vocabulary scores and hopefully this is the product of variation in the degree of skill with which learners can marshal their knowledge when faced with the kind of communicative and academic tasks that formal examinations present. Equally, it might also be the result of the kind of imprecision that subjectively assessed criteria introduce into the testing system.

Richards *et al.* (2008) investigate this relationship further among learners of French as a foreign language. They compare not just overall scores on the X-Lex vocabulary size test to the grades that emerge at GCSE and are predicted at 'AS' level, but also examine how each 1000 word band interacts with these grades. Their results are summarised in Table 8.7.

Superficially, it appears that vocabulary size predicts grades in both examinations equally well, but the breakdown of the relationship with the 1000 word bands suggest that the relationship is more subtle. The GCSE grade is predicted by knowledge of the first 1000 words only and no other frequency band. With vocabulary size so small among GCSE learners, generally less than 1000 words, and with knowledge concentrated in the first frequency band, perhaps this result is not surprising. AS grades are predicted by all the frequency bands, but the strongest relationship is with the fourth and fifth 1000 word frequency bands. It appears that knowledge of relatively infrequent vocabulary is a requirement of doing well in the AS examination. Richards *et al.* (2008) also manage to demonstrate very modest, but nonetheless statistically

Table 8.7 Spearman rank order coefficients and statistical significance of correlations between X-Lex scores and GCSE and predicted AS grades

	GCSE grade	*Predicted AS grade*
Adjusted total score	0.43 (0.020)	0.43 (0.020)
Raw score on first 1000	0.55 (0.004)	0.35 (0.049)
Raw score on second 1000	0.29 (ns)	0.43 (0.021)
Raw score on third 1000	0.32 (ns)	0.35 (0.050)
Raw score on fourth 1000	0.32 (ns)	0.58 (0.002)
Raw score on fifth 1000	0.23 (ns)	0.49 (0.009)

Source: Richards *et al.* (2008: 204)

significant correlations between D, a measure of lexical richness, and GCSE and 'A' level grades.

Rule of thumb

The better a learner knows the most frequent 1000 words in French, the better he or she is likely score in GCSE French in the UK.

The presence of French data placed alongside the EFL data in this way, raises challenging questions as to the degree to which vocabulary sizes, and standards more generally, vary across different examinations and in the assessment of level in different languages. It is notable that progress beyond elementary to intermediates levels in EFL generally seems to require a vocabulary of over 2000 or 2500 words. The data for French as a foreign language collected in the UK suggest that learners at intermediate level, those taking GCSE and 'A' level examinations, know far fewer words. GCSE is intended as an intermediate level examination and yet learners routinely take and pass the examination knowing less than 1000 words in French. How can this be explained? Does French really require far fewer words for communicative fluency than English, or is the examination system badly out of alignment? This is exactly the kind of question, and the kind of confusion, that the CEFR has been established to address.

Vocabulary Size and the CEFR

With vocabulary size linked to the level of particular examinations, and as these examinations are tied into the CEFR framework, it is possible to link vocabulary size to the CEFR. It might be expected, following the work mentioned earlier in this chapter on *Threshold* and

Waystage wordlists, that the scale of vocabulary knowledge associated with each level would equate to some degree with the size of these lists. Meara and Milton (2003: 8) have built EFL vocabulary size scores, based on the results of testing using X-Lex with a ceiling of 5000 words, into the framework. The vocabulary guides they produce appear robust when compared with the data from learners taking EFL examinations in Greece and Hungary, described in Chapter 4. The vocabulary scores at each CEFR level are shown in Table 8.8.

While considerable EFL vocabulary knowledge is required to get beyond the initial A1 level, thereafter progress with each level appears fairly consistent, with gains of 500 words or so associated with each successive CEFR level. It seems that the CEFR is able to provide an effective common framework in EFL, as the two countries, one using its own examination system and the other using the external Cambridge examination system, have independently been able to arrive at very similar standards where their examinations are placed at the same level in the CEFR. In many ways, this regularity is quite surprising. The CEFR was overlaid onto existing examination formats and levels, and little thought can have been given to whether each successive level of difficulty could be made regular in some objectively measured way. In part, this regularity, even across the 5000 most frequent words in English, reveals the degree to which learners of this language have to grow a very considerable vocabulary in order to achieve levels of ability and fluency in a foreign language. Not all languages need behave this way. Also, the quantities of vocabulary associated with EFL in the CEFR need not be replicated in other languages. Nonetheless, in the base of English, it appears that learners need to know about 60–70% of the test corpus, some 3000 words or more, before they can progress from elementary (A1 and A2) to intermediate levels (B1 and B2). They need to know about 80% of the corpus, perhaps 4000 words, before they can become truly advanced (C1 and C2).

Table 8.8 Mean EFL vocabulary size scores and the CEFR

CEFR level	Wordlist size	X-Lex	EFL Greece	EFL Hungary
A1		< 1500	1477	
A2	1000	1500–2500	2156	
B1	2000	2500–3250	3264	3136
B2		3250–3750	3305	3668
C1		3750–4500	3691	4340
C2		4500–5000	4068	

> **Rule of thumb**
> Learners of EFL will probably need to know 2500 or more of the most
> frequent 5000 words to move from CEFR A2 to B1. They will probably
> need 3750 words or more to move from CEFR B2 to C1.

French as a foreign language is discussed in Chapter 3. While the
similarity of coverage, and other indicators such as the similarity of
Threshold and *Waystage* wordlist sizes, suggest that at the lower levels of
competence EFL and French may be quite similar, at higher levels the
two languages may be different. The absence in French of an equivalent
to the Academic Word List in English suggests that learners of French
may not need to add vocabulary in the same way as EFL learners in
order to increase their proficiency. Speakers of French as a foreign
language can use their more frequent French vocabulary in the formal
and academic environments in a way that is impossible in English.
Vocabulary size estimates, using a French version of X-Lex, have been
made among learners in both the UK (Milton, 2006b) and Greece and
Spain (Milton & Alexiou, 2009), and have been tied back through
examination level and course materials to the CEFR. These figures are
shown in Table 8.9.

The figures from Greece and Spain in particular tell a cogent story with
vocabulary size increasing at each successive level of the CEFR. The Greek
and Spanish figures are also notably similar to each other and, at A2 and
B1 levels, quite different from the figures for the learners of French in the
UK. The fact that A2 and B1 share the same score is an artefact of the UK
examination system, which allows learners to take the GCSE examination
at age 16 at either of these levels and data collection to date has not
distinguished between the two. In the UK, however, the placement of
national examinations at B1 and B2 levels within the CEFR has been
criticised as misleading (Milton, 2006b) and on the basis of these figures it

Table 8.9 French as a foreign language vocabulary size scores and the CEFR

CEFR level	Wordlist size	French in the UK	French in Greece	French in Spain
A1			1160	894
A2	1000	850	1650	1700
B1	2000	850	2422	2194
B2		1920	2630	2450
C1			3212	2675
C2		3300	3525	3721

is possible to see why. It seems unlikely that a learner in the UK with 850 French words will be as communicative as learners in Spain with double the French vocabulary at their disposal. Other evidence reported in Chapter 4 suggests that the standards of foreign language examinations are slipping, and these vocabulary scores lend weight to this belief.

The French vocabulary sizes are broadly similar at A1, A2 and, to a lesser extent, B1 level to the EFL scores at the same CEFR levels. But, thereafter, French appears to require less vocabulary for progress than English. Chapter 3 notes the differences in coverage for French and English and it seems quite likely that this is partially the effect of French reusing highly frequent words in academic discourse while English requires additional, less frequent lexis. The effect of this is that if the data from UK learners of French is discounted, then learners probably need to know 2000 words or more from the most frequent 5000, some 40% of the test corpus, to progress from the elementary level of French (IA1 and A2) to intermediate standard (B1 and B2). Learners probably need to know about 3500 words, or 70% of the test corpus, before they can become advanced level (C1 and C2).

Rule of thumb

Learners of French as a foreign language will probably need to know 2000 or more of the most frequent 5000 words to move from CEFR A2 to B1. They will probably need 3000 words or more to move from CEFR B2 to C1.

There are some figures available for learners of Greek as a foreign language, learning in Greece, and these are presented in Table 8.10.

Again, these figures suggest that vocabulary increases with CEFR level. Learners, as in EFL, appear to require some 3000 words, 60% of the test corpus, before progressing from elementary (A1 and A2) level to intermediate (B1 and B2). It is not clear from this data exactly how much vocabulary is required of advanced (C1 and C2) level language users in Greek, but it would appear to be over 4000 words or 80% of the test corpus. It would appear that greater vocabulary demands are made of learners of Greek as a foreign language than is the case for either English or especially French.

Rule of thumb

Learners of Greek as a foreign language will probably need to know 2500 to 3000 or more of the most frequent 5000 words to move from CEFR A2 to B1. They will probably need 4000 words or more to move from CEFR B2 to C1.

In all the data sets collected here the importance of vocabulary knowledge to CEFR level is clear. Milton and Alexiou carry out a series of regression analyses to emphasise and quantify these points and the results are shown in Table 8.11.

It appears that in Spain and Greece the CEFR levels that learners are placed at are particularly sensitive to the vocabulary size of the learners. Some 60–70% of variance in CEFR levels can be explained by vocabulary size. In the UK, there is also a moderate relationship and over 40% of variance can be explained in this way. This observation fits well with other observations (e.g. Milton, 2006b; Richards *et al.*, 2008) that examination success in foreign languages in the UK is related to vocabulary size. Only in Hungary does the strength of this relationship diminish. It is not immediately obvious why these data should be so very different from the others.

I have argued that in English and in French there appears to be some agreement as to how much vocabulary is required at the various CEFR

Table 8.10 Greek as a foreign language vocabulary size scores and the CEFR

CEFR level	Greek as a foreign language
A1	1492
A2	2238
B1	3338
B2	4013
C1	
C2	

Source: Milton and Alexiou (2009)

Table 8.11 Linear regression modelling the relationship between vocabulary size and CEFR level

Learners	R	R^2	Adjusted R^2	SE of estimate
EFL learners in Greece	0.842	0.708	0.705	0.9465
EFL learners in Hungary	0.417	0.174	0.168	0.5229
French FL learners in the UK	0.664	0.441	0.437	0.7065
French FL learners in Greece	0.809	0.654	0.648	0.8562
French FL learners in Spain	0.825	0.681	0.675	1.0519
Greek FL learners in Greece	0.844	0.713	0.708	0.8480

Note. All regressions are statistically significant

levels. Nonetheless, the disparity between the different languages reviewed is quite clear. It is made plain when the mean scores obtained in all the countries and for all the languages are conflated in a single table, as in Table 8.12.

I believe that the UK data from French learners is aberrant and is the product of misplacement rather than a reflection of systematic differences in the vocabulary requirements of French, English and Greek. But the manner in which French requires less vocabulary knowledge, and Greek more, than English as the CEFR levels increase does require explanation. One possible reason has already been suggested and lies in the way coverage figures differ from one language to another. Coverage figures for English, French and Greek were plotted up and compared in Chapter 3 (Figures 3.5 and 3.6). These suggest that crucial threshold levels of coverage required for gist understanding and complete comprehension are different in these three languages. The differences appear to mirror the vocabulary loadings in the CEFR reported here, and French vocabulary provides rather more coverage with less vocabulary than English, while Greek provides less coverage. This may provide a rationale for why learners can achieve higher CEFR levels with less vocabulary than learners of other languages.

This whole area of matching vocabulary levels to CEFR grades requires more investigation with more learners and more languages, but differences in these coverage figures may provide a way of moderating the vocabulary loading required in different languages at the six CEFR levels. The value of this kind of undertaking can be seen in the difficulties the UK system has in finding a correct placement for their French as a foreign language examinations. Objective style data that vocabulary size can provide would help these placements to be made rather more securely.

Table 8.12 Summary of mean scores for each CEFR level in three foreign languages

CEFR level	French in the UK	French in Spain	French in Greece	EFL in Greece	EFL in Hungary	Greek in Greece
A1		1160	894	1477		1492
A2	850	1650	1700	2156		2238
B1	850	2422	2194	3264	3136	3338
B2	1920	2630	2450.	3305	3668	4013
C1		3212	2675	3691	4340	
C2	3300	3525	3721	4068		

I am conscious in making this evaluation, that I have deliberately simplified the whole process in merely reporting mean scores for the groups at each CEFR level. This has helped make sense of the way vocabulary and language levels interact, but does little justice to the complexity of the way these things interact in reality. In fact, the mean scores hide very considerable individual variation, and learners manage to find their way into classes or pass examinations at each of the CEFR levels with vocabulary knowledge which can be different from the scores reported here. Part of this will be due to the way data has been collected, as the level of every student could not be meticulously checked in every case and learners can find themselves in classes or taking examinations for a wide variety of reasons in addition to level of attainment. Year group might be kept together in school, for example, even though over the course of several years' study the most able might far outstrip the least able in levels of knowledge. But, it may reflect too the fact that learners are likely to vary not only in their knowledge, but in the use they can make of their knowledge. Some learners may need comparatively less lexical information before being able to jump to understanding compared with other learners who may need to recognise every word in a text before comprehension occurs. Some learners may be more imaginative and risk-taking in their use of limited lexical resources than others and achieve greater communicability. We have very little understanding of how this kind of variation works and interacts with knowledge.

Conclusion

I think the data presented in this chapter suggests very strongly that vocabulary size can be connected to examination levels and to the CEFR in a plausible way. In fact, vocabulary size appears very strongly connected to these levels. As such, it appears that it can be a quick and useful way to assess the overall level of knowledge and proficiency of a foreign language learner, lending credence to placement tests such as Nation's Vocabulary Levels Test (1990) and Meara and Milton's X-Lex (2003). There does not seem to be any good reason why schools, learners and examination boards should not make more use of this kind of information. In the UK, for example, where we use the full panoply of the formal examination system to regularly test the progress of learners throughout their school careers, it is worth questioning whether the kind of quick, unintrusive and relatively low-stakes testing that the vocabulary size tests exemplify might provide the same information at far less cost, effort and disruption to the educational process for schools and learners alike. At the very least, it can provide a much more tangible justification for examination placements, or to demonstrate the consistency of standards of an examination over time.

In particular, the virtue of building vocabulary levels into frameworks and syllabus descriptions is that it can help protect them against the kind of slippage in standard that the UK GCSE and 'A' level examinations are accused of. The results presented here suggest very strongly that the placement of UK foreign language examinations in the CEFR framework is inappropriate and is likely to mislead most users of this information across the rest of Europe. Vocabulary sizes can help suggest much more appropriate CEFR levels for these examinations. They suggest too that these examinations have declined in standard over time.

Vocabulary size estimates can clearly be very useful in dealing with examination systems and with large groups of learners. The relationship between groups of learners and the examination and levels hierarchy is relatively predictable. But, it must be admitted that the kind of ordered regularity seen among groups of learners may not be reflected in the performance of every individual. We still understand very little of the way individuals vary in their vocabulary size and yet can still emerge at the same level in formal examinations or other placements. This may be a problem with the examination system itself, which is less than perfect and relies heavily on the subjective judgement of examiners. But, it may also reflect differences in the way learners use the words they have available to them in a foreign language and which we have little understanding of at present. This individual variation, however, should not blind us to the importance of vocabulary in language learning: you cannot be good in a foreign language without lots of words and, within reason, the more words you know the better you are likely to be.

Chapter 9
Vocabulary Acquisition and Classroom Input

This chapter will examine the measurements we have of what learners gain from the vocabulary input that they receive from:

- *the textbooks they read and use;*
- *the oral input they receive from their teachers.*

This need not be the only source of vocabulary input for learners, but for many learners in foreign language settings it will be the principal source of the words they learn. It might be thought that the words learners are exposed to should influence the words they learn, but there is a school of thought that suggests the influence of this formal input is small. The evidence suggests, however, that lexical input can vary a good deal and this does have a major input on what learners learn and the levels of language ability they achieve.

In this chapter, I will examine the measurements we have which show the effect that classroom language input, in its various forms, can have on vocabulary acquisition. This need not be the only source of vocabulary input for many learners. Learners in many second and foreign language environments can be exposed to their foreign language from other sources, and for learners of English as a foreign language (EFL) in particular, these sources can be many and varied. English can be very pervasive through popular culture such as songs, films and advertisements. Anecdotal evidence from students suggests they do, indeed, target these media for access to English language use. Learners of other languages are not so fortunate. Learners of French in the UK, for example, will have to work harder to find French language films with subtitles and neither these, nor French popular songs, will have the same cachet to young learners as their English equivalents. For many foreign language learners, therefore, the principal and sometimes the only source of foreign language vocabulary will be from the language they are exposed to in the classroom; the textbooks and the teacher's language.

This is another area where Harold Palmer (1917) offered suggestions about what he thought should be in textbooks and how they should be organised. He seems to suggest that as we become more scientific in our study of language learning and teaching, we should be able to find an optimal sequence for the presentation of this kind of material; 'In every programme there is generally a place where a word may be introduced to best advantage' (Palmer, 1917: 126). He implies that textbooks and syllabuses ought to resemble each other in their selection of vocabulary and other things as they conform to an optimal sequence. The selection of vocabulary should be important because if choices are made inappropriately then this may hinder learning. Historically, it seems, there has been very little similarity in the choice of lexis for inclusion in foreign language textbooks and their contents have been highly idiosyncratic. Milton and Benn (1933: 147) in a study of 29 beginner French course books, for example, note that of the more than 6000 types used, only 19 were common to all the books. They note the tendency in these books for frequent vocabulary, apparently so important to language, to be underrepresented. They note too, the difficulty this variety creates both in measuring progress in any uniform way, and in the selection of content for more advanced learning materials when the learners, apparently, had so little in common to build on (Milton & Benn, 1933: 148). Even in the 1920s and 1930s, it seems that writers were adjusting their selection of vocabulary according to frequency criteria, and Robson (1934: 265) draws explicit attention to *Longman's Modern Method French Book*, where the contents are derived in this way. The major modern publishers now have their own corpora on which to draw and, although it is not always entirely clear how they select their contents and vocabulary, frequency criteria are often specifically identified (e.g. Rixon, 1990: 5).

There is a school of thought that suggests that formal vocabulary instruction through textbook and classroom language is not so very important to learners. Harris and Snow (2004: 55), for example, claim that 'few words are retained from those which are "learned" or "taught" by direct instruction', and R. Ellis (1994: 24) suggests that 'most L2 vocabulary is learned incidentally, much of it from oral input'. The influence of classroom materials may vary with level, as the time available in class for formal instruction will inevitably be limited, then the more advanced learners may be expected to take individual responsibility for expanding their knowledge through reading and other activities. But it would be very surprising if elementary learners gained only 'a few words' from the classes they attend. The evidence of Chapter 3 further suggests it would be very hard to build a large vocabulary purely from oral interaction and that written materials would provide far greater access to the quantities of infrequent vocabulary needed for this task. Nonetheless, the claim made by Harris and Snow is potentially very important and raises many questions. What does the vocabulary content of textbooks really look like? Does it reflect the sort of frequencies which normal language possesses, as we understand it from frequency lists derived from corpora? And, crucially, what do learners actually gain from this language exposure? Do learners acquire a substantial core of important and frequent vocabulary, which common sense tells us they should be learning, or almost nothing, as Harris and Snow suggest?

What does Theory say about Vocabulary Input?

There are two key issues to be addressed in the selection of vocabulary for textbooks. One is what vocabulary is to be chosen for teaching and the second, as these words cannot all be taught all together, is how is this material to be spread out over the course of teaching?

The vocabulary content of a course or textbook is, as O'Dell (1997) points out, something that has escaped the detailed attention of most syllabus theorists over the last 50 years or so. The attention of syllabuses may have moved from a grammar orientation to a communicative one, or from a product to a process orientation, but the specifics of the vocabulary content are almost always missing. In the case of the process syllabus, the selection of vocabulary may be determined by the choices of the learners, which would defy the kind of prescription that a syllabus implies and is something Gairns and Redman (1986: 56) characterise as potentially anarchic. A more recent interest in vocabulary has seen the development of the idea for a lexical syllabus (e.g. Lewis, 1993). Sinclair and Renouf (1988) suggest that learners should be taught the words that native speakers most use, which can be derived from frequency and concordance data. There seems to be a general acceptance that frequency criteria should be fairly prominent. Gairns and Redman (1986: 58) place frequency at the top of their list of criteria for vocabulary selection, as do White (1988: 48–50) and O'Dell (1997: 269).

Even within the framework of a lexical syllabus, however, there is little agreement on what this frequency orientation might imply. Sinclair and Renouf (1988: 142–143) suggest this need not require a large vocabulary to be taught, especially initially, while Lewis seems to be in favour of giving lexis more prominence and teaching a large number of lexical items. Whatever the overall scale of the lexicon to be taught, there is one figure that is repeated several times and this is the importance, at least in English, of teaching the 2000 most frequent words or something very like them. Gairns and Redman (1986: 58) and Nation (2001: 16) repeat this figure. While high frequency in a word does not guarantee its usefulness to every learner, it is the best guide to general usefulness that seems to exist, as these words contribute so massively to coverage in general texts. Beyond these words, and in addition to this material, there are other factors that govern the words for teaching. These include factors not unrelated to frequency, such as range and coverage (White, 1988: 48–50), and others such as availability, learnability and words that are opportunistically available or are related to the learners' level or needs and interests. If any degree of fluency is sought, then it seems likely that several thousand of these words will need to be taught, provided, of course, the time is available for such volumes of learning to occur.

The second issue is how to control the introduction of so large a volume of materials, as it cannot all be taught, or learned, in one go. Gairns and Redman (1986: 66) suggest an average of 8 to 12 productive items as representing reasonable input, which might lead to over 1000 items being presented in 125 hours of tuition. They seem resigned to the fact that not all of these will be learned and the evidence presented in Chapter 4 confirms that uptake, at least of the most frequent vocabulary, appears to be much slower. Gairns and Redman imply that input, therefore, should best be fairly regular. Scholfield (1991: 17) points out that there will almost certainly have to be a cyclic element in the presentation of vocabulary, as only some lessons can be expected to be dedicated to this aspect of the language while other lessons will need to focus on grammar or skills or on recycling, revising and testing materials already introduced. Scholfield, in an imaginary and optimum course that introduces, on average, nine new items per lesson, draws up a hypothetical plot of the way new words might be introduced in a course. This is shown in Figure 9.1.

This model of vocabulary introduction is entirely theoretical and real books are unlikely to look exactly like this. They may not look like this at all as the content and sequencing of textbooks is likely to be driven more by the practical concerns of constructing a workable text and less by such theory as exists. The content and sequencing of textbooks is likely to be driven more by the practical concerns of constructing a workable text and less by such theory as exists.

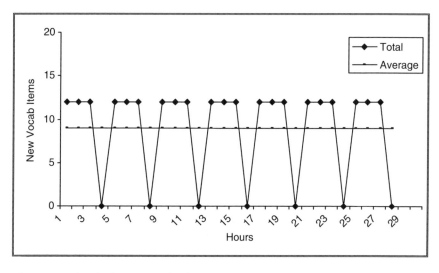

Figure 9.1 Vocabulary rate plot for an imaginary course (Scholfield, 1991: 27)

> **Rule of thumb**
> An effective textbook is probably going to introduce vocabulary at regular intervals and probably with some kind of cyclic element for recycling and practice.

If little thought on the level of theory has been given to the vocabulary content of textbooks, even less attention has been paid by academics and by theory to the vocabulary of the teacher. We know that the vocabulary of spoken language can be significantly different to that of written language, and that the language of the teacher must be a significant source of input for the learner, but there are few guidelines as to how this language might be optimally structured for vocabulary learning. We might assume that the teacher would want to speak and exemplify the words that form the thematic content of the textbook. We might assume that the teacher will want to issue oral instructions to the learners and handle classroom management through the medium of the foreign language wherever possible. We might assume also that oral practice and recycling of lexical material would be an aim for the teacher. The selection and volume of vocabulary in teacher talk might be assumed to be similar or the same as that selected for the textbook, therefore. However, anecdotal reports from teachers suggest that in addition to recycling the vocabulary of the textbook, some also like to expand this material and add synonyms and antonyms or other related words. We certainly do not know whether this occurs and whether it is effective in terms of vocabulary uptake. How often these words are to be spoken in class is a mystery and we have no idealised vocabulary rate plots for teacher talk as we do for textbook materials.

What Happens in Books in Reality? Vocabulary Exposure

In practice, how have course book writers and teachers handled the vocabulary content of classes? As O'Dell (1997: 264) points out, the writers of successful course books have followed a more eclectic approach to vocabulary selection than theory suggests. What emerges by way of teaching materials is a compromise drawn from competing priorities in the syllabus, and from sheer practicality in writing attractive and motivating material. However desirable it is to introduce a good volume of the most frequent vocabulary in beginner materials, for example, these materials must also have thematic content. Frequency lists are not conveniently organised by theme or idea and if a teaching text is to have any coherence then its vocabulary will have to be selected from across the frequency levels. Both textbook and teacher language would contain a combination of frequent and structural vocabulary and infrequent lexical vocabulary, therefore. This material will have to be balanced with other elements of the syllabus, forcing the introduction of new lexis to be constrained.

We have some idea of how vocabulary is treated in reality. O'Dell (1997: 264–268) reviews a number of widely used courses and points out that *Kernel Intermediate* (O'Neill *et al.*, 1971), true to its time, focuses on the presentation of grammatical items and treats vocabulary learning inexplicitly. Vocabulary is not entirely ignored but learners are, instead, taught how to handle unfamiliar words by attempting to guess meaning from context or by ignoring them. Swan and Walter's (1984–1987) *The Cambridge English Course*, includes vocabulary as the first of its eight main syllabuses but, O'Dell notes, disappears from the Teacher's books, although vocabulary inevitably occurs in other syllabuses such as Notions and Topics. Perhaps vocabulary is still not seen as a topic worthy of explicit teaching. O'Dell notes that in *Headway* (Soars & Soars, 1993), while the vocabulary syllabus does include the intention to teach new words, rather more attention is paid to encouraging effective vocabulary learning habits and to introducing students to systems of vocabulary.

Scholfield (1991) has applied his vocabulary rate plot idea to real texts, including the Swan and Walter text referred to above, and this certainly gives a very practical insight into how the volumes of vocabulary introduced are treated in the course of teaching. Figure 9.2 shows a plot of Book 1 of *The Cambridge English Course*, which would assume no prior knowledge of any English vocabulary.

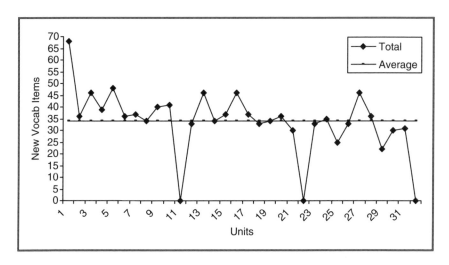

Figure 9.2 Vocabulary rate plot for *The Cambridge English Course Book* 1 (Scholfield, 1991: 27)

This book, it seems, introduces a total of 1082 new words and it appears that Scholfield (1991: 14–15) is not counting lemmatised types here, although compounds, phrasal verbs and idiomatic expressions are counted as single lexemes. This may well be a higher count than a lemmatised count, but in terms of trying to estimate the learning burden for absolute beginners, this may be a useful way to approach things. Absolute beginners will not be familiar with even the most routine ways of inflecting words in the foreign language and each new form of a word will, initially, have to be learned as a new item. *The Cambridge English Course Book* contains the cyclic element Schofield expected to see. There are three cycles in this material and at the end of each cycle there are units, 11, 22 and 32, which contain no new vocabulary. Scholfield (1991: 18) also points to other elements within the cycle as new vocabulary is loaded in units at the beginning of each cycle. Units 1, 3 and 5, for example, in the first cycle, and units 13 and 16 in the second cycle are particularly heavily loaded. There is also an overall trend as the number of new vocabulary items decreases over the course. All the plots in the first cycle are above the average line, for example, while in the third cycle, all but two are below this line. In principle, the reduction of new vocabulary in this way should allow previously introduced vocabulary to be recycled. Scholfield also analyses a further four courses and not all of them appear to be constructed in so obviously principled and systematic a way as the Swan and Walter course. Figure 9.3 shows a

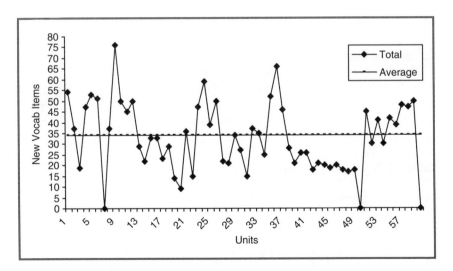

Figure 9.3 Vocabulary rate plot for *American Language Course 2101* (Scholfield, 1991: 28)

plot from the American Language Course 2101 at the Defense Language Institute, where it is harder to discern any consistent trend or cycle.

Scholfield's results suggest that there is considerable variation and rather more vocabulary is introduced in some textbooks than we have imagined. Not every unit lasts an equal length in these books, and it is not always clear how long a teacher might spend on a unit, but an average of 58 new words per unit in *Access to English: Starting Out* (Coles & Lord, 1975), suggests to me that about 20 words per classroom hour are being introduced on average, perhaps double the figures suggested by Gairns and Redman and in Scholfield's imaginary course. By contrast, *Integrated English 1* (Methold & Tadman, 1986) contains 15 units with an average of 21 words per unit, a vocabulary loading one third the size of Swan and Walter's Cambridge Course, although, almost certainly, it is not designed to occupy so many classroom hours. If a vocabulary loading of over 1000 words for a beginners' course seems high, Orosz (2008) reports a beginners' course book with more than double this content.

This variation in loading is nothing new and Robson's (1934) study of 16 first year French courses revealed that input ranged from 212 to 1112 words. Nor is it confined to EFL. Tschichold (2008) reviews the vocabulary contents of the first four volumes of *Encore Tricolore* (Honnor & Mascie-Taylor, 2000, 2001a, 2001b; Mascie-Taylor *et al.*, 2002), a popular French as a foreign language course book used in UK schools. She examines both the glossaries provided by the course writers and the contents of the course itself. Table 9.1 shows the numbers of lemmatised types contained in each volume, the numbers of new types introduced and the likely volume of vocabulary learning per contact hour (based on figures in Milton [2006b] where the school concerned used this course).

The fact that the volume of vocabulary introduced each year can vary from 562 to nearly double this figure (1065) is mitigated by the way the hours available for learning change from year to year. The rate of vocabulary exposure to learners appears reasonable, and even quite consistent, if at the upper end of the range suggested by Gairns and

Table 9.1 Vocabulary content in *Encore Tricolore*

Volume	Types in glossary	New types	New types per contact hour
1	928	928	11.9
2	1220	562	9.6
3	1676	726	12.4
4	2740	1065	13.7

Redmond. Given the small amount of vocabulary knowledge revealed by tests of learners using this course (Milton, 2006b), these figures are something of a surprise. Interestingly, Tschichold notes that the glossaries can include a substantial volume of vocabulary not actually present in the text of the course book itself. In volume 4 of *Encore Tricolore*, 126 of the 1065 items in the glossary did not appear in the text.

Rule of thumb
An effective textbook is probably going to introduce vocabulary in very large quantities.

Modern textbooks vary in the volumes of vocabulary they choose to introduce and it appears that they also vary in the choice of vocabulary. This observation is not restricted to EFL courses, but extends to French as a foreign language. It appears that the huge differences noted by Milton and Benn (1933) nearly 80 years ago still exists between course books intended for the same learners at a single level. Most of the information we have is still restricted to beginner courses.

What Happens in Books in Reality? Selection of Vocabulary

Milton and Vassiliu (2000: 448) review the contents of three beginner textbooks and compare their choice of vocabulary. They construct a Venn diagram to illustrate the volumes of lexis that these courses share and this is shown in Figure 9.4.

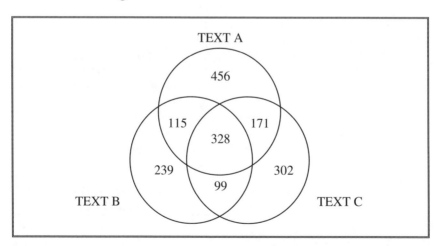

Figure 9.4 Vocabulary common to three beginner EFL textbooks (Milton & Vassiliu, 2000: 448)

Text book A contains 909 unlemmatised types, textbook B 964 and textbook C 1175 types. These figures confirm the type of vocabulary loading which Scholfield notes, and the suspicion that EFL learners are exposed to much more vocabulary than we have suspected is confirmed in this case, as it is known that these texts combined comprised a 100-hour beginners course. Milton and Vassiliu tidy up the corpus to remove personal names and other materials not relevant to the study. Of the remaining 1710 types, only 328 are common to all three texts.

This finding is not unusual it seems, and Milton and Benn's (1933) observation that course books for the same level can have surprisingly little in common, is as true today as it was 75 years ago. Alexiou and Konstantakis (2007) review the lexical content of five Junior A and a further five Junior course books – books designed for the first two years of instruction to learners who will be about 7 years of age. Their results are summarised in Table 9.2.

The numbers of vocabulary items common to all books is very low. What makes this surprising as a result is the general agreement that highly frequent vocabulary is very important and should feature prominently in course books. This should include structure and functional words such as propositions and the verb *to be*, which would be hard to avoid, it might be thought. If course book writers are really trying to select from this highly frequent material, than rather more common items might be expected. But if writers are being so varied, how much of this highly important, very frequent material is there in textbooks?

Tschichold (2008) compares the corpus of French as a foreign language course book material against the *français fondamental* levels 1 and 2 to gauge whether learners are being denied access to the highly frequent structural and functional vocabulary. The four-book corpus contains 3341 lemmas and is about the same size as the *français fundamental* lists, which is approximately 3500 words. The comparison is summarised in Figure 9.5.

More than half of the *français fundamental* contents is contained in the *Encore Tricolore* teaching materials. It is not absolutely clear what an ideal figure would be, but this seems reasonable. *Français fundamental* is an intelligently constructed list containing highly frequent items that are

Table 9.2 Total number of types and common types in beginner level course books

	Total number of types in all five books	*Number of common types in all five books*
Junior A	949	108
Junior B	1551	54

Source: Alexiou and Konstantakis (2007)

essential for communication and progress in French. It is also apparent from Richards *et al.*'s (2008) study that GCSE grades are dependent to a degree on knowledge of the most frequent vocabulary. It might be expected that a course designed to raise learners from beginners to a Threshold level, about B1 in the Common European Framework of Reference for Languages (CEFR), should contain a significant proportion of these items. Given the scale of the vocabulary content of the four *Encore* books, it would be impossible to include the whole of the *français fundamental* list, and a balance of highly frequent and structural vocabulary and less frequent lexical vocabulary that is about equal seems common in beginners' textbooks. The problem of vocabulary selection within the UK foreign language syllabuses appears to be growing more acute. *Encore Tricolore* is now a rather old textbook and more recent foreign language course books contain substantially less vocabulary overall (Häcker, 2008).

Milton and Vassiliu analyse the three textbooks in Figure 9.4, which make up a first year course for EFL beginners and lemmatise their corpus in order to make a calculation of the words in the highest frequency bands. The 1710 unlemmatised types were reduced to 1396 lemmatised types by this process and the lemmas that emerged were compared with Nation's (1984) vocabulary lists. The results are shown in Table 9.3.

Several things emerge from this analysis. One is that, similar to Tschichold's French materials, roughly equal volumes of highly frequent and structural vocabulary, and less frequent thematic vocabulary are introduced, despite the pressures from the need for thematic content and to cover other elements of the syllabus, and despite the fact that this material is designed for only two years' work rather than four. A total of

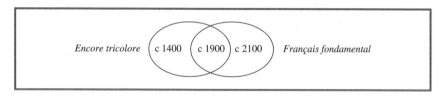

Figure 9.5 Common vocabulary between *Encore Tricolore* and *français fundamental* (Tschichold, 2008)

Table 9.3 Beginner text vocabulary content by frequency range

Nation's levels	Level 0	Level 1	Level 2	Level 3+
% Lemmas	8	40	6	46
No. of lemmas	105	558	84	649

Source: Milton and Vassiliu (2000: 449)

663 out of 1150 level 0 and level 1 words are introduced. But the need for thematic content is apparent in the inclusion of 649 words from outside of the most frequent levels, levels 0, 1 and 2. About 46% of the vocabulary syllabus, therefore, is made up of infrequent vocabulary and it may appear surprising just how many of these infrequent words there are. In between these two elements, the proportion of words in the second 1000 vocabulary band appears small. Only 84 of these words are introduced, about 6% of the total vocabulary loading. Vassiliu (1994) in a review of two different texts has noted the same characteristic. Häcker's concern that foreign language course books in the UK contain an excessive quantity of infrequent items appears misplaced, although her point that the quality of these words, long lists within limited domains, may be correct and the vocabulary taught may be less broadly useful for communication as a result.

Alexiou and Konstatakis (2007) look at this in a slightly different way and investigate the coverage provided by highly frequent lexis in the 10 course books they investigate (Figure 9.6).

These course books appear reassuringly like normal English in the proportions of text, which is comprised of the most frequent 2000 words. But, again, it is not clear if this is an essential or even a desirable quality in the books, as the need in beginners' learning text to recycle elementary structure might be expected to raise the proportions of the most frequent lexis.

Rule of thumb

An effective textbook is probably going to introduce frequent and infrequent vocabulary in roughly equal amounts. It will probably be thematically very diverse.

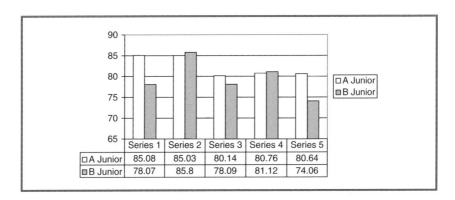

	Series 1	Series 2	Series 3	Series 4	Series 5
□ A Junior	85.08	85.03	80.14	80.76	80.64
▣ B Junior	78.07	85.8	78.09	81.12	74.06

Figure 9.6 Percentage of coverage for the A and B Junior course books according to the BNC lists

It is hard to say, in the absence of information about the uptake of the items, whether these proportions strike the right balance to allow learners to make good language progress or not. Fortunately, Milton and Vassiliu (2000) and Vassiliu (2001) have investigated the learning of individual items within these lists to investigate just this question.

Vocabulary Uptake from Classroom Input

Vassiliu (2001), in several studies, has addressed the question of how much of the textbook vocabulary was learned by his students. He tested 45 young learners, aged seven and eight, taking a 100-hour course and using the three textbooks whose content is illustrated in Table 9.4 and Table 9.5. He used a Yes/No test similar in design to those described in Chapter 4. The 180-item test contained 120 items randomly selected from the textbooks and 60 pseudo-words used to adjust the scores for guesswork and overestimation. Learners were presented with these words both orally and in writing. Vassiliu extrapolates the results of this test to calculate the number of words, and these are tokens rather than lemmatised types, his learners have added to their passive receptive lexicons. The results he obtained are presented in Table 9.4.

At this point, it is worth revisiting Harris and Snow's (2004: 55) claim that 'few words are retained from those which are "learned" or "taught" by direct instruction', because the evidence of real learners taking real courses suggests that nothing could be further from the truth. The learners in this study acquired a receptive vocabulary, on average, of over 900 unlemmatised words formally presented as part of their course

Table 9.4 Vocabulary learning from 100-hour beginner course

n	Target vocabulary	Min	Max	Mean	SD
45	1710	137	1385	913	285

Source: Vassiliu (2001: 136)

Table 9.5 Vocabulary learning from three beginner courses with differing vocabulary loadings

	n	Target vocabulary	Min	Max	Mean	Mean as%	SD
Course A	63	1556	155	1276	863	55.46	239
Course B	29	1323	252	998	746	56.41	196
Course C	18	1009	182	945	669	66.28	205

Source: Vassiliu (2001: 146)

in one academic year of instruction. Vassiliu suggests, having reworked his data as lemmatised types, that these learners acquire 6.5 to 8 new words per contact hour. The best learners have acquired even more. There are 15 scores of over 1000 words in this data and a highest score of 1385, some 77% of the total vocabulary loading of the textbook. The lowest score is 137, but this is, by some way, an outlier. Learners have not become familiar with the entire corpus of words presented to them, however. Large though the figures for learning are, 900 unlemmatised words represents just over half (53%) of all the words presented.

Rule of thumb
Learners should learn large quantities of the vocabulary presented in their course books.

Vassiliu revisits this issue in a further experiment both to check whether this volume of vocabulary learning can be replicated, and to investigate whether presenting such large volumes of vocabulary may be counter-productive. Vassiliu (2000: 141) reasons that it would be strange to introduce vocabulary if there is no intention for it to be learned. If vocabulary is included in the textbook and if even the best learners cannot master it, then perhaps they are being overwhelmed. If the lexical loading of textbooks were reduced, to exclude some of these items nobody learns, then perhaps learning might even be improved. Time spent fruitlessly trying to learn items that cannot later be recalled, could be spent on something else. Therefore, he examines three different beginner courses, A, B and C, in three different Greek schools using textbooks that carry different vocabulary loadings. Course A contained unlemmatised 1556 types, course B 1323 types and course C 1009 types. He designed tests to investigate the vocabulary uptake from each of these courses and the results he obtained are presented in Table 9.5.

It is hard to be completely certain of the implications to be drawn from these results. While the length of the course, approximately 100 classroom hours, was similar in each case, the groups could not be completely controlled for the abilities of the students, the nature of the classroom input, the quality of the various texts used and a whole host of other factors that may potentially influence the success of vocabulary learning. Nonetheless, it seems clear that substantial amounts of vocabulary learning are normal, at least in Greece. Again, acquisition appears to be at a rate of between 6 and 7.5 lemmatised types per contact hour. The most able learners continue to acquire around 1000 new vocabulary items and the mean vocabulary gains are in the region of 600–800 items. The results suggest that presenting learners with less vocabulary does lead to a greater proportion of the target vocabulary being learned. As the target vocabulary decreases in number, so the mean number of words learned, expressed as a percentage of the target vocabulary, increases. But this does not appear to help learners in terms of the amount of vocabulary learned. The mean vocabulary scores decrease as the vocabulary targets get smaller. Even though learners learn proportionately more of the vocabulary being presented to them, they end up, on average, learning less vocabulary. And despite the lower vocabulary target, even the best learners still have not mastered all the vocabulary of the textbook. It is possible to argue that reducing the volumes of vocabulary being presented has limited the achievement of the most able learners. The target vocabulary of course C is lower than the vocabulary learning achieved by one third of the learners in Vassiliu's original experiment and the best learners in course C learn 30–40% fewer vocabulary items.

> **Rule of thumb**
> The more vocabulary that is presented in course books, the more vocabulary learners seem to acquire. Learners do not appear to get overloaded in this area of acquisition.

The conclusion to be drawn from these results is that the vocabulary selection and loading of textbooks is far from being an immaterial concern in language learning nor one which has little impact on learning. It appears to have a very direct bearing on what and how much vocabulary is learned. Learners, if they make progress at all, can learn large amounts of the vocabulary formally presented to them. They appear to acquire it in volumes and at a rate that suggests, if it were to continue over the course of classroom learning, it is very possible to master the thousands of words needed for communicability and some semblance of fluency. For the most able learners, it would seem, there is a good case to be made for pushing vocabulary in large numbers at them, as they can learn this material and move rapidly to more autonomous language use as a result. In order for this to happen, the textbooks would have to continue to select and grade their material very carefully, and continue to add substantial quantities of infrequent vocabulary. This ought to mean that well graded and sequenced textbooks include progressively more infrequent vocabulary; that they will become more and more lexically sophisticated. Again, the evidence of well-constructed textbooks suggests that this is what does happen in some carefully constructed textbook series. Figure 9.7 shows an analysis of the reading comprehension texts taken from the *Upstream* series of course books (Evans & Dooley, 2001a, 2001b, 2002a, 2002b) and shows the percentage of lemmatised types which fall outside the General Service Wordlist and the Academic Word List.

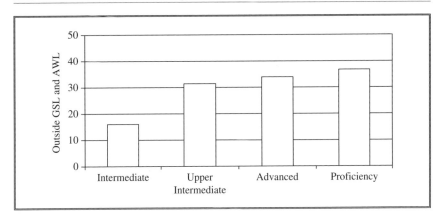

Figure 9.7 Percentage of infrequent lexis in *Upstream* reading comprehension texts

The proportion of words in a text that fall outside the 2000 most frequent words can be taken as an indication of lexical sophistication (Daller *et al.*, 2007: 13). Figure 9.7 suggests that as the textbooks in the series become more and more advanced, they also become progressively more lexically sophisticated. As learners progress through the series, therefore, increasingly infrequent lexis is loaded into the teaching material and is available for learning. I have suggested elsewhere (Milton, 2004: 8) that relatively normal text in English might have a lexical sophistication score of about 20–25%. The Intermediate level book, therefore, appears quite lightly loaded in terms of the volumes of infrequent vocabulary, which is probably appropriate for learners of this level although it is comparable with the Beginner textbooks reported in Figure 9.6. Learners at Cambridge Advanced and Proficiency levels would expect to handle quite challenging and academic style text, and the lexical sophistication scores of around 35% suggest that this is exactly what is happening.

Orosz (2008), however, in an analysis of three sets of course books used in the Hungarian state system suggests that the progressive vocabulary loading of course books may not always work as well as might be expected. Her figures suggest that the kind of high vocabulary loading found in the first year of learning is not sustained. It is not that the textbooks do not contain large volumes of vocabulary, but rather that the same vocabulary recurs year after year, and long after, she reports, most of it has been mastered.

The information on vocabulary uptake from textbooks has concentrated thus far on learners of EFL for the simple reason that we know far less about course book content and vocabulary learning in other languages. We have some information about French as a foreign language learners in the UK, however, and in Chapter 4, I have already touched on the very low rates of vocabulary learning among these learners. It might reasonably be questioned whether this is connected to the vocabulary provided for them in the textbook, which may lack sufficient breadth and richness to allow learners to progress. The evidence we have from Tschichold's study reported above suggests that learners are exposed to a relatively modest volume of vocabulary in *Encore Tricolore*: about 3300 lemmatised types over the first four years of study. The volume of highly frequent vocabulary also appears small with only some 1900 of the 3500 vocabulary items in *français fundamental* included. Milton's (2006b) study of learners who use this book reported that learners after four years had an average vocabulary size of 592 lemmatised words (a figure confirmed in David, 2008a), which suggests an uptake of available vocabulary much less than Vassiliu's EFL learners displayed. Vassiliu's learners, on average, learned about half of the vocabulary made available to them in their textbooks, the French learners in Milton (2006b) may be displaying vocabulary uptake of less than 20%. Whatever problems the UK learners of French may have, including issues with the textbook, it does not appear that the textbook's vocabulary loading is a cause.

Vocabulary Recycling in Books and Acquisition

It is an axiom of good teaching that new material must be recycled and repeated if it is to be satisfactorily learned. Vocabulary teaching is no different, and writers, if their course books are to be good, will need to consider recycling their lexical vocabulary. It is probably impossible to avoid repeating much functional and structural vocabulary, which is essential to well-constructed language, so this is much less of a problem to writers. Nation suggests (1993) that few textbook writers actually do recycle vocabulary systematically and, with the large volumes of vocabulary being presented in course books, which the previous section has suggested, it may not even be possible to recycle every item systematically. Nonetheless, the evidence suggests that this can be an important element of success in learning. Palmberg (1987), for example, reports that two thirds of the words produced by his Swedish EFL learners comprised lexis regularly repeated in their course books. Kachroo (1962) reports that most words repeated more than seven times in the Indian course books he studied were learned, while words occurring only once were not. Saragi *et al.* (1978) recommend at least 10 encounters for each new word to aid learning. Gairns and Redman (1986: 94) even suggest when new words should be repeated; after one day, one week, one month and after six months. If recycling of words is not always systematic in textbooks, this may explain the effect Vassiliu noted above, that several hundred words, present in the course book, appear never to be learned. These may be the words that are not recycled.

Vassiliu (2001) has investigated this and re-examined the data from his three course books summarised in Table 9.6 and Figure 9.8, and tested the vocabulary uptake of 47 learners using this material. He divides the vocabulary contained in the textbooks he used into eight bands according to frequency, and tested 15 words from each band using the Yes/No format described above.

Broadly, the results are what might be expected. The more an item is repeated in the textbook, and presumably the more the learners are exposed to it, the more likely it is to be learned. But even very high repetition does not guarantee learning. One learner in Vassiliu's sample failed to recognise the word *is* even though it was repeated 1355 times in the text. Similarly, low repetition in the course book does not guarantee that a word will not be learned. A surprisingly high proportion of the words repeated only once or twice were learned, despite the absence of recycling. It has to be noted that a large proportion of the unlemmatised types in this text are only infrequently repeated. Sixty-four percent of the types are repeated five times or fewer.

Several factors may be at play here. There is more to learning than the content of the course book. One factor may be the effect of oral presentation and recycling that should, at least in principle, supplement the contents of the textbook. Vassiliu notes (2001: 161) that some words with low repetition in the textbook, such as *welcome* and *door*, were generally known by students possibly because they formed part of an

Table 9.6 Repetition and vocabulary learning

Frequency band	No. of words	Repetition rate	Min (%)	Max (%)	Mean (%)	SD
1	109	36–1355	66.6	98.3	87.83	8.06
2	19	31–35	66.6	100	89.12	9.18
3	23	26–30	60.0	100	89.12	9.69
4	43	21–25	53.3	100	87.12	10.33
5	66	16–20	45	100	84.28	11.18
6	111	11–15	51.6	100	83.15	11.48
7	245	6–10	40.0	95	68.40	14.39
8	1094	1–5	40.0	100	65.38	19.42

Source: Vassiliu (2001: 157)

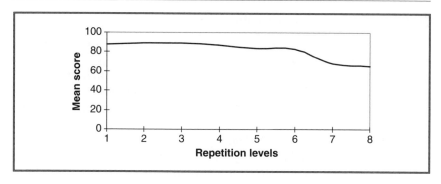

Figure 9.8 Repetition and vocabulary learning (Vassiliu, 2001: 158)

oral routine used by the teacher. Other factors affecting learning may include the elements of word difficulty discussed in Chapter 2. Thus, some words with high learning rates but low course book repetition, such as *dolphin* and *actress*, are highly imageable, which ought to aid recall. Other words were cognate to Greek, such as *acrobat*, and the learners may have found these types of words more accessible. A further factor may have been that not all the vocabulary of a textbook is available to be read in the same way as these words. Some of the most frequently repeated expressions in the textbook occurred as part of written instructions for exercises and these had comparatively low rates of recognition. Possibly, where the activity was obvious, the instructions did not need to be read, or even explained, and these vocabulary items were not accessed by learners, even though present in the textbook. Orosz (2008) adds further to the complexity by suggesting that even at low levels, learners are sufficiently highly motivated in Hungarian schools to take extra classes and learn vocabulary extensively outside the classroom. This possibility is examined in Chapter 10.

> **Rule of thumb**
> Repetition and recycling seems to have a beneficial effect on the likelihood that a word will be learned, but it is not, necessarily, an essential condition of learning. Words that are almost never recycled are also learned in considerable numbers.

The conclusion to be reached here is that measurements of real learners confirms that repetition really can play a role in helping the acquisition of a large vocabulary, even if it does not tell the whole story. A well-constructed textbook with a good choice of vocabulary and which includes some recycling, can enhance learning and help lead to the growth of large vocabularies, even if everything cannot be recycled.

Teacher Talk and Acquisition

We know much less about the effect of teacher talk on vocabulary acquisition than we know about the content of teaching texts. This is despite the fact that it appears quite commonly believed that this type of language input 'is the most crucial factor in determining language acquisition' (Håkansson, 1986: 83) and I have already repeated R. Ellis's (1994: 24) assertion that 'most L2 vocabulary is learned incidentally, much of it from oral input'. The relevance of the study of the oral language of teachers takes on a greater salience when it is considered how many children now learn a foreign language at an age when they are still learning to cope with reading and writing in their first language. As Donzelli (2007) points out, more than 80% of children in Europe currently study a foreign language from or before the age of eight. For these learners, the quality of their oral input from teachers must be even more important than for older learners. Chapter 8 has further drawn attention to the importance of the knowledge of phonological word form in examination success in foreign languages.

Older studies of teacher talk (e.g. Gaies, 1977; Chaudron, 1978; Håkansson, 1986) concentrate on the complexity of the language used by teachers and these suggest that teachers are able to simplify their language for low-proficiency learners and adjust it as proficiency increases. Only more recently is the vocabulary content of teacher talk examined. Meara *et al.* (1997) examine the vocabulary in the speech of 10 ESL teachers in Quebec's French immersion courses. Analysis of a 30-minute sample of classroom teacher talk from each teacher revealed that, on average, 85% of the language used fell within the 1000 most frequent words in Nation's 1986 wordlists. Only 3% fell outside the most frequent 2500 words; substantially different from the course book vocabulary reported earlier in this chapter. It would be hoped that input of this kind would be accessible to low-level learners, but it is hard to see how learners could grow large vocabularies on the basis of it. A study by Tang and Nesi (2003) confirms the impression that teacher talk can provide a very poor lexical environment for learners, although much depends, it seems, on the degree of autonomy that teachers are allowed to exercise.

Donzelli (2007) examines both the vocabulary content of teacher talk and the vocabulary content of the textbook used, and then goes on to try to calculate the degree to which the vocabulary presented in these two ways is learned. Teacher talk, it transpires, has some very different characteristics to those of the textbook. Donzelli creates a vocabulary rate plot for 55 successive classes examined over the course of a complete year of instruction, and shows the number of different word types spoken by the teacher in each class. This is shown in Figure 9.9.

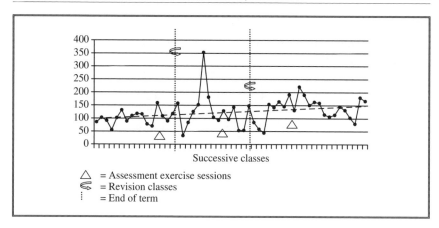

Figure 9.9 Spoken word types in a low-level EFL class in Italy (Donzelli, 2007: 111)

The amount of teacher talk per class can vary from 33 types up to 353. Donzelli's analysis of this suggests that the kind of cyclic features that Scholfield (1991) noted in the vocabulary of course books are repeated here. Revision classes, where no new items would be introduced in the textbook, are associated with large numbers of different word types used by the teacher as the vocabulary introduced in previous classes is recycled. Assessment classes, where no new material is introduced and pupils are busy writing, are associated with very small numbers of words used by the teacher. Donzelli points out that the teacher adopts a term-pattern, and term ends are shown in Figure 9.9. The number of different word types used by the teacher appears to increase over the course of a term, there is a slump during assessment, followed at the end of term by a big increase as all this vocabulary is recycled. It is to be noted that as the number of new vocabulary items diminishes, class by class, over the course of the whole year, in the teacher's speech the number of different words used per class increases. Oral input is therefore increasing over the year.

It appears too that the teacher is not merely repeating and recycling the language of the textbook. The vocabulary used by the teacher is not only greater in quantity than that contained in the course book, but it is also more varied. Considerable vocabulary is introduced which does not occur in writing in the textbook. Over the course of the year, the textbook introduces some 740 words types, but the teacher orally introduces more than double this with some 1322. This is not restricted to a particular cycle or to a handful of classes, it appears to be a continuous trend over the whole year. Figure 9.10 shows this trend.

Rule of thumb
A good teacher appears to recycle the textbook vocabulary in class and expand upon it to give a rich lexical environment to the learners.

Donzelli's teacher appears a fairly modest talker compared to others. Orosz (2008) notes that one class she recorded included over 3000 words of teacher talk in a 35-minute class; effectively a non-stop monologue. An analysis of the teacher talk and the textbook vocabulary suggests that Donzelli's teacher mirrors the textbook in the frequency distribution of the vocabulary used. A breakdown of these two corpora is given in Table 9.7.

These figures suggest that the vocabulary loading of the textbook would be similar to the ideals that Scholfield and Gairns and Redman suggest. This 55-hour course introduces 740 different types at an average rate of about 13 words per hour. Donzelli notes that the frequency distributions are similar to those noted by Vassiliu (2001) with about 50% of the vocabulary being from the first 1000 most frequent vocabulary band and approximately 30% of the words being infrequent lexis. The teacher's oral input mimics these proportions in her input almost exactly, although a greater vocabulary is used and the language can scarcely have been prepared. Together these input suggest a very rich lexical environment with some 24 new words introduced on average per contact hour in either written or oral format. It is not surprising that all of this vocabulary is not retained by learners, and in a test that presents words both orally and in writing it appears that learners could, at the end of the year, recognise on average about one third of this input (Donzelli, 2008).

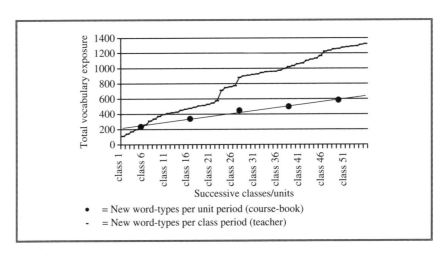

Figure 9.10 Comparison between written and oral vocabulary exposure (Donzelli, 2007: 113)

Table 9.7 Teacher and textbook vocabulary divided by frequency band

	Level 1	*Level 2*	*AWL*	*Other words*	*Total types*	*Total tokens*
Input from teacher	667	235	14	406	1322	32096
Input from course book	304	97	6	176	740	4218

An average of 463 of the words suggests an uptake of 8.4 words per contact hour, which compares very favourably with those obtained by Vassiliu (2001), and substantially better than adolescent learners of French in the UK (Milton, 2006b).

Donzelli continues her investigation to ask what the benefit of the oral input is and tries to calculate the degree that words which are both heard and seen are better recalled that those which are only heard, or are only seen on the page. Her results suggest that there was no statistically significant difference between the numbers of words that were learned in each condition. Words that were both seen and heard were not more likely to be retained (Donzelli, 2008). No correlation between the number of oral repetitions of a word and the likelihood that it would be learned could be found in this data. Further, some of the features of difficulty in word learning, such as cognateness, could not be found to affect the learning of words on this course. Her learners were very young, 6 or 7 years old, and perhaps one of the lessons to be taken from this study is that the models of learning we are familiar with for adult learners need to be reassessed with these young learners in mind. But also, this research suggests that the oral language learners are exposed to is a rich source of vocabulary for learners, but that we know very little of how learners interact with this material.

Conclusion

A lot of information has been presented here, and yet there are still a lot of unknowns. We have very little good information on the vocabulary loading of course books and classroom talk, the organisation of this vocabulary and how these factors relate to learning. It is an area that cries out for more systematic study. In the absence of this, we are left with largely unsupported assertions of how things should be done: repetition is good or even essential, and introducing 8 to 12 words per lesson is about right. However, these issues are complex, and calculating the effect of the course book and teacher talk on vocabulary learning is clouded by other factors that can affect whether the vocabulary presented to learners is learned and about which we also have very little knowledge. Some potentially useful pieces of information have emerged, however.

In real course books, it seems, there is lots of variety. These books can present a surprisingly large amount of vocabulary, thousands of words in a short space of time even to absolute beginners. And they can also choose from a very wide variety of thematic areas, so the most frequent words are often taught alongside substantial amounts of infrequent vocabulary. If this seems far from ideal, then the product of these books, vocabulary learning by students, suggests otherwise. At least in EFL it seems that the learners appear able to soak up this vocabulary, and the more they are exposed to, the more they learn and the more progress they make in English. This sort of volume and variety of vocabulary exposure seems to allow good students to be challenged and to progress well, without absolutely overwhelming any but the least able. Successful EFL course books and teachers appear to strike a balance between frequent and non-frequent vocabulary that allows learners to progress well. That balance appears to be about 50% frequent vocabulary and 50% infrequent thematic material in the earliest course books. This balance allows the text to retain the characteristics of normal language at least as far as coverage by the most frequent words is concerned. The rather less successful French foreign language course books examined here appear to present similar proportions of frequent and infrequent lexis and it is not clear why, from the point of view of the vocabulary content of teaching, why vocabulary uptake should be so markedly different.

Successful courses, also, do not recycle all their vocabulary systematically as is widely thought essential for learning. While there is a relationship between word repetition and learning, it appears simply impractical to recycle every vocabulary item the required number of times and still retain a useful course book. Despite the relationship between repetition and learning, it seems that large numbers of words that are presented only once are still learned. This may be related to the characteristics of the words themselves and some may be especially memorable, but may equally be related to other things that successful learners do, often outside the classroom, such as learn wordlists.

Successful course book series also manage the addition of vocabulary and introduce progressively greater and greater loadings of infrequent vocabulary, so the texts that learners use become progressively more and more lexically sophisticated. Elementary texts may be relatively unsophisticated while more advanced texts might be quite challenging even for native speakers. This last observation may seem like obvious good sense, you do not want to overwhelm beginners, but it challenges too dogmatic an adherence to authenticity of materials in the classroom. Authentic materials can, of course, be used in the classroom, but it would be an advantage if they were selected with care for the right vocabulary characteristics.

For once, it seems that Harold Palmer was wrong, and good books can vary enormously in order to reflect the interests of learners, and there is no ideal sequence for all vocabulary learning. It seems likely that functional and structural vocabulary must be taught early, but most vocabulary items can be added at whatever time meets the interests of the students. Perhaps good growth in vocabulary is a product of this variety.

The under-researched aspect of teacher oral input suggests that this too can be much richer than we have suspected, but it is still not clear how oral and orthographic lexical presentation can be most beneficially combined to expedite learning. Interestingly, the probably rather good teacher Donzelli (2007) investigated was able to mirror the frequency of the textbook input with equivalent oral input, and adjust the amount of oral input to mirror the new materials in the textbooks. She provided a surprisingly rich lexical environment for her learners. Her learners were successful and perhaps this practice was, in part, responsible.

Overall, the impression is given that a quality classroom learning environment can contribute very directly to the learning of vocabulary and to very large amounts of it. Harris and Snow (2004) and R. Ellis (1994) are probably wrong to suggest that the classroom plays little or no part in vocabulary learning. For many learners, it seems that the classroom and textbook are very important in their input and can be a condition of success. This does not mean, necessarily, that there is no learning outside the classroom and from oral and informal input. Chapter 10 investigates what can be learned from this type of material.

Chapter 10
Vocabulary Acquisition and Informal Language Input

This chapter tries to answer the question of what vocabulary learners learn from non-formal language activities: the kind of incidental learning and exposure that some writers think is so important. The measurements we have of learning in these contexts suggest that:

- *Learners may get very little from unfocused and undirected work of this kind.*
- *But learners can learn large amounts of vocabulary from well-structured and focused activities.*

The same might be reported of study abroad programmes where, despite the enormous opportunities for communication and learning:

- *learners can avoid language use and learning in some circumstances;*
- *but may benefit when placed in more conducive circumstances.*

The opening of the last chapter reported a number of assertions that vocabulary can be learned implicitly. R. Ellis (1994: 24) even reports that 'most L2 vocabulary is learned incidentally, much of it from oral input'. This chapter will examine the measurements of vocabulary learning we have, where the learners have been engaged in non-formal language activities, outside the classroom. This will help determine whether incidental exposure really is as effective as these assertions appear to suggest, and whether the large lexicons necessary for fluency in a foreign language are gained this way.

Tackling the question of whether this type of learning is effective is made difficult by the confusion of terminology that surrounds it. As Rieder (2003) points out, in language learning, the concept of implicit learning is insufficiently well distinguished from the concept of implicit learning in psychology. In psychology, there is a crucial distinction made between implicit and explicit learning, where implicit learning requires the absence of conscious operations in the learning process; the learner by this definition is not deliberately testing a hypothesis or searching for a structure in the language he or she is exposed to. This is something which language learning terminology often ignores. Language teaching further blurs the distinction between incidental and implicit learning with the two terms often used almost interchangeably. Thus, Kerka (2000) describes incidental learning as 'unintentional or unplanned learning', an explanation which might include learning that is implicit in the psychology sense, and involving no deliberate intention to analyse language or to learn, as well as learning which might be intentional on the part of the learner even if not part of an organised syllabus. Snow (in Harris & Snow, 2004: 55) is even clearer in connecting incidental learning with implicit learning, in the psychology sense, when he contrasts the explicit teaching of words by the teacher with the 'subconscious absorption of words as they crop up incidentally' in other activities. These definitions seem to imply that one way to learn vocabulary in a foreign language, even a good way, is through something akin to purely passive exposure, where the learners need not be expected to take much part in the learning process. The learning that occurs is a side-effect of another activity and the learners themselves may even be unaware of learning taking place.

Perhaps a more widely accepted definition would be Huckin and Coady's definition, where incidental vocabulary acquisition is the learning of new words as a by-product of a meaning-focused communicative activity, such as reading or listening, and interaction. It occurs through 'multiple exposures to a word in different contexts' (Huckin & Coady, 1999: 185). The learner is clearly active in this, but it is a moot point whether the learner is engaged in the conscious operation of searching for structure or testing hypotheses, where learning would be explicit, or not, where it would be implicit. This has implications for testing and measuring vocabulary knowledge because it has been suggested that different aspects of vocabulary knowledge will be learned differently, some explicitly and some implicitly. N. Ellis (1994a, 1994b) suggests that recognition of the phonological form, for example, might be acquired implicitly through mere exposure. Learning the meaning of new words, however, would require conscious processing at the semantic and conceptual levels. The form of a word has to be deliberately noticed and connected to meaning. If this were true then measurements of vocabulary knowledge made using passive receptive vocabulary size tests would show considerable vocabulary gains from simple language exposure, while exposure would not yield gains if knowledge were measured by a translation test.

There is an argument that all successful vocabulary learning has to be explicit, given some of the features that are necessary for any learning to take place at all. Laufer and Hulstijn (2001: 3) draw attention to Schmidt's (2000: 9) noticing hypothesis, since 'attention... appears to play a crucial role in both implicit and explicit language learning'. This raises the question of learner motivation. In order to notice anything in a language, the learners must be sufficiently willing to take part in the language activity in a meaningful sense. Laufer (2005: 223) further argues that meaningful input might be a requirement of language learning, but is insufficient for acquiring vocabulary and that *focus on form* is an additional essential component of successful learning. The evidence of studies which investigate the guessing of unknown words suggests that where the meaning of an unknown word is obvious from the context, then the word is not easily recalled subsequently (Mondria & Wit-de Boer, 1991); by moving so directly to meaning, the form of a new word is missed and learning of that new word cannot take place. Laufer and Hulstijn (2001: 11) note several further studies, which suggest that where words have to be looked up, or where attention is paid to the form of the word, then recall is enhanced. Laufer and Hulstijn specifically attempt to identify tasks, or elements of tasks that are conducive to this kind of learning. Like Huckin and Coady (1999), I would expect that motivation and the degree and nature of attention paid to vocabulary would vary not so much according to the activity itself, but according to the intentions of the individual learner, and even according to the individual words and word contexts he or she is exposed to. It is quite impossible to second guess what the learners' intentions really are on every exposure to every word contained in studies of these activities.

Despite the confident assertions that these informal activities, such as reading and listening, result in vocabulary learning, historically, it has been difficult to find unequivocal examples of very large amounts of vocabulary being gained in this way. Horst and Meara (1999) suggest two major factors which plague research in this area. One is the absence of a predictive or explanatory model for vocabulary learning from informal activities, and I think this is, at least in part, addressed in papers such as Laufer's (2005) and Laufer and Hulstijn's (2001), with their consideration of focus on form and task-induced involvement. The second is the absence of an experimental methodology capable of detecting learning if, or where, it occurs. It has already been noted above that the choice of an inappropriate testing method might result in the failure to detect vocabulary learning even where it does occur. Horst *et al.*'s (1998) review of studies of incidental learning concludes that while studies such as Pitts *et al.* (1989), Day *et al.* (1991) and Hulstijn (1992) confirm that some words are learned through reading, the results are actually far from impressive and that uptake is slight; two or three words per reading passage. While most studies drawn on reading uptake from short passages, Horst *et al.* investigated vocabulary uptake from a 21,000 word simplified novel and concluded that an average of only five words were acquired, although there may have been sampling problems with the 45 item test.

Rule of thumb

Little vocabulary is probably learned from genuinely incidental language learning activities.

In a more recent review, Laufer (2005) compares a number of studies where it is possible to separate out on the one hand, tasks which focus on form and, on the other hand, those which focus on meaning and where a surprise vocabulary test follows. To aid comparison, Laufer converts the results, the words learned, into a percentage of the new words to which the learners were exposed. Laufer (2005: 243) is able to conclude that the focus on form is effective and it appears that vocabulary uptake, where a new word is linked to meaning, is generally higher in this condition. She is also able to report (Laufer, 2005: 244) that where vocabulary learning is decontextualised for various focus on form exercises, this contributed to even better vocabulary learning, suggesting that treating words as a specific object of study can be beneficial. In the rush to engage learners in meaningful and communicative activities, it seems that the benefits of traditional vocabulary exercises, such as learning wordlists, have almost been forgotten.

In all of these activities it is hard to infer the scale of learning which is described and what effect it might have on the learning of a whole lexicon. Learning is clearly occurring, which is good, but is the vocabulary uptake observed sufficient to account for the very large foreign language vocabularies that fluent users appear to have mastered? Can the evidence really support the claims that learners grow their vocabularies largely from these sources of input and activity? This is the kind of methodological problem that Horst and Meara (1999) refer to. In this chapter, I intend to cut across the debate as to learners' intentions to learn and the nature of their engagement with the words they are exposed to, and ask a far simpler question. What measurements of learning do we have from these informal language-related activities and where we can estimate the volumes of learning that occur in relation to the expected size of a learner's lexicon? There are some studies that will allow tentative conclusions to be drawn.

Vocabulary Learning from Reading Comic Books

In Horst and Meara's (1999) study, a single, adult, English native-speaking learner of Dutch was asked to read an extended text once a week for several weeks. The learner agreed to avoid all other exposure to Dutch during the period of the study. The text was read through each Saturday and the subject was tested once a week on the following Wednesday. The subject had no formal training in Dutch, but had gained his knowledge from reading and travel. While the subject described himself as at low-intermediate standard, he was an experienced and successful foreign language learner, fluent in several other European languages. The text used for the study was a Dutch version of the Tenderfoot episode in the *Lucky Luke* comic book series (Dargaud, 1976).

While the text itself is some 6000 words long, and a substantial read therefore, the story is told almost entirely through dialogue and pictures with occasional lines of narration. Each picture has, on average, about 15 words providing considerable support to illustrate meaning and help to the language learner. The subject estimated it took him about an hour to read, but 6000 words is a lot to read in a foreign language for an intermediate-level learner and I surmise it took longer and that the subject was rather better than his low-intermediate self-evaluation.

The text was analysed in order to construct a sizable test capable of detecting learning and avoiding sampling problems. The text contained 617 words that occurred once only and 300 of these were chosen for the test. The test was delivered by a computer programme, which randomly presented each of these words in turn. The subject had to respond to these by estimating his knowledge of the word using the vocabulary knowledge scale given in Figure 10.1.

The subject carried out the procedure of reading and testing for eight weeks. Ten weeks after the final week, a ninth test was carried out to check attrition. While this test relied on self-reporting, which appears inherently unreliable, on conclusion of the study, the subject was asked to provide translations of the words he identified as known and, even after a period of several months, could still provide these for over 90% of the words rated at 3 in week 8. The results and the vocabulary gained are reported in Table 10.1.

The study shows, as might be expected, that with each successive week the proportion of words in state 0, not known, goes down, while the words in state 3, definitely known, increases. Many of these words appear to pass through the intermediate states, 1 and 2, on the way to being known. One hundred and forty one of the test words entered state 3 by the end of the study, indicating they had been learned. This is a figure Horst and Meara were able to predict with some accuracy on the basis of the first week's uptake using a model for lexical growth. When extrapolated to the 617 singly occurring words in the text, this suggests that well over 200 words may have been learned over the course of eight weeks. A recalculation of the scale of vocabulary growth in terms of the

---

0 – I definitely don't know what this word means
1 – I am not really sure what this word means
2 – I think I know what this word means
3 – I definitely know what this word means

Figure 10.1 Vocabulary knowledge scale (Horst & Meara, 1999: 316)

Table 10.1 Vocabulary growth from reading a comic book

		No. of words in state			
		0	1	2	3
Pre-test		114	50	54	82
Week	1	81	51	47	119
	2	72	27	37	164
	3	57	33	37	173
	4	48	30	41	181
	5	40	30	39	191
	6	43	26	31	200
	7	39	24	28	209
	8	30	20	27	223

Source: Horst and Meara (1999: 319)

time spent on the activity suggests that learning may have been of the order of 30–36 words per hour (Milton, 2008: 230). This may be an underestimate, as this count excludes words that occurred more than once in the text. A proportion of these are also likely to have been unknown to the learners at the start of the project.

There are several interesting features to this study. One is that it involves the reading of a substantial text rather than the short texts available for intensive study that form the basis of most estimates of vocabulary learning from reading. Another is that it involves the reading and rereading of a text several times so that singly occurring words in the text should have been encountered eight times in the course of the study. This is not normal practice in most modern language teaching methodologies, but repetition is an important factor in learning and this activity has clearly provided it. The size of the text involved has meant that the learner can return to the text several times and take something new from it each time. Table 10.1 shows that week after week, the subject was learning new vocabulary missed in the previous readings. While the greatest gains are to be found at the outset of the study, substantial learning continued to occur over the full eight weeks of the study. The result is that it appears that hundreds of words have been learned from a reading activity, compared with the handful of words which are reported in most reading studies. An uptake rate of over 30 words per hour forces a rethink about the scale of the challenge facing language learners in developing the vocabulary size necessary for fluency. At this rate of vocabulary learning, a fluent user's lexicon of several thousand items becomes a realistic target within the confines of a few hundred hours of formal classroom instruction with added reading activities; something that seemed less likely when only uptake in class was considered.

This study has used a methodology which asked the subject to identify words and self-assess the degree to which they were known. It might be thought that this methodology is picking up on the ability to recognise the form of the word, as N. Ellis has suggested might be possible from purely passive exposure, and fails to reveal any deeper and more useful learning. However, the Vocabulary Knowledge Scale was devised to allow greater depth of knowledge to be investigated and the translation test suggests that the learning that has occurred is deeper than passive word recognition. As a result of this activity, learning is more complete and includes meaning.

The study also includes an attempt to model attrition and the degree to which words, once learned, remain in the mental lexicon. As time passes, it must be expected that some of the items gained from the activity will drift out of memory and will be lost. After a 10-week gap from reading *Lucky Luke*, the subject retook the test and 198 words remained in state 3, definitely known, which suggests about 10% of the words were lost. Using the same model, Horst and Meara suggest that, without further Dutch input, attrition would continue for a time, but stabilise at a point where about 127 of the learned words remained in the lexicon. Both of these figures suggest that the learning that occurs is far from ephemeral.

There are caveats to be considered in this study. One is the nature of the learner, who was clearly very good indeed having already mastered several European languages. This learner would almost certainly have made impressive vocabulary gains from almost any kind of language exposure, including formal classroom study, and the scale of his achievement is unlikely to be typical of a more average learner, such as a teenager learning at school. A second is the nature of the task and the learner's commitment to it. The nature of the reading task with a weekly vocabulary test attached to it makes this a far remove from the types of implicit or incidental learning discussed at the opening of this chapter. The learner was not imbibing vocabulary sub-consciously, but must have become heavily focused on the words of the text in addition to the general story line. This type of learning appears much closer to the focus on form condition that Laufer (2005) discusses. It requires sufficient motivation and effort from the learner to commit to several hours study a week, and the weekly reading and testing format means that it is controlled and monitored, if only by the learner himself. However, the activity appears to have been sufficiently interesting and enjoyable for the subject to willingly do this.

Vocabulary Learning from Singing Greek Songs

The vocabulary gains from the Horst and Meara study are sufficiently impressive to merit replication. If vocabulary learning on this scale can be routinely derived from relatively informal language activities, then the potential obstacle of building large vocabularies can be viewed in a very different light. One attempt I have made to see whether large vocabulary gains can be made relatively informally, uses song as the basis of the language input and is reported in Milton (2008).

In this study, a single, adult, native-English-speaking learner of Greek was asked to listen to a CD of Greek songs once a week for several weeks. The learner agreed to avoid all other exposure to Greek during the period of the study. The songs were listened to with the accompaniment of a set of Greek lyrics and a fairly literal English translation that made the meaning of the lyrics plain. The subject had attended evening classes in Greek and rated himself as at high-beginner or low-intermediate standard, and was an experienced serial language learner with 'get-by' capability in several languages. The text used for the study was a CD of songs taken from Greek films of the 1950s and 1960s, selected because the subject liked them and because many of the songs were slow ballads where the words could be clearly distinguished and sung along with. A second CD of songs where the learner knew only 60% of the tokens was rejected because the subject felt it was too difficult to take anything from. The Greek lexis of the songs comprised 2225 tokens and 574 unlemmatised types. In a preliminary test, the subject was asked to identify the words he knew using the Vocabulary Knowledge Scale in Figure 10.1. This showed that the subject knew 1765 (79%) of these tokens and 260 (45%) of the types in the corpus. Three hundred and fourteen types fell into states 0 and 1, not known by the subject, and 100 of these were selected for testing. In a pencil and paper test, the subject was presented with each of these 100 words in turn and asked to indicate on the Vocabulary Knowledge Scale how well they were known.

In addition to the weekly tests to estimate the vocabulary added to the subject's lexicon, three additional tests were added. In week 4, test of a different 100 words was added to gauge whether the learning that occurred was the product of the listening activity alone or the extra focus and repetition of the particular words which the test included. A translation requirement was added to the Vocabulary Knowledge Scale in week 4 to check the accuracy of the subject's self-evaluations and to check whether meaning was being learned in addition to the recognition of word form. Finally, a post-test was administered three months after the end of the study to check retention and attrition of the items learned. The results obtained from this study are given in Table 10.2.

Table 10.2 Vocabulary growth from listening to Greek songs

		No. of words in state			
		0	*1*	*2*	*3*
Pre-test		93	7	0	0
Week	1	77	1	7	15
	2	65	6	7	22
	3	59	4	4	34
	4	43	3	4	49
	5	43	3	1	53
	6	40	4	0	56
	7	33	3	0	64
	8	22	1	0	77
Post-test		54	1	4	41

As in the Horst and Meara study, each successive week the proportion of words in state 0, not known, goes down, while the words in state 3, definitely known, increases. This learner made little use of the possibility for intermediate levels of knowledge and decided that, overwhelmingly, words were either known or not known. This feature is noted in Chapter 7, and it may be that the scale functions, in effect, as a binary Yes/No test, however, Grabe and Stoller (1997: 114) suggest that it is not that these states do not exist or are not used, but that, for some learners, words pass through them very quickly. By the end of the eight-week study, 77% of the words that were not known at the outset, fell into state 3. If extrapolated to all the unknown words in the text, this suggests a volume of a rate of learning similar to the subject in the *Lucky Luke* study; over 200 words learned at a rate of over 30 words per hour spent on the activity.

It was unclear from the original Horst and Meara study how much of this learning was due to the presentation and repetition of words in the texts which were being used, and how much additional learning was being generated by the tests which focused on particular words in the texts and gave them additional repetition and prominence. The second test in week 4, in which a different set of unknown words from the text was also tested, helps to provide an answer to this. Words that were tested were only marginally better recognised by the subject than those that were not tested; 49% for tested words and 48% for untested words. This suggests that the presence of a vocabulary test each week, focuses the learner's attention on the lexis of the texts being studied, rather than on the lexis of the test. Learning is not restricted, or even concentrated, on the words in the test.

As in the original, this study included a translation test as a check on the accuracy of self-reporting and a check on whether the exposure had resulted purely in recognition of form or in deeper learning of meaning. Again, the results are strikingly similar to Horst and Meara's original. The subject was able to provide translation equivalent to over 90% of the items in state 3. The post-test suggested, however, that retention for this subject was not as strong as in the original with only 41% of items staying in state 3, three months after the input had finished, a drop of over 40%. It appears that the words that were retained had some very particular characteristics in the input. An analysis of the uptake and attrition of the words in the study, in relation to their frequency of occurrence in the text, is shown in Figure 10.2.

Words that occurred four times or more in the text tended to be noticed and learned rather more quickly than those that occurred less frequently. The relationship between repetition and learning has already been noted in the previous chapter. However, there is a striking difference in the rate of attrition. The words repeated four times have a 100% retention rate even after three months with no Greek input at all, while those repeated less often are more likely to be forgotten. The relationship between long-term retention and repetition in the text is very striking and appears to be an almost straight line relationship.

Rule of thumb
Multiple repetition may not help the initial learning of words, but may help them stay in the memory after learning.

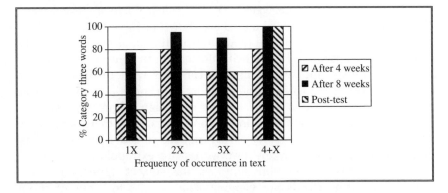

Figure 10.2 Frequency and vocabulary uptake (Milton, 2008: 231)

It is not clear whether the difference in attrition is a feature of the particular learner's experience, or is a product of the song method, or the subject matter of the songs. It seems quite likely, however, that if other language input had continued in this period, even if it were different, through a regular class for example, then vocabulary loss might have been different. Nonetheless, the conclusions to be drawn from this study are broadly those to be gained from Horst and Meara's original. It appears that informal input of this kind can produce very considerable vocabulary gains over several weeks, where the material is graded to provide sufficient opportunity for this, and where the learner is sufficiently engaged in the activity to put in the time necessary for such learning to occur.

Vocabulary Learning from Watching DVDs with Subtitles

In a further study reported in Milton (2008), the same subject from the study in learning from Greek songs, subsequently took part in a further replication where the input used subtitles in Greek to a film on DVD. In this reworking of Horst and Meara's (1998) study and the previous study, the subject selected a DVD of *Xena Warrior Princess* to form the basis of language input. The learner watched the film with English audio and Greek subtitles, and the film was paused when required to allow the subtitles to be read. The film lasted about 100 minutes, but with pauses for reading, winding and rewinding, the exercise of watching this film took about two and a half hours per viewing. The Greek subtitles contained 2390 tokens which, given the two and a half hour exercise, represents a less dense exposure to the foreign language than in the previous studies. A pre-test on the Greek lexis identified the numbers of known and unknown words. Three hundred and eighty two separate lemmatised types, occurring once only in the text, were unknown to the learner and 100 of these were selected for testing. The learner watched the film and was tested once a week for four weeks. The 100 test words were tested using Yes/No format. The results obtained are shown in Table 10.3.

Film is a somewhat different medium from the songs and comic books of the previous two studies. Much information in film is conveyed by image and music, and whole minutes can pass without dialogue as a scene is set or some visual action unfolds. Both songs and comic books seem to be more dense in the occurrence of foreign language vocabulary presented in speech bubbles or in the song lyrics. Nonetheless, as in the previous two studies, the exercise has produced considerable vocabulary gains. If the results from the test words are extrapolated to all the unknown words in the film subtitles, the subject appears to have acquired about 40 words per viewing. This equates to a rate of about 16 words per hour of study.

Table 10.3 Vocabulary growth from watching a DVD with Greek subtitles

		Unknown	*Known*
Pre-test		100	0
Week	1	78	22
	2	70	30
	3	63	37
	4	59	41

Source: Milton (2008: 233)

Rule of thumb

Learners can learn very large amounts of vocabulary from informal tasks they enjoy doing – provided vocabulary learning is a focus of the activity.

Vocabulary Learning from Wordlists

Learning vocabulary from bilingual wordlists is something that has become acutely unfashionable in the UK in recent years, although it was a standard learning technique in my days learning languages at school, and persists in many other countries. The technique is simple enough in essence. Learners take a list of words, usually with their translations alongside, and try to memorise them. For some learners, these lists are easy to remember and have a remarkable power to stay in the memory. A colleague of mine can still recite lists of tree names and the names of birds in English and French nearly 50 years after learning them at school and giving up French thereafter. He has no idea what many of these birds and trees look like, but can remember all the names. Other learners find this kind of task incredibly hard. In a recent study, Fitzpatrick *et al.* (2008) attempt to measure the volume of learning and retention that can take place from a technique of this kind, and also try to measure the effect of progressive loading. Essentially, they are asking the question whether learners become overwhelmed by decontextualised words learned in this way and suffer diminishing returns from the activity.

In Fitzpatrick *et al.*'s study, a learner was asked to learn a vocabulary of 300 high-frequency Arabic words over a period of 20 days. The words were presented on cards that contained the English transcription of the Arabic form of the word, and its English translation. The cards also contained 20 numbered boxes, one for each day of the learning period, so that the learner could indicate on which days she had encountered or revised each word. She spent a maximum of 30 minutes each day on the learning task and was expected to learn 15 new words each day, and to revise any words that she had learned previously. She also kept a diary of her learning and the strategies that she employed, and these records indicate that she spent 25–30 minutes on the task each day. At the end of the learning period, four test sessions were administered, each with two parts: a test of productive knowledge of the 300 words, and a test of receptive knowledge. The tests were translation tasks. The productive knowledge test (recall test) was taken first, with the learner being asked to provide the Arabic translation (transcribed in Roman script) of English cues. In the receptive test (recognition test), English transcriptions of Arabic words were given and the learner provided the English translation. The tests were administered immediately after the last learning session, and two weeks, six weeks and ten weeks after the first test. A summary of the results of this test is given in Table 10.4.

What emerges from this data is that the learner had little difficulty in acquiring almost all of the 300 words presented to her, and she was able to retain these words as long as she was allowed to revisit and rehearse them. The expectation that the cumulative effect of learning a new set of words, day after day, would eventually cause a drop off in performance does not seem to have been fulfilled. However, as in the Horst and Meara (1999) and Milton (2008) studies reported above, there is some evidence that once revisiting and rehearsal stops, there is attrition. Of the 286 words that the subject recognised immediately after the learning period, only 219 were still recognised after 10 weeks. There is some evidence that the number of words recognised at this point is beginning to plateau out, suggesting that the words that remain after this period of attrition will remain fairly permanently in memory. For productive vocabulary, as might be expected, rather fewer words are initially retained, with just over half of the 283 words correctly produced at the end of the learning period and only 149 words still capable of being recalled after 10 weeks. Matrix modelling suggest that long term, about 78% of the 300 target items would be retained receptively and about 35% productively. If that last figure seems disappointingly small, remember that the studies in Chapter 6 suggest that the relationship between productive and receptive vocabulary size is generally of this order.

Table 10.4 Number of correct responses at four test times after wordlist learning

	T1	*T2*	*T3*	*T4*
Recognition test	286	262	221	219
Recall test	283	191	135	149

The rates of learning reported here are very similar to those reported in the previous studies, at something like 30 words per hour if extrapolated up. Fitzpatrick *et al.* conclude that wordlist learning, far from being an old-fashioned and outdated technique, appears to be a very valuable way of progressing to the levels of vocabulary needed for threshold communication and beyond.

Rule of thumb
Far from being outmoded and ineffective, the learning of lists of translation pairs can be very effective in acquiring large amounts of vocabulary very quickly.

Vocabulary Learning on Study Visits Abroad

The benefits of living or working in the country where the foreign language you are learning is spoken, are thought to be so self-evident that they require almost no explanation or investigation. It is almost an article of faith. Snow (Harris & Snow, 2004: 78), for example, comments, 'a[n overseas] visit does indeed contribute to vocabulary extension', although he offers no evidence for this. But it is easy to suggest what, in theory at least, the benefits should be. It should provide ample exposure to the foreign language, as everyone will speak the foreign language and all interactions will be carried out in it. There should be the opportunity for extensive meaningful interaction both informally in everyday life, going shopping, getting tickets, doing the laundry, or socialising with native speakers, and formally through the lectures and tutorials that often form part of the exchange. The volumes of interaction and the intensive nature of exposure that are possible on an overseas trip cannot possibly be recreated in the few hundred hours that may be available for foreign language classroom learning. The benefits are so obvious, it seems, that it has not been necessary to investigate or measure them. Prior to Milton and Meara's (1995) study, only two published investigations into language learning on foreign placements could be unearthed from the literature and neither addresses questions of vocabulary acquisition.

The 1995 study, however, was directly concerned with assessing the volume of English as a foreign language (EFL) vocabulary growth that students from various European countries experienced during an academic year's exchange in a UK university. Fifty-three students on European LINGUA and ERASMUS exchange programmes were tested in October on entry to the UK university for their year's study, and then again in April the following year as the academic year drew to a close. There was no attempt to pre-select students by English language level for these exchange programmes, although, in principle, the students should have had a language level making them capable of studying alongside English native-speaking home undergraduates. Most were taking degrees in management science and attended classes in this subject. In practice, the students displayed a wide variety of language levels, from intermediate up to highly advanced.

The students were tested with Meara and Jones's (1990) Eurocentres Vocabulary Size Test, which estimates learners' knowledge of the most frequent 10,000 words in English. A score of about 10,000 words is considered to indicate native-like standards of knowledge by its authors. Given the nature of the test, it was thought that the difference between the entry and exit scores on this test should give a good estimate of the growth in vocabulary size, within the 10,000 word range, that the learners experienced during their stay in the UK. In addition, the students provided details of the number of years they had spent learning English prior to arrival in the UK, the hours they spent studying while at university in the UK, their native language, and their friendship patterns while in the UK.

Milton and Meara express the results of this investigation in two ways. One is as an estimate of mean vocabulary growth in the six months stay in the UK, which can be compared with mean vocabulary growth for the same period prior to arrival on exchange. The results are summarised in Table 10.5.

The figure for vocabulary growth while at school and prior to the exchange suggests an annual vocabulary growth of about 500–600 words per year, which is similar to the figures for annual growth that have emerged in earlier chapters in this book. It is a rate of progress that allowed them, over a period of years, to become sufficiently able and communicative to study through the medium of English at university in the UK. The period on exchange in the UK, however, produced much greater gains, and students on average gained 1325 words in the six months of their exchange visit, which suggests that vocabulary learning might be in the region of some 2600 words per year. This rate of progress is similar to the figures that emerge from the literature for first language vocabulary growth and which Nagy and Herman (1987: 21) describe as 'astounding' and 'a tremendous volume of word learning'.

Table 10.5 Comparison of vocabulary growth rates of six-month periods at home and on exchange

	At home	*On exchange*	*% Increase*
Mean vocabulary growth	275	1325	23
SD	88	1058	

Source: Milton and Meara (1995: 22–23)

The additional information collected from the students in this study suggested how the learners achieved such progress. No significant relationship could be found with the scores the students provided for their friendship patterns. It seems that mixing with native speakers, even having a native-speaking girl or boy friend does not link with vocabulary improvement. These learners tended to mix with other non-native speakers, as friendship patterns would already be well established among home students at the host university, by the time the exchange students arrived. Nonetheless, among these learners from such a heterogeneous language background, it seems that English was the preferred common language and learners may have had the opportunity to use their English much more than they would at home, despite the absence of native speaker contact. Significant correlations, albeit modest in scale, were found with the learners' estimates of the time they spent in formal and informal study. This will have included time spent in lectures, carrying out background reading and in completing written assignments. One feature of the students' study programme that is worth emphasising is that they were all voluntarily attending two hours a week of explicit EFL classroom instruction and were preparing for Cambridge First Certificate and Proficiency examinations. For these learners, it seems that it was the formal study element, both studying the language and studying in the language, which predicted progress, rather than the degree of informal language exposure and use.

It may be that this figure for vocabulary growth, large though it is, is actually an underestimate since, as with any frequency-based test, there may be ceiling effects. A second presentation of the results hints at this. Milton and Meara (1995: 25) note that the vocabulary level the students displayed at the beginning of the exchange programme can explain half of the variation in vocabulary growth. The lower the vocabulary knowledge in October, the more vocabulary they appeared to learn. This relationship can be seen in Figure 10.3, where vocabulary growth scores have been divided into groups by score on entry.

Not only do students who enter with the lowest vocabulary scores make the most gains, it seems, but students who enter the university with scores of 8000 or more make no measurable progress at all. The inverse relationship between the entry vocabulary score and vocabulary growth is almost a straight line. It might be thought that university level courses in subjects such as Business Studies would contain a high preponderance of infrequent, technical and semi-technical vocabulary, and that students whose vocabulary levels are already substantial would concentrate their learning in these areas. Ceiling effects are not the only factor that might explain this effect, however, and there is evidence that the lexical sophistication of Business Studies course books and journals is not that large and that business-related courses are not heavily loaded in

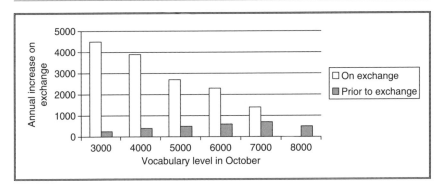

Figure 10.3 Vocabulary increases divided by starting vocabulary

this way with infrequent vocabulary. An analysis of the content of this material suggests that a knowledge of the most frequent 6000 words only would be sufficient to provide 95% coverage of almost all business-related course books and journal articles in half the business-related subject areas (Milton, 2007b). An alternative explanation is that learners who have high vocabulary levels no longer need to expand their vocabulary breadth for the purposes of communication even in the relatively sophisticated domain of academic discourse. A knowledge of 8000 of the most frequent 10,000 words in English suggest knowledge approaching native-like standards. If vocabulary knowledge is increasing for these students, it is quite likely that it is in the areas of depth or fluency.

Rule of thumb
An educational exchange can lead to large vocabulary gains, but these are probably conditional upon: learners being fully integrated into an L2 speaking community, language support being offered, the presence of formal learning goals that focus learners' attention on language.

A study visit abroad does not inevitably lead to vocabulary gains, however. The study of the lexical growth in students of French as a foreign language passing through UK school and university reported in Milton (2006c) contains a cohort of learners who are equivalent to the EFL learners in the Milton and Meara study. These learners attended university in the UK to study French either as a single or a joint honours subject and, as part of their course, took a period abroad at universities in France under the ERASMUS exchange programme. The growth in vocabulary for these students is shown in Figure 10.4.

The university students in this study gained approximately 500 words per year on a test of the 5000 most frequent words. At the end of their

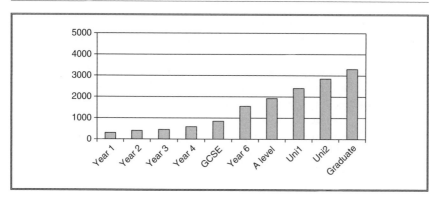

Figure 10.4 Vocabulary growth through the UK school and university system (Milton, 2006c)

second year of university study, when they were preparing for their intercalary year, these students had average vocabulary sizes of 2900 words. Students who had completed the intercalary year and who were graduating had average vocabulary scores, on the same test, of 3300 words. If learners continued after the intercalary year to make the kind of progress they did before the year abroad, then it appears that vocabulary growth during this year was almost zero. From these figures, it is hard to discern any gain at all from the intercalary year, let alone increases on the scale that the EFL students in the UK exhibited. This is not an isolated observation and David (2008a) reports almost identical figures for the students she studied passing through university.

There may be several reasons why this result may have been obtained and they suggest that this area of language study for learners is well worth investigating in greater detail. One possibility is that the differences between French and English, described in Chapter 3, mean that there is less need for learners of French to gain the large vocabularies that academic English students require. The test used was also different with a ceiling of only 5000 words rather than the 10,000 that the original study of EFL learners used. However, whatever the impact of these factors, it seems unlikely that almost no progress in terms of vocabulary development is visible. A rather more obvious explanation of the difference lies in the experience of the learners. While questionnaire data from these learners was not collected, we have plenty of anecdotal evidence to fall back on. It seems that like their EFL counterparts, these learners were unable, as a rule, to break into the already established friendship system that existed in their host universities and that they mixed predominantly with other non-native speakers. However, the common preferred language was again English, so these learners will not have had the amounts of informal foreign language use which the EFL learners had during their year abroad. It appears too that the learners in France are not routinely provided with formal language instruction leading to examinations, nor were they required to attend lectures and complete assignments for credit, in the way the EFL students were. Their French language level, which appears quite modest, may have made this impossible for them to do in many cases. It seems likely that despite being in France, these students experienced a far less rich foreign language environment than their counterparts in the UK, and one less conducive to learning. It seems that living and even studying in a foreign country need not lead inevitably to language progress.

Conclusion

The principal conclusion that emerges from the kind of studies reviewed here is that learners can acquire very large volumes of vocabulary from language activities even if they are relatively informal and are conducted outside the classroom. But none of the successful activities appears to resemble the kind of 'sub-conscious absorption of words' that Snow (Harris & Snow, 2004: 55) describes; rather, learners have been deliberately targeting vocabulary or general language development. The key factor appears to be that of time. Successful learners here have chosen to devote many hours, in addition to classroom interaction, engaged in a meaningful foreign language activity with a focus on learning something useful. It should not be surprising if these learners are more successful in the long run than those who only attempt to learn vocabulary in class where the time available is much more restricted and much of that time is devoted to other aspects of language learning. But, a goal of language learning has to be building a vocabulary large enough to communicate successfully, and informal activities of the kind described here can be very successful for dedicated and able learners. It is now possible to hypothesise how foreign language learners can gain the very language volumes of vocabulary that enable them to become fluent when classroom time alone does not permit this.

One thing that these studies have in common is their concentration on assessing vocabulary knowledge through tests of the written form of words and not phonological word knowledge. It is conceivable that, particularly for learners on trips abroad whose interaction may be predominantly oral, progress and fluency have been missed by tests of this kind. Differently constructed studies may prove insightful. Nonetheless, it still seems unlikely that R. Ellis's claim (1994: 24) that most vocabulary is learned incidentally and from oral input is incorrect. Studies of incidental vocabulary learning suggest very little gain from such activities and oral language is probably not sufficiently rich for learners to develop a large lexicon. These activities work not least because they involve written texts.

Another feature of these successful activities worth emphasising is the way the foreign language words or texts are revisited several times, even to the point where whole songs are learned verbatim. Modern communicative methodology would hardly endorse this and it is not the kind of thing we routinely train foreign language teachers in, but it is a feature of some more traditional learning. The literature reveals that successful learners can and do use rote learning and learning texts by heart, to help their foreign language development (Stevick, 1989). This kind of revisiting and learning is often based on the study of comparatively large texts, thousands of words, which are far larger than the texts usually selected for intensive study, but the virtue of such texts is the way learners are able to revisit them and still find something new they had not learned before. Learning may appear to drop off with this repetition, but it may contribute to the long-term retention of words.

Finally, the studies reported here have challenged the commonly held idea that a period spent abroad will inevitably lead to foreign language progress and to vocabulary gains in particular. It appears that learners can benefit form this but, as with the other activities in this chapter, they must meaningfully engage with the language and will benefit from some direction and control. The evidence of UK undergraduates abroad suggests that it is all too possible for native English speakers in particular, to avoid using the foreign language with the not unexpected result that language gains are not made. Given the low language levels that many of these learners possess, it seems that more attention needs to be given to the nature of the environment and the activities that these learners are introduced to. Throwing learners into an environment where they understand nothing is unlikely to result in language development.

Chapter 11

Implications for Learning and Teaching: Theory and Practice

This chapter will briefly consider what the measurements of vocabulary reported in this book can tell us about the theories which underpin our understanding of language learning and especially vocabulary learning. In particular, it looks at:

- *The way words are stored in the mental lexicon.*
- *The frequency model that underpins so much vocabulary testing.*
- *The role of individual variation.*

It will also consider what these measurements might mean for the practice of teaching vocabulary.

Measurements of vocabulary knowledge draw on theories and models of the mental lexicon, and how learning occurs, to provide them with validity. We use models, like the frequency model of learning, to justify the selection of the vocabulary we use for testing, and argue that this is a well-directed test that will give us the most useful information in consequence of this. A test that consistently provided incomprehensible results might be drawing on an inappropriate model of learning and be testing the wrong things (of course, there are many other things that might be going wrong). But vocabulary measurements also provide results that can inform us about the validity of these theories and more general theories of language acquisition. If, for example, our measurements of vocabulary acquisition consistently told us that the most frequent lexis does not tend to be learned early in the course of learning, then we would have to reconsider the frequency model. The intention of this final chapter, therefore, is to go back to the starting point of the book and reconsider what the results of vocabulary measurements can tell us about the accuracy and validity of the theories we like to draw on for testing and for teaching.

There are a number of ideas to consider here. One is the question of lexical storage: how do we organise words in the brain and access and use them? Are we really using the right model to test words in the right form to arrive at useful conclusions about learning? A second is the way we rely on frequency data. Researchers in the field of vocabulary draw on this information to an unusual degree and much more so than researchers in other areas of language acquisition. Vocabulary test construction often tends to, if not ignore, then disregard other features of words and of language learning generally, which might affect learning. Are tests constructed in this way really characterising learning satisfactorily? A third question lies in the assumption that all theories tend to make, which is that all learners are likely to behave in the same way. What can vocabulary measurements tell us about the degree of uniformity that learners display in acquiring a language? What can it tell us about the levels of knowledge and performance we should expect of learners?

In this chapter, the intention is to consider each of these questions in turn and then address other points and questions that have also arisen.

Vocabulary Storage and the Definition of a 'Word' for Testing

The most widely used vocabulary tests we have, tend to draw on lists of single words that have been lemmatised or reduced to word families. These words can be tested in isolation or in context, receptively or productively. But the assumption is that if we test one form of a word, then learners are likely to know other forms of a word within the same lemma or word family and this reflects the way second language (L2) learners really handle and store words: as a base form with regular inflections and derivations. Is this right? Do learners really store their words and handle them this way?

Broadly, it seems that they do and the information we have, summarised in Chapter 5, suggests that the most frequent and regular inflections and derivations, which would generally form a lemma, tend to be learned early, while the less frequent derivations are added later in the course of learning. This kind of finding lends credence to broader theories of language learning, such as Pienemann's processability theory. Pienemann's (1998) model, which is based on Lexical Functional Grammar (Kaplan & Bresnan, 1982) and on Kempen and Hoenkamp's (1987) procedural account of language generation, also starts from the premise that the acquisition of grammar is driven by word learning. In his model, access to the lemmas is the first step in the processability hierarchy, without which no further learning can take place. In a recent version of generative grammar, the Minimalist Program, the differences between languages are seen to be mainly lexical in nature. Thus, Cook (1998) suggests that the Minimalist Program is lexically driven; the properties of the lexical items shape the sentence rather than lexical items being slotted into pre-existent structures. This has implications for language acquisition, because it suggests that the task the language learner faces is mainly one of learning the lexicon, both lexical and functional vocabulary. The acquisition of these items in sufficient quantity triggers the setting of universal grammatical parameters. This approach is reflected in the Lexical Learning Hypothesis (N. Ellis, 1997), according to which vocabulary knowledge is indispensable to acquire grammar. These theories place the learning of words at the very heart of language learning; something without which the acquisition of other aspects of language cannot occur. This is a far cry from the structuralist approaches to learning and teaching which I describe in the Introduction to this book, where vocabulary appears to be a thoroughly dispensable part of language learning and where the numbers of vocabulary items taught could be limited to those needed to exemplify language structures.

In the measurements of vocabulary breadth described in this book, one figure has cropped up again and again which gives a sense of scale to the vocabulary learning requirements of language. A 2000–3000 word threshold in English keeps recurring. It gives about 80% coverage of most texts, it is the minimum required to allow learners to gain some kind of gist understanding, and to allow the beginnings of independent communication in authentic language situations. This figure may vary from one language to another, but the implication that syllabuses should teach and require in testing, large volumes of vocabulary is one that is general to all languages. To achieve real fluency, learners needs thousands more words and, in English again, figures approaching 10,000 are common. In this light, some frequently adopted aims of language teaching can be called into question. Teaching the use of compensation strategies, to be used where vocabulary knowledge is deficient, is not an adequate substitute for knowing the vocabulary.

If this seems an obvious lesson to point out, it must be remembered that there are some language syllabuses, and the UK foreign language syllabus in schools is one example, which seem to have forgotten this. Learners are very heavily dependent on the language they are exposed to in textbooks and in class, and there is reason for thinking that UK foreign language learners may have a very odd input compared to the English as a foreign language (EFL) style of input that researchers in the field tend to be most familiar with. Häcker (2008) suggests the input for UK learners may be restricted in scale, and in the structures used. As a colleague, Brian Richards, that pointed out to me EFL texts and old modern foreign language teaching materials in the UK always had substantial texts to read, but a feature of the modern foreign language texts used in the UK is that lengthy texts for intensive study are avoided and very brief spoken exchanges are substituted. This is almost certainly done in the name of authenticity but, paradoxically, the adherence to authenticity has produced a form of language that displays, in terms of word frequencies, something very different from normal language. It seems likely that much high frequent vocabulary and many frequent word forms are missing. Learners cannot learn what they do not encounter. The normal language that learners will need to master to become fluent is not exemplified to them in any quantity and consequently, it is not learned. Authenticity in materials can cover a range of things, and in language teaching there is no substitute for well-written materials for learners that exemplify language within the knowledge limitations of the learners, and challenge them sufficiently to develop. It may be that the UK modern foreign language teaching materials are not providing this well, hence the slow pace of development that is a feature of recent measurements of vocabulary learning in the UK.

Vocabulary Frequency as a Model for Learning

A second assumption that underpins the measurements we have of vocabulary learning, is that learners are especially sensitive to the frequency of words and that this will be reflected in the way words are added to the L2 lexicon. Tests draw on frequency lists because frequent words are more likely to be encountered by learners. To learn a word you have to encounter it, and you are more likely to encounter these frequent words, and encounter them repeatedly, than with less frequent words. This seems very straightforward and yet the idea causes problems to many academic linguists. Tschichold (2007) is a recent example of the validity of frequency information being questioned in relation to language learning and testing. The sort of things that concern Tschichold include the age of the corpus; we still often draw on West's (1953) General Service Word List and an example of this would be the background work on Coxhead's Academic Word List (2002). Questions are also raised about how to handle multi-word units, polysemy and the unit of counting. To this list might be added the influence of word difficulty factors such as length, transparency and cognateness, all of which might be expected to dilute the impact of frequency of the words a learner acquires.

Despite all these concerns, the tests which use frequency information, and I have described many of them in this book, emerge as remarkably robust and workable. It seems that tests based on the lemma as the unit of counting give insightful results which clearly demonstrate a frequency effect: frequent lemmas really are learned in greater numbers than less frequent lemmas. This fact is not influenced significantly by the age of the corpus or its size, once you get beyond about a million words in a reasonably well-constructed corpus. The most frequent words in a corpus are not likely to change radically over time even with the addition of further material to a corpus. The frequency effect even extends, McGavigan (2009) suggests, to highly infrequent multi-word units. Any count that is consistent and based on a reasonably intelligent definition of what is being counted appears to reveal this effect. It is so powerful that word difficulty features, commonly accepted as influential in determining whether or not a word will be learned, fail to significantly impact on this effect (Milton & Daller, 2007). Despite the doubts, the importance of frequency in vocabulary learning is as near to a fact as it is possible to get in L2 acquisition.

One conclusion that is drawn from this, is the importance of repetition to learning or at least learning the type of automatisation of use that is important to fluent language use (Hilton, 2008). Repetition still carries a lot of negative connotations. Hilton (2008: 162) even describes it as 'a pedagogical heresy' to many teachers. This is due to the rather mindless and painful drilling which characterised the audio-lingual method and which many learners felt was so unsatisfactory. Yet, as Vassiliu (2001) demonstrates, good EFL teaching materials do routinely recycle much high frequent lexical material and this material is then learned by most learners.

Perhaps we should be looking more closely, and at a theoretical level, into the importance of repetition in teaching. There is a paradox in asserting the importance of repetition in vocabulary learning because it is clearly impossible to repeat and recycle every item of vocabulary systematically. There is insufficient time, even in the most generously timetabled foreign language class, for this to occur. And yet people do learn large amounts of foreign language vocabulary and do become fluent in using comparatively infrequent words that they appear to have encountered only once or twice. The evidence of successful textbooks is that a wide range of the most frequent lexis is recycled, while the specialist, thematically related and less frequent vocabulary tends not to be. Perhaps this is the best compromise that can be achieved, and allows fairly normal forms of frequent words and their combinations to be encountered and automatised. The less frequent lexis requires more individual input from the learners themselves. Successful learners, it seems, employ strategies, like linkword systems to aid memory, but also create their own opportunities for exposure and repetition; even if it is no more than repeating and learning wordlists. Evidence suggests this can be a very successful way to develop a sizable L2 lexicon.

How Much do Learners Vary in the Vocabulary They Learn?

A third assumption that has underpinned discussion in this book is that all learners are pretty much the same and will follow the same kinds of processes in language learning. We assume that all learners will be better able to learn repeated materials, for example. Of course, this does not have to be the case. One of the features of the measurements of vocabulary learning presented here is the huge variety of learning and progress that learners make. Learners can sit in the same class, be exposed to the same materials, do the same exercises and still come up with very different vocabulary learning outcomes. Some learners make huge progress and others do not. There may be many reasons for this. Learners are differently motivated, for example, and you cannot make anyone learn a foreign language who does not want to. Nevertheless, while we understand something about how groups of learners grow vocabulary in a foreign language, we really do not understand and cannot yet predict how individuals will behave. We have not satisfactorily linked vocabulary learning with explanations of individual differences in learning to produce a model that can account for the variation in vocabulary learning. All we do know is that variation in learning languages is normal and that the kind of variation we see in vocabulary learning, which can be quantified, is enormous. We have some evidence that different aptitudes can predispose learners to acquire subtly different types of vocabulary.

Studies of language learning aptitude studies have a long history, but have rarely been specifically applied to the learning of a lexicon. In Carroll and Sapon's (2002) highly influential Modern Language Aptitude Test (MLAT), aptitude is broken down into four sub-elements: Phonemic Coding Ability, Grammatical Sensitivity, Inductive Language Learning Ability and Rote Learning Ability. The last, Rote Learning, is of interest here because it is tested via a rote memorisation test of vocabulary paired associates: testees are presented with 40 pairs of words, one in the native language and the other in an unknown language, and these must be memorised in a short space of time. Testees are then asked to recall as many of these word pairs as possible. The more that can be recalled by learners, the greater their memory and the greater their aptitude. There is an assumption that people's memory, in particular, will vary and this ought to make for differences in a learning task such as learning thousands of foreign language words. But rote memory ability alone probably cannot explain the nature of variation in vocabulary learning that was reported in Chapter 2, where about 60% of learners produced regular frequency profiles while the remainder produced irregular profiles. The volumes of vocabulary learned could be the same, but the nature of the vocabulary known could vary considerably from one individual to another. Some learners are described as *level 2 deficit* learners, where knowledge of the second 1000 word frequency band is lower than expected, while others have a *structural deficit* and lack knowledge of the most frequent 1000 words. The profiles these learners produce are shown in Figure 11.1 and Figure 11.2.

Milton (2007a) investigated 21 Greek learners who took two tests from the Meara *et al.* (2001) range of aptitude tests. These were LAT_B, a paired associates learning task designed to test memory in language

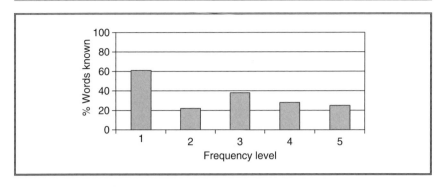

Figure 11.1 Frequency profile illustrating level 2 deficit (Milton, 2007a: 51)

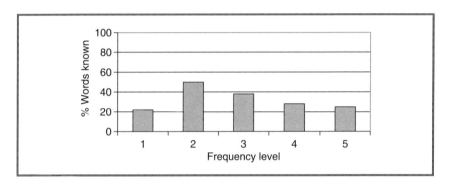

Figure 11.2 Frequency profile illustrating structural deficit (Milton, 2007a: 52)

learning, and LAT_C, a language rule recognition task designed to test inductive and analytic language learning skills. The learners were grouped according to their profiles, 10 normal profiles and 11 level 2 deficit, and their scores on these aptitude tests calculated. Mean scores are presented in Figure 11.3.

It appears that differences in aptitude can influence the nature of the vocabulary that is learned. The difference in the mean score for the memory test is particularly marked and the learners who scored higher on the memory test, LAT_B, tended to display level 2 deficit. Those learners who displayed normal profiles did comparatively less well on the memory test, although their scores on the analytic test were marginally higher. The results suggested that there were both group and test effects that were statistically significant. These results suggest that different learning strengths and styles really can influence the foreign language vocabulary that learners acquire in class, and that this effect is particularly noticeable in the degree to which vocabulary in the

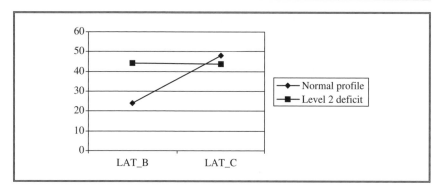

Figure 11.3 Mean scores on aptitude tests for two groups of learners with different vocabulary profiles (Milton, 2007a: 55)

first two 1000 word frequency bands is learned. This being said, it appears that the importance of frequency reasserts itself in the overall profiles that both these types of learners display.

Learners can vary in other ways. One is the way in which learners develop automaticity in the use of the foreign language. For example, Kroll *et al.* (2006) point out that even fluent bilinguals will be slower in picture-naming tasks when compared to monolingual speakers. This is an interesting area of study, as the work here suggests a way to handle individual variation in making sense of the kind of measurements this study produces. Segalowitz (in for example, Segalowitz, 2003; Segalowitz & Freed, 2004; Segalowitz *et al.*, 2004) notes that individuals can vary in the speed and automaticity with which they read and recognise words in their first language (L1), and this has the effect of undermining attempts to make good use of measurements of automaticity in L2 learning. Individual variation in the automaticity of word processing has the effect of disguising the kind of systematic progress that learners will make as they improve in knowledge and fluency in their foreign language. Foreign language learners become more automatic in their language use as they improve, but it seems there is no set level of performance that characterises advanced language users over less proficient users, as even the most able learners will vary enormously in this facet of performance. Segalowitz's way of handling this is to take a measure of learners' automaticity in their L1 to provide a base line against which performance and progress in the L2 can be measured. Learners' progress in their L2 can then be measured against their own L1 performance rather than against a single external standard of performance that may not be appropriate or useful. The results this approach produces appear to make much more sense of learning.

This kind of approach might help us make sense of other aspects in vocabulary learning where variability is a prominent characteristic of testing. Even something like the vocabulary sizes that I have been suggesting are requirements for certain levels of performance, might be reconsidered in this light. We tend to assume that all native speakers have very large vocabularies and that learners will compare poorly with this level of knowledge until such time as they can acquire a large vocabulary. Goulden *et al.*'s figure of 17,000 word families as an average for native speakers tends to be taken as a standard that will characterise all English native speakers, for example. However, my own use of this test suggests there is much, and fairly systematic variation around this figure. Native-speaking undergraduates entering university tend to score about 9000 words on this test, post-graduates about 13,000–14,000 and faculty members over 20,000. Even among our undergraduates, there is variation, as the monolingual English speakers score on average 9500 while the bilingual Welsh-English score about 8000 (remember they will also have, presumably, a correspondingly large vocabulary in Welsh) with a marked deficiency in the area of Coxhead's Academic Word List. But all of these are native speakers who function at a high level through English. And while the figures for the vocabulary needed for coverage and understanding of texts cannot be discounted, perhaps, as with automaticity, we should expect learners to grow vocabularies in a foreign language equivalent in scale to their L1 rather than aspiring to a single set size that even native speakers may not attain in many instances. This would certainly be in line with Fitzpatrick's current thinking on word association tasks.

Individual Variation and the Dimension of Vocabulary Depth

A further aspect of individual variation already touched upon in Chapter 6 is the way individuals handle word associations. This has implications for the way we view word knowledge in the L2 learner and the importance of developing vocabulary depth in addition to vocabulary breadth. The assumption underlying the organisation of the lexicon in L2 learners is that it is quantitatively and qualitatively different from that of native speakers, and that as the learner grows in competence, knowledge and skill, the lexicon will become more native-like. The evidence of Fitzpatrick's (2006) study is that there is probably not a single native-like structure or size to which learners can develop; native speakers will vary in their preferences for associations and their organisation. The analysis of the nature of associations between lexical items (Henriksen, 2008) further suggests that many of these links are not particular to a first or a second language, but are language general, so the task in the L2 is to develop sufficient breadth of vocabulary that these links can be demonstrated. Many of the links being carefully noted and counted in vocabulary depth tests, such as V-States (Wolter, 2005), are unlikely to tell us much about the developing L2 depth dimension. They may inform us about the number of words a learner has, so they can produce the language general associations Henriksen describes, or they may tell us about the way a learner is progressing towards rebuilding their L1 association preferences which, in the absence of detailed information about a learners' L1 association responses, will tell us little about their development.

I think this tells us something about how we should view this dimension of vocabulary depth which may prove to be a less useful idea and less informative than we have hitherto thought. The very wide range of links that are usually included in this dimension may tell us very little about the L2 lexicon, as these can only mimic the L1 lexicon. Testing the existence of these links in the L2 may only tell us whether these words exist in the L2 lexicon and nothing novel about the state of the lexicon. There are other issues, such as the handling of multi-word units which, McGavigan suggests, may be learned and handled in such a way that they are treated as single lexemes and should really be included within vocabulary breadth anyway. From an L2 learning perspective, the interest is really much narrower than most definitions of depth suggest, and focuses only on those aspects where the links are different from the L1. This might mean that depth is usefully restricted to collocations such as those that Gyllstad tests, where your L1 is unlikely to tell you which verb (from *make*, *take* or *do*) you would need to link with *bath*, or connotations where the secondary meanings of words may be different. This, in turn, makes the creation of a general test of vocabulary depth for learners of all languages very difficult.

Individual Variation, Age and Word Difficulty

One final idea that has cropped up in this book but has not been touched on, is the degree to which learners will vary in terms of their age and cognitive development. Traditionally, learners were either mature adults or adolescents in school, but increasingly language learning is being systematically, and not so systematically, introduced to much younger learners. Some of the assumptions we make about the learners themselves and the nature of the learning process ought to change as a consequence.

One very important difference between very young learners and adult learners is the degree of literateness they possess. Adult learners of a foreign language will, for the most part, be skilled and experienced readers who are able to use strategies such as predicting ideas and words that will occur in a text and recognising words by shape rather than by spelling. Young learners will be very different and will be far less fluent both in word recognition and moving from word to meaning. Young learners, it seems to me, are likely to be much more reliant on oral language input than adults. It seems inevitable that these two types of learner will process, learn and store words very differently. It is noted in Chapter 5 that beginners tended to favour phonological word learning over orthographic, suggesting they favour phonological storage. Perhaps part of the underlying issue here is that beginners will tend to be much younger and they have to store new words in a foreign language this way because they lack the armoury of skills and experience to store them orthographically. As learners improve in their foreign language ability, they inevitably become older and better able to handle the orthographic form of words in both or all their languages. The trend that was noted for learners to move from a phonologically loaded to a heavily orthographically loaded lexicon may, therefore, be a feature of age and cognitive development as much as of language level.

The same idea should force us to challenge some of the long cherished notions of what makes words easy or difficult. I have already noted in Chapter 2 that word features such as cognateness and length, assumed to affect difficulty and learning, have proved elusive when their impact on the learning of a whole lexicon is examined. Features that appear important at the micro-level of individual word learning, disappear at the macro-level of the lexicon. If I doubt their importance at any level of learning, there are particular reasons for doubting their importance with very young learners. Cognateness requires learners to have an extensive L1 vocabulary and to have the insight to recognise that a word in the L1 can have a similar translation in the L2 if they choose to set about handling language in this way. I am by no means certain that very young learners handle the vocabulary-learning task with this degree of insight or sophistication and they certainly have L1 lexicons that are still developing and will be much smaller than highly educated adults. All of the theories we use in language learning will need to be rethought if they are to apply to young learners with the same relevance they do to adults.

Implications for the Practice of Teaching Vocabulary

A goal of measuring vocabulary uptake and progress must be to feed information back into the learning and teaching process so that the time spent on these activities can be optimised. The measurements outlined in this book confirm much that would be accepted practice in teaching and confirm what common sense often tells us we should be doing. But, in some instances, it also contradicts long cherished ideas about the learning process.

The principal lesson that emerges from the study of vocabulary learning in foreign languages is that learners need to learn lots of vocabulary if they are to achieve any level of independent communicability. The volumes may vary slightly from one language to another, but thousands of words are needed and it will take hundreds of hours to achieve this kind of learning. It would probably be a benefit to everyone involved in the language learning process if some of these goals were made explicit in courses and syllabuses, so learners can begin to understand where they are in relation to these, rather more tangible goals, of language learning. This seems to be an area where there are no short cuts to learning.

Successful learners, and by implication good courses, manage to organise the acquisition of vocabulary so that it is learned in regular amounts over extended periods of time. It seems to be a feature of successful course books that they include, not surprisingly in light of the above, lots and lots of vocabulary, and new vocabulary is introduced at regular intervals. A feature of successful courses in EFL is that they display great thematic variation and perhaps this allows learners to be engaged and motivated sufficiently to enable learning to take place, as well as providing an opportunity for fresh vocabulary to be introduced. There does not seem to be an upper limit (within reason) to the amounts that can be presented and the volumes that good learners will learn, provided the materials allow at least some of the topics and the vocabulary they contain to be revisited from time to time. Interestingly, a feature of UK modern foreign language books is the way they lack this huge variety of thematic coverage, as well as presenting rather less vocabulary. It may be no coincidence that foreign language vocabulary learning is so problematic in UK schools.

It is a standard of good teaching practice that both the spoken and written forms of new words should be presented to learners and the evidence of real learners shows how important both phonological and orthographic word form knowledge is for success in later examinations. But the evidence also shows that these examinations require, in the long run, rather greater orthographic vocabulary knowledge than phonological for success. It seems to be quite satisfactory for learners to learn merely sight recognition of much infrequent vocabulary.

In the Introduction, I commented that it seems to be a commonly held belief that learners do not retain much vocabulary from what is taught explicitly, from the textbook, in class. This belief is dangerously misleading, as learners seem to learn much of the most frequent vocabulary, and considerable infrequent vocabulary, explicitly from the content of course books. But the books do not restrict themselves only to the most frequent words. A feature of successful course books is that there seems to be an equal mixture of the most frequent (the 2000 most frequent words in corpora) and less frequent thematic materials. It appears as though the volumes and repetition of frequent vocabulary builds up over the years, so learners manage to cover and master most of it. Research also suggests that learners do not acquire words implicitly without conscious effort, as has been suggested, but they can, using informal tasks they like and where vocabulary learning is a target of the activity, acquire huge amounts of words from activities like listening to songs, reading comics and watching films in the foreign language. It has been good practice to advocate these activities for many years, but the research suggest these can be much more effective in vocabulary learning than any of us had really imagined. A combination of good classroom practice and well-directed effort outside class can begin to explain how learners acquire very large vocabularies of thousands of words, so they can achieve functional fluency. The idea that teachers do not have to teach and learners do not have to try to learn vocabulary, however, is nonsense. It requires deliberate effort and considerable time on the part of the learner.

There is very little evidence on what impact the teacher's oral contribution to learning is, but it must be important where this is a prime source of input for the phonological realisation of the words learners are acquiring. Received wisdom says a lexically rich environment is good for learning and Donzelli's teacher, who we think is a very successful teacher, managed to exemplify the words in the textbook and go beyond this to provide a very rich environment (Donzelli, 2007).

Research linking vocabulary size to examinations and the Common European Framework of Reference for Languages (CEFR) is beginning to fit guideline figures for these levels and standards, helping to provide both learners and teachers with clearer goals in managing the learning process. From 2000 to 2500 words (of 5000) in English seems to be a threshold for moving from beginner to intermediate level, where language use can start to become independent. From 6000 to 7000 words are needed for oral fluency and 8000–9000 for written fluency and for attaining the kind of proficiency needed for examinations at the C2 level of the CEFR. In this context, I think there is much to be said for expanding the use of informal and low-stakes testing. The virtue of tests that are quick and easy to administer and which are easy to mark is that the stress, the expense and the disruption caused by high-stakes formal testing can be avoided, while useful feedback about level and progress can still be accessed.

Conclusion

These considerations have suggested that the more we understand of the vocabulary learning process, the more important it seems to be to the whole of the language learning process. Vocabulary learning is not something that can be sidelined, nor can the volume of vocabulary be reduced to minute levels to suit the convenience of a course, if the ability to communicate in the foreign language is the goal of learning. The systematic presentation of vocabulary, and in large quantities, should provide a very different environment for the creation of language syllabuses than has been the case for the last 50 or 60 years, although these insights are taking some time to work their way into the language-teaching mainstream. The measurements we are able to make of vocabulary breadth in particular, suggest that vocabulary might also have an important role to play in language assessment, as growth in vocabulary is a principal factor in the development of communication skills. It should also have a much more important role in assessment, as it can add a degree of objectivity to the language assessment process which is subjective and impressionistic only.

Measurements of vocabulary have also suggested the importance of corpora and frequency studies both in learning and in the design of tests to measure learning. Using frequency-based tests, it is possible to suggest with some confidence what vocabulary knowledge groups of learners will possess after certain amounts of language input or at specified levels of performance. This is reassuring, but should not blind us to the fact that frequency cannot predict or explain all vocabulary learning and, in particular, we have very little to explain how individuals can vary even when groups behave relatively predictably. Perhaps the focus of attention in measuring vocabulary learning should shift from group studies to that of the individual to help address this shortcoming.

I have suggested that the measurements we have of vocabulary have challenged some of the dimensions we have used to try to conveniently characterise vocabulary knowledge. In particular, vocabulary depth may not be so useful or insightful an idea as has become popular in vocabulary studies in the last few years. Consideration of other aspects of vocabulary knowledge and performance would merit more systematic investigation; to pluck just one idea to illustrate this, Kamimoto's (2005) investigations into the degree of confidence learners have in their vocabulary knowledge is the kind of idea that falls outside the usual dimension of lexical knowledge, but where investigation might tell us much about why learners gain the scores they do on vocabulary tests. This leads, I think, to how this might impact on vocabulary teaching.

I have suggested that clear and large-scale vocabulary goals should be a principal feature of any good teaching syllabus. The process of measuring vocabulary learning allows us to be fairly sure that this is a requirement of language learning success. We also have some idea on how the words might optimally be presented to learners and how they have to be engaged with in order to expedite learning. However, the study of the content of course books, and of teacher talk in class, is really in its infancy and we have some way to go before we really understand how and why learners acquire exactly the words they do, while failing to learn others. I am conscious that teachers often feel the need to teach depth of knowledge explicitly and, in light of the doubts expressed about the conceptual validity of the dimension, I would question whether time explicitly spent on these tasks, at the expense of expanding the learners' lexicons, is time well spent. A condition of improving vocabulary depth, however defined, is to increase vocabulary breadth to provide sufficient words for a complex network to develop. An appropriate final word on measuring vocabulary in foreign language learning would seem to be that when in doubt about what to do in class, the teacher cannot go far wrong in teaching more vocabulary.

Appendix 1

Vocabulary Breadth Tests

A note on scoring

Each test presented here contains 20 words randomly selected from each of the first five 1000 word frequency bands found in each language. It also contains 20 false words, which are designed to allow the amount of over-estimation that any forced answer test produces to be calculated and the scores adjusted. To make the contents clear to users, words from the first 1000 word band are presented in column 1 of the test. Words from the second 1000 word band are presented in column 2, and so on. False words are presented in column 6. It is usually good practice to randomise the presentation of test words.

To enable an estimate of the words a learner knows out of the most frequent 5000 lemmatised words in each language, scoring is as follows. Award 50 for each real word checked by the testee and total these to produce a *raw score*. From the *raw score* deduct 250 for each false word, which is checked to produce an *adjusted score* and the estimate of words known.

253

X-Lex Vocabulary Test

Please look at these words. Some of these words are real English words and some are invented but are made to look like real words. Please tick the words that you know or can use. Here is an example.

dog ✓

Thank you for your help.

that	both	cliff	sandy	lessen	darrock
with	century	stream	military	oak	waygood
before	cup	normal	impress	antique	kennard
person	discuss	everywhere	staircase	chart	gazard
feel	park	deny	daily	limp	fishlock
round	path	shot	essential	permission	cantileen
early	tower	refer	associate	headlong	gillen
table	weather	independent	conduct	violent	pardoe
question	wheel	feeling	relative	fade	frequid
effect	whole	bullet	upward	rake	hobrow
market	perform	juice	publish	trunk	candlin
woman	pity	nod	insult	mercy	litholect
stand	probable	gentle	cardboard	anxious	gumm
believe	signal	slip	humble	pedestrian	alden
fine	dish	diamond	contract	arrow	treadaway
instead	earn	press	mount	feeble	sumption
produce	sweat	provide	tube	sorrow	horozone
group	trick	drum	moreover	brighten	hyslop
arrive	manage	reasonable	crisis	dam	manomize
difficult	mud	boil	jug	outlet	horobin

X-Lex Vocabulary Test

Please look at these words. Some of these words are real English words and some are invented but are made to look like real words. Please tick the words that you know or can use. Here is an example.

dog √

Thank you for your help.

had	govern	system	interval	mosquito	warboy
which	industry	position	overcome	proceed	cordonise
little	frequent	knowledge	border	rot	skemp
just	grass	relation	dozen	manly	trudgeon
turn	perform	rabbit	pat	opponent	stillhard
word	plenty	steady	style	sneeze	astell
open	wire	drag	reference	overlook	inertible
wife	worry	steam	previous	enclose	gallimore
take	climb	miserable	manager	screen	surman
main	combine	serve	squeeze	enigmatic	chicorate
bring	thick	vain	upset	wedge	eckett
meet	wet	educate	odd	network	varney
person	collar	prepare	leadership	simplicity	widgery
you	cap	castle	liner	dial	callisthemia
low	excite	sleeve	display	dip	postherent
wrong	faint	recommend	instant	cord	moffant
prepare	artificial	goat	qualify	native	troake
boy	audience	flag	sum	troublesome	waggett
interest	nurse	property	frank	forwards	gorman
girl	pan	envelope	fog	sake	murrow

X-Lex Vocabulary Test

Please look at these words. Some of these words are real English words and some are invented but are made to look like real words. Please tick the words that you know or can use. Here is an example.

dog √

Thank you for your help.

there	inform	law	structure	lobby	oestrogeny
would	origin	amuse	heap	tighten	captivise
because	responsible	director	mystery	compose	spalding
go	warm	criminal	apartment	risk	vickery
bring	rain	inform	snowy	restore	effectory
kind	slip	precious	boundary	sip	claypole
hear	crop	tail	muscle	offense	peritonic
certain	curtain	shoulder	origin	plaster	antile
short	encourage	behave	final	idle	nickling
read	harbour	admire	leisure	creep	clarinate
evening	avoid	collect	scatter	budget	tindle
decide	bone	choice	confuse	sauce	mabey
sudden	cow	curious	select	solemn	obsolation
easy	cream	postpone	performance	plunge	quorant
start	fierce	sense	reaction	item	hammond
peace	fond	likely	volume	harden	mealing
suggest	beat	willing	spill	ensure	gammonary
spend	blade	terrible	decrease	curl	utting
write	pour	dive	calculate	junction	encopulate
build	pump	guest	keeper	roast	ashment

French X-Lex Vocabulary Test 1

Please look at these words. Some of these words are real French words and some are invented but are made to look like real words. Please tick the words that you know or can use. Here is an example.

chien ✓

Thank you for your help.

que	clair	dessus	brouillard	buffle	crétale
dont	octobre	grouper	tante	innocent	abjecter
devenir	complexe	élu	proximité	animation	arguable
ville	bouche	toit	paire	habileté	euplain
nuit	inconnu	classer	habiller	vieillesse	eltrisse
oui	centaine	négliger	déchirer	éther	défaulter
docteur	spécialiser	progresser	vol	régir	formirique
époque	pareil	silhouette	metteur	brûlé	disabilité
malgré	contemporain	avancé	disparition	habillé	signard
marché	accomplir	muscle	montage	originaire	dour
aussitôt	défaut	collaborateur	terrestre	épanouir	écourt
connu	causer	formuler	vigoureux	fronce	gestide
air	revue	tasse	malin	sauvegarder	précont
lendemain	odeur	auditoire	véritablement	comtesse	jerette
ton	peser	précipiter	contribuable	élaboration	entrance
soi	plage	fatiguer	intégral	grillage	diroir
admettre	rendement	judiciaire	pastoral	modéré	lifrer
métro	réduit	signal	requête	radio	expecter
rare	bataille	accrocher	retrait	remise	nadoir
saison	réduction	caché	vernis	adjudant	tirôt

French X-Lex Vocabulary Test 2

Please look at these words. Some of these words are real French words and some are invented but are made to look like real words. Please tick the words that you know or can use. Here is an example.

chien ✓

Thank you for your help.

je	ouest	inspirer	détenir	concurren	fronter
temps	transformer	paquet	accélérer	mouiller	naçon
chaque	formule	mélange	suprême	bavarder	garmente
fin	sien	proclamer	élimination	raser	giste
revenir	faveur	distinction	avenue	divorce	piédeur
fils	agent	débarrasser	purement	pardon	outrir
fort	chasse	perce	rgant	ascenseur	grasper
anglais	observation	creuser	remporter	cravate	triparoix
âge	mériter	fleuve	insuffisant	lucide	joyance
lever	empire	prudence	border	tenture	froise
bientôt	fameux	menace	amiral	hautemen	liabilité
faible	passé	miel	étiquette	pneu	abtrâte
actuellement	immeuble	substance	teneur	célébrité	litéracie
sécurité	courant	logique	chaire	différemment	luvois
prévoir	fonctionner	barbe	fureur	fragment	malignant
entrée	angoisse	décoration	mentir	inconcevable	ministeur
charge	debout	procédure	récolter	pochoir	pédiment
revoir	inétressé	coude	taverne	ruelle	prévieux
presse	extrêmement	psychologie	ultime	succession	permissable
mise	liste	taureau	vernis	tumeur	soupaire

French X-Lex Vocabulary Test 3

Please look at these words. Some of these words are real French words and some are invented but are made to look like real words. Please tick the words that you know or can use. Here is an example.

chien √

Thank you for your help.

de	distance	abattre	absurde	achevé	manchir
aussi	intellectuel	argument	résolution	habitation	vernique
jamais	oreille	teinte	lame	voler	gillais
long	contrôle	publication	juré	financer	ultimation
plusieurs	quantité	congruence	salarié	lassitude	talenté
regarder	catégorie	sportif	exploiter	soupçon	satisfactoire
lequel	maximum	agiter	voulu	cracher	brigeable
divers	futur	équipage	survivre	prêcher	reparlance
début	tromper	baser	pistolet	coiffé	houroux
solution	respect	coutume	entamer	indignation	provocatif
genre	résistance	insecte	analogie	sonde	spirité
existence	solide	tourneé	consommateur	valve	porvent
possibilité	douter	domestique	défi	pelouse	slendre
structure	entretenir	pot	guérir	réflexe	touceul
révéler	bombe	panneau	séduire	attachement	statutorie
source	acteur	déplacement	antiquité	débrouiller	rescuer
participer	aile	trésor	entrevue	équivaloir	aperne
soudain	étoile	étonné	objection	localement	vicinité
style	baisser	outil	pourcent	opportun	introis
procédé	spécialement	financement	taxi	serpent	siéve

Greek X-Lex Vocabulary Test

Please look at these words. Some of these words are real Greek words and some are invented but are made to look like real words. Please tick the words that you know or can use. Here is an example.

αστυνομία √

Thank you for your help.

ο	ανάλογος	ρούχο	περιγραφή	αστυνόμος	αλογομένη
μόνο	έπειτα	πίνω	υπερβολή	προβλεπόμενος	νερολός
μικρός	διεύθυνση	προτεραιότητα	συγκρότηση	ισόβιος	βιλός
πόλη	πλησιάζω	βίος	ψωμί	υπότιτλος	κολίμας
προσπαθώ	ανά	μωρό	βεβαιότητα	χριστιανικός	απέριος
βέβαια	ξεχωρίζω	απόπειρα	σκάζω	διακύμανση	ζόλος
αλλάζω	αδυναμία	χτύπημα	μελωδία	εποπτεία	φελί
διαθέτω	προοπτική	έξοχος	φράγκο	πρωτοτυπία	τρε
εκατομμύριο	προκριματικός	ιδίως	ιθύνων	κατάμεστος	τέτριο
όριο	καθορίζω	μήνυση	ξυλένιος	πρωτοπορία	σερό
βγάζω	μελετώ	ασφαλής	εμμονή	επιμελητής	στρίμα
συγκεκριμένος	μόνιμος	προσόν	αντιληπτός	μεραρχία	σκελίκα
εις	κάμερα	προορισμός	εορτή	δημοτική	ματριτάκι
νιώθω	συμβάλλω	εργάτης	τιμόνι	ξαφνιάζω	αρχεότηχος
υποβάλλω	πλανήτης	εμπνέω	εφικτός	μετανάστευση	τραπεζόλ
κύκλος	ρεύμα	δρομολόγιο	μετανιώνω	κινητήρας	γεραντοπολίο
ουσιαστικά	προσωπικά	συντήρηση	αποδοκιμασία	επιλύνω	δενερή
σπουδαίος	πλάνο	ικανοποιητικός	υπονομεύω	επιζητώ	τεποταπολίο
σωστός	στρατηγική	ψυχρός	λεσχη	ρητορικός	μυχανίο
πείθω	σπάνια	χείλος	διχάζω	αφοσιώνομαι	βατορά

Appendix 2

Lex30

Instructions

Look at the words below. Next to each word, write down any other words that it makes you think of. Write down as many as you can (more than three, if possible). It doesn't matter if the connections between the word and your words are not obvious; simply write down words as you think of them.

1	attack	
2	board	
3	close	
4	cloth	
5	dig	
6	dirty	
7	disease	
8	experience	
9	fruit	
10	furniture	
11	habit	
12	hold	
13	hope	
14	kick	
15	map	
16	obey	
17	pot	
18	potato	
19	real	
20	rest	
21	rice	
22	science	
23	seat	
24	spell	
25	substance	
26	stupid	
27	television	
28	tooth	
29	trade	
30	window	

References

Adamopoulou, R. (2000) The equivalence of a computer-delivered and a paper-delivered Yes/No vocabulary test. Unpublished MA thesis, University of Wales Swansea.

Adolphs, S. and Schmitt, N. (2003) Lexical coverage of spoken discourse. *Applied Linguistics* 24 (4), 425–438.

Aizawa, K. (2006) Rethinking frequency markers for English-Japanese dictionaries. In M. Murata, K. Minamide, Y. Tono and S. Ishikawa (eds) *English Lexicography in Japan* (pp. 108–119). Tokyo: Taishukan-shoten.

Akande, A. (2003) Acquisition of the inflection morphemes by Nigeria learners of language. *Nordic Journal of African Studies* 12 (3), 310–326.

Al-Akloby, S.A.A. (2001) Teaching and learning vocabulary in Saudi Arabian public schools: An exploratory study of some possible reasons behind students' failure to learn English vocabulary. Unpublished PhD dissertation, University of Essex.

Albrechtsen, D., Haastrup, K. and Henriksen, B. (2008) *Vocabulary and Writing in a First and Second Language: Processes and Development.* Houndsmill, Basingstoke: Palgrave.

Alderson, J.C. (2005) *Diagnosing Foreign Language Proficiency: The Interface between Learning and Assessment.* London: Continuum.

Alexiou, T. and Konstantakis, N. (2007) Vocabulary in Greek EFL young learners' course books. Paper delivered to ESCR Seminar: *Models and concepts, practical needs and theoretical approaches in modelling and measuring vocabulary knowledge.* Swansea University, July.

Al-Hazemi, H. (1993) Low-level EFL vocabulary tests for Arabic speakers. Unpublished PhD thesis, University of Wales Swansea.

Anderson, J.R. (1983) *The Architecture of Cognition.* Cambridge, MA: Harvard University Press.

Anderson, R.C. and Freebody, P. (1981) Vocabulary knowledge. In J.T. Guthrie (ed.) *Comprehension and Teaching: Research Reviews* (pp. 77–117). Newark, DE: International Reading Association.

Arnaud, P.J. and Savignon, S.J. (1997) Rare words, complex lexical units and the advanced learner. In J. Coady and T. Huckin (eds) *Second Language Vocabulary Acquisition: A Rationale for Pedagogy* (pp. 157–173). Cambridge: Cambridge University Press.

Barnard, H. (1961) A test of PUC students' vocabulary in Chotanagpur. *Bulletin of the Central Institute of English* 1, 90–100.

Baudot, J. (1992) *Fréquences d'utilisation des mots en français écrit contemporain.* Montréal: Les Presses de l'Université de Montréal.

Bauer, L. and Nation, I.S.P. (1993) Word families. *International Journal of Lexicography* 6 (3), 253–279.

Broeder, P., Extra, G. and van Hout, R. (1993) Richness and variety in the developing lexicon. In C. Perdue (ed.) *Adult Language Acquisition. Volume II: The Results* (pp. 145–163). Cambridge: Cambridge University Press.

Brown, R. (1973) *A First Language*. Cambridge, MA: Harvard University Press.

Burns, G. (1951) An investigation into the extent of first-year vocabulary in French in boys' grammar school. *British Journal of Educational Psychology* 21, 36–44.

Cambridge ESOL (2008) On WWW at http://www.cambridgeesol.org/teach/ ielts/general_training_writing/data/public_writing_band_descriptors.pdf. Accessed 28.8.08.

Carroll, J.B., Davies, P. and Richman, B. (1971) *The American Heritage Word Frequency Book*. Boston, MA: Houghton Mifflin.

Carroll, J.B. and Sapon, S. (2002) *Modern Language Aptitude Test: Manual 2002 Edition*. Bethesda, MD: Second Language Testing, Inc.

Carver, R.P. (1994) Percentage of unknown vocabulary words in text as a function of the relative difficulty of a text: Implications for instruction. *Journal of Reading Behavior* 26, 413–437.

Chaudron, C. (1978) *English as the Medium of Instruction in ESL Classes: An Initial Report of a Pilot Study of the Complexity of Teacher's Speech*. Modern Language Centre, Ontario: Institute for Studies in Education.

Cobb, T. and Horst, M. (2004) Is there room for an AWL in French? In B. Laufer and P. Bogaards (eds) *Vocabulary in a Second Language: Selection, Acquisition, and Testing* (pp. 15–38). Amsterdam: John Benjamins.

Coles, M. and Lord, B. (1975) *Access to English: Starting Out*. Oxford: Oxford University Press.

Collins Cobuild (1995) *Dictionary of Idioms*. London: Harper Collins.

Cook, V. (1998) Review of Skehan, P. (1998) *A Cognitive Approach to Learning Language*. Oxford: Oxford University Press. On WWW at http://homepage.ntl world.com/vivian.c/Writings/Reviews/SkehanRev.htm. Accessed 16.2.7.

Coste, D., Courtillon, J., Ferenczi, V., Martins-Baltar, M. and Papo, E. (1987) *Un Niveau Seuil*. Paris: Editions Didier.

Council of Europe (2001) *Common Framework of Reference for Languages*. Cambridge: Cambridge University Press.

Coxhead, A. (2000) A new academic word list. *TESOL Quarterly* 34 (2), 213–238.

Coxhead, A. (2002) The Academic Word List: A Corpus-based word list for academic purposes. In B. Ketteman and G. Marks (eds) *Teaching and Language Corpora (TALC) 2000 Conference Proceedings* (pp. 73–89). Atlanta, GA: Rodopi.

Daller, H., Milton, J. and Treffers-Daller, J. (eds) (2007a) *Modelling and Assessing Vocabulary Knowledge*. Cambridge: Cambridge University Press.

Daller, H., Milton, J. and Treffers-Daller, J. (2007b) Editors' introduction: Conventions, terminology and an overview of the book. In H. Daller, J. Milton and J. Treffers-Daller (eds) *Modelling and Assessing Vocabulary Knowledge* (pp. 1–32). Cambridge: Cambridge University Press.

Daller, H., van Hout, R. and Treffers-Daller, J. (2003) Lexical richness in spontaneous speech of bilinguals. *Applied Linguistics* 24 (2), 197–222.

Daller, H. and Phelan, D. (2007) What is in a teacher's mind? Teacher ratings of EFL essays and different aspects of lexical richness. In H. Daller, J. Milton and J. Treffers-Daller (eds) *Modelling and Assessing Vocabulary Knowledge* (pp. 234–244). Cambridge: Cambridge University Press.

Daller, H. and Xue, J. (2007) Lexical richness and the oral proficiency of Chinese EFL students. In H. Daller, J. Milton and J. Treffers-Daller (eds) *Modelling and Assessing Vocabulary Knowledge* (pp. 150–164) Cambridge: Cambridge University Press.

Dargaud Benelux (1976) *Lucky Luke: Tenderfoot*. Brussels: Dargaud.

David, A. (2008a) Vocabulary breadth in French L2 learners. *Language Learning Journal* 36 (2), 167–180.

David, A. (2008b) A developmental perspective on productive lexical knowledge in L2 oral interlanguage. *Journal of French Language Studies.* 18, 315–331.

David, A., Myles, F., Rogers, V. and Rule, S. (2009) Lexical development in instructed learners of French: Is there a relationship with morphosyntactic development? In B. Richards, H. Daller, D. Malvern, P. Meara, J. Milton and J. Treffers-Daller (eds) *Vocabulary Studies in First and Second Language Acquisition: The Interface Between Theory and Application.* (pp. 147–163) Houndsmill, Basingstoke: Palgrave.

Day, R., Omura, C. and Hiramatsu, M. (1991) Incidental EFL vocabulary learning and reading. *Reading in a Foreign Language* 7, 541–551.

Diack, H. (1975) *Test your own Word Power.* London: Paladin.

Dolch, E.W. (1927) *Reading and Word Meanings.* Boston, MA: Ginn.

Donzelli, G. (2007) Foreign language learners: Words they hear and words they learn, a case study. *Estudios de Lingüística Inglesa Aplicada (ELIA)* 7, 103–126.

Donzelli, G. (2008) Young learners and foreign language learning: The words they hear and the words they learn. Unpublished PhD dissertation, Swansea University.

Ellis, N. (1994a) Consciousness in second language learning: Psychological perspectives on the role of conscious processes in vocabulary acquisition. In J. Hulstijn and R. Schmidt (eds) *Consciousness in Second Language Learning. AILA Review* 11, 37–56.

Ellis, N. (1994b) Vocabulary acquisition: The implicit ins and outs of explicit cognitive mediation. In N. Ellis (ed.) *Implicit and Explicit Learning of Languages* (pp. 211–282). London: Academic Press.

Ellis, N. (1997) Vocabulary acquisition: Word structure, collocation, word-class, and meaning. In N. Schmitt and M. McCarthy (eds) *Vocabulary: Description Acquisition and Pedagogy* (pp. 122–139). Cambridge: Cambridge University Press.

Ellis, R. (1994) *The Study of Second Language Acquisition.* Oxford: Oxford University Press.

Erigna, D. (1974) Enseigner, c'est choisir: Vocabulaire-verwerving. *Levende Talen* 306, 260–267.

Evans, V. and Dooley, J (2001a) *Upstream Intermediate B2.* Newbury: Express.

Evans, V. and Dooley, J. (2001b) *Upstream Upper Intermediate B2+.* Newbury: Express.

Evans, V. and Dooley, J. (2002a) *Upstream Advanced C1.* Newbury: Express.

Evans, V. and Dooley, J. (2002b) *Upstream Proficiency C2.* Newbury: Express.

Eyckmans, J., Van de Velde, H., van Hout, R. and Boers, F. (2007) Learners' response behaviour in Yes/No vocabulary tests. In H. Daller, J. Milton and J. Treffers-Daller (eds) *Modelling and Assessing Vocabulary Knowledge* (pp. 59–76). Cambridge: Cambridge University Press.

Fitzpatrick, T. (2006) Habits and rabbits: Word associations and the L2 lexicon. In S. Foster-Cohen, M. Medved Krajnovic and J. Mihaljevic Djigunvic (eds) *EUROSLA Yearbook 6 (2006)* (pp. 121–145). Amsterdam: John Benjamins.

Fitzpatrick, T. (2007) Productive vocabulary tests and the search for concurrent validity. In H. Daller, J. Milton and J. Treffers-Daller (eds) *Modelling and Assessing Vocabulary Knowledge* (pp. 116–132). Cambridge: Cambridge University Press.

Fitzpatrick, T., Al-Qarni, I. and Meara, P. (2008) Intensive vocabulary learning: A case study. *Language Learning Journal* 36 (2), 239–248.

Fountain, R.L. and Nation, I.S.P. (2000) A vocabulary-based graded dictation test. *RELC Journal* 31, 29–44.

Gaies, S.J. (1977) The nature of linguistic input in formal second language learning: Linguistic and communicative strategies in ESL teachers' classroom language. In H.D. Brown, C.A. Yorio and R.H. Crymes (eds) *On TESOL '77: Teaching and Learning English as a Second Language* (pp. 204–212). Washington, DC: TESOL.

Gairns, R. and Redman, S. (1986) *Working with Words: A Guide to Teaching and Learning Vocabulary.* Cambridge: Cambridge University Press.

Gass, S.M. and Mackey, A. (2002) Frequency effects and second language acquisition. *Studies in Second Language Acquisition* 24, 249–260.

Glahn, E., Håkansson, G., Hammarberg, B., Holmen, A., Hvenekilde, A. and Lund, K. (2001) Processability in Scandinavian second language acquisition. *Studies in Second Language Acquisition* 23, 389–416.

Goulden, R., Nation, I.S.P. and Read, J. (1990) How large can a receptive vocabulary be? *Applied Linguistics* 11, 341–363.

Grabe, W. and Stoller, F.L. (1997) Reading and vocabulary development in a second language: A case study. In J. Coady and T. Huckin (eds) *Second Language Vocabulary Acquisition* (pp. 98–122). Cambridge: Cambridge University Press.

Guiraud, P. (1954) *Les caractères statistiques du vocabulaire.* Paris: Presses Universitaires de France.

Gyllstad, H. (2007) *Testing English Collocations – Developing Receptive Tests for Use with Advanced Swedish Learners.* Lund: Lund University, Media-Tryck.

Häcker, M. (2008) Eleven pets and twenty ways to express one's opinion: The vocabulary learners of German acquire at English secondary schools. *Language Learning Journal* 36 (2), 215–226.

Håkansson, G. (1986) Quantitative aspects of teacher talk. In G. Kaspar (ed.) *Learning, Teaching and Communication in the Foreign Language Classroom* (pp. 83–98). Aarhus: Aarhus University Press.

Hall, C.J. (2002) The automatic cognate form assumption: Evidence for the parasitic model of vocabulary development. *International Review of Applied Linguistics in Language Teaching* 40 (2), 69–87.

Harris, V. and Snow, D. (2004) *Classic Pathfinder: Doing it for Themselves: Focus on Learning Strategies and Vocabulary Building.* London: CILT.

Hatzigeorgiu, N., Mikros, G. and Carayannis, G. (2001) Word length, word frequencies and Zipf's law in the Greek language. *Journal of Quantitative Linguistics* 8 (3), 175–185.

Henriksen, B. (2008) Declarative lexical knowledge. In D. Albrechtsen, K. Haastrup and B. Henriksen (eds) *Vocabulary and Writing in a First and Second Language: Processes and Development* (pp. 22–66). Houndsmill, Basingstoke: Palgrave.

Hilton, H. (2008) The link between vocabulary knowledge and spoken L2 fluency. *Language Learning Journal* 36 (2), 153–166.

Hindmarsh, R. (1980) *Cambridge English Lexicon.* Cambridge: Cambridge University Press.

Honnor, S. and Mascie-Taylor, H. (2000) *Encore Tricolore 1.* Cheltenham: Nelson.

Honnor, S. and Mascie-Taylor, H. (2001a) *Encore Tricolore 2.* Cheltenham: Nelson.

Honnor, S. and Mascie-Taylor, H. (2001b) *Encore Tricolore 4* (2nd edn). Cheltenham: Nelson.

Horst, M., Cobb, T. and Meara, P. (1998) Beyond a Clockwork Orange: Acquiring second language vocabulary through reading. *Reading in a Foreign Language* 11, 207–223.

Horst, M. and Meara, P.M. (1999) Test of a model for predicting second language lexical growth through reading. *The Canadian Modern Language Review/La Revue canadiennne des langues vivantes* 56 (2), 308–328.

Hu, M. and Nation, I.S.P. (2000) Unknown vocabulary density and reading comprehension. *Reading in a Foreign Language* 13 (1), 403–430.

Huckin, T. and Coady, J. (1999) Incidental vocabulary acquisition in a second language. *Studies in Second Language Acquisition: A review* 21 (1), 181–193.

Hulstijn, J. (1992) Retention of inferred and given word meanings: Experiments in incidental vocabulary learning. In P.J.L. Arnaud and H. Bejoint (eds) *Vocabulary and Applied Linguistics* (pp. 113–125). London: MacMillan.

Ishikawa, S., Uemura, T., Kaneda, M., Shimizu, S., Sugimori, N. and Tono, Y. (2003) *JACET8000: JACET List of 8000 Basic Words.* Tokya: JACET.

Johnson, W. (1944) Studies in language behavior: I. A program of research. *Psychological Monographs* 56, 1–15.

Kachroo, J.N. (1962) Report on the investigation into the teaching of vocabulary in the first year of English. *Bulletin of the Central Institute of English* 2, 67–72.

Kamimoto, T. (2005) The effect of guessing on vocabulary test scores: A qualitative analysis. Paper presented at The European Second Language Association (EuroSLA) Conference 15, Dubrovnik, Croatia.

Kaplan, R. and Bresnan, J. (1982) Lexical-functional grammar: A formal system for grammatical representation. In J. Bresnan (ed.) *The Mental Representation of Grammatical Relations* (pp. 173–281). Cambridge, MA: MIT Press.

Kawaguchi, S. (2000) Acquisition of Japanese verbal morphology: Applying processability theory to Japanese. *Studia Linguistica* 54 (2), 238–248.

Kempen, G. and Hoenkamp, E. (1987) An incremental procedural grammar for sentence formulation. *Cognitive Science* 11, 201–258.

Kerka, S (2000) Incidental learning. *Trends and Issues Alert* no. 18. On WWW at http://www.cete.org/acve/docgen.asp?tbl = tia&ID = 140. Accessed 5.10.07.

Kesslar, C. and Idar, I. (1979) Acquisition of English by a Vietnamese mother and child. *Working Papers on Bilingualism* 18, 66–79.

Kilgariff, A. (2006) BNC database and word frequency lists. On WWW at http://www.kilgariff.co.uk/bnc-readme.html#lemmatised. Accessed 5.2.07.

Kirby, A. (2004) Parrot's oratory stuns scientists. On WWW at http://news.bbc.co.uk/hi/sci/tech/3430481.stm. Accessed 16.3.07.

Kiss, G.R., Armstrong, C., Milroy, R. and Piper, J. (eds) (1973) *An Associative Thesaurus of English and its Computer Analysis.* Edinburgh: University Press.

Konstantakis, N. (2007) Creating a business word list for teaching Business English. *Estudios de Lingüística Inglesa Aplicada (ELIA)* 7, 103–126.

Krizsán, E. (2003) *Mozaik Kerettanterv az Általános Iskolák számára. Angol nyelv 3–8. évfolyam.* On WWW at http://www.mozaik.info.hu/Homepage/NAT2003/Doc/Angol3-8doc. Accessed 29.1.08.

Kroll, J., Bobb, S.C. and Wodnieczka, Z. (2006) Language selectivity is the exception, not the rule: Arguments against a fixed locus of language selection in bilingual speech. *Bilingualism, Language and Cognition* 9 (2), 119–135.

Kuçera, H. and Francis, W.N. (1967) *A Computational Analysis of Present-Day American English.* Providence, RI: Brown University Press.

Kwon, E-Y. (2005) The "Natural Order" of morpheme acquisition: A historical survey and discussion of three putative determinants. *Teachers' College Columbia Working Papers in TESOL and Applied Linguistics* 5 (1), 1–21.

Larsen-Freeman, D. (1996) An explanation of the morpheme acquisition order of second language learners. *Language Learning* 26, 125–134.

Laufer, B. (1989) What percentage of text is essential for comprehension? In C. Lauren and M. Nordman (eds) *Special Language; from Humans Thinking to Thinking Machines* (pp. 316–323). Clevedon: Multilingual Matters.

Laufer, B. (1990) Words you know: How they affect the words you learn. In J. Fisiak (ed.) *Further Insights into Contrastive Linguistics* (pp. 573–593). Amsterdam: John Benjamins.

Laufer, B. (1991) Knowing a word: What is so difficult about it? *English Teachers' Journal* 42 (May), 82–88.

Laufer, B. (2005) Focus on form in second language vocabulary learning. In S. Foster-Cohen, M.P. Garcia Mayo and J. Cenoz (eds) *EUROSLA Yearbook* 5 (pp. 223–250). Amsterdam: John Benjamins.

Laufer, B. and Hulstijn, J. (2001) Incidental vocabulary acquisition in a second language: The construct of task induced involvement. *Applied Linguistics* 22 (1), 1–26.

Laufer, B. and Nation, I.S.P. (1995) Vocabulary size and use: Lexical richness in L2 written production. *Applied Linguistics* 16 (3), 307–322.

Laufer, B. and Sim, D.D. (1985) Reading and explaining the reading threshold needed for English for academic purposes texts. *Foreign Language Annals* 18, 405–411.

Le, Q.H., Sicilia-Garcia, E.I., Ji, M. and Smith, F.J. (2002) Extension of Zipf's law to words and phrases. In *Proceedings of the International Conference on Computational Linguistics*, 1 (pp. 1–6). Morristown, NJ: Association for Computational Linguistics.

Levelt, W. (1989) *Speaking: From Intention to Articulation.* Cambridge, MA: MIT Press.

Lewis, M. (1993) *The Lexical Approach.* London: LTP.

Li, H. (2007) Can vocabulary be judged discretely in story-telling tasks? Paper delivered to ESCR Seminar: *Models and concepts, practical needs and theoretical approaches in modelling and measuring vocabulary knowledge.* Swansea University, July.

Lightbown, P. and Spada, N. (1999) *How Languages are Learned.* Oxford: Oxford University Press.

Lorenzo-Dus, N. (2007) The best of both worlds: Combined methodological approaches to the assessment of vocabulary in oral proficiency interviews. In H. Daller, J. Milton and J. Treffers-Daller (eds) *Modelling and Assessing Vocabulary Knowledge* (pp. 220–233). Cambridge: Cambridge University Press.

Lorenzo-Dus, N. and Meara, P. (2005) Examiner support strategies and test takers' vocabulary. *International Review of Applied Linguistics* 43, 239–258.

Mackey, W. (1965) *Language Teaching Analysis.* London: Longman.

MacWhinney, B. (2000a) *The CHILDES Project: Tools for Analyzing Talk* (3rd edn, Vol. 1: *Transcription Format and Programs*). Mahwah, NJ: Erlbaum.

MacWhinney, B. (2000b) *The CHILDES Project: Tools for Analyzing Talk* (3rd edn, Vol. 2: *The Database*). Mahwah, NJ: Erlbaum.

Malvern, D.D. and Richards, B.J. (1997) A new measure of lexical diversity. In A. Ryan and A. Wray (eds) *Evolving Models of Language* (pp. 58–71). Clevedon: Multilingual Matters.

Malvern, D.D. and Richards, B.J. (2002) Investigating accommodation in language proficiency interviews using a new measure of lexical diversity. *Language Testing* 19, 85–104.

Marsden, E. and David, E. (2008) Vocabulary use during conversation: A cross-sectional study of development from year 9 to year 13 amongst learners of Spanish and French. *Language Learning Journal* 36 (2), 181–198.

Mascie-Taylor, H., Spencer, M. and Honnor, S. (2002) *Encore Tricolore 3*. Cheltenham: Nelson.

McCarthy, M. (1990) *Vocabulary*. Oxford: Oxford University Press.

McCarthy, M. (1998) *Spoken Language and Applied Linguistics*. Cambridge: Cambridge University Press.

McGavigan, P. (2009) The acquisition of fixed idioms in Greek learners of English as a foreign language. Unpublished PhD dissertation, Swansea University.

Meara, P. (1980) Vocabulary acquisition: A neglected area of language learning. *Language Teaching and Linguistics: Abstracts* 15 (4), 221–246.

Meara, P. (1982) Word association in a foreign language: A report on the Birkbeck vocabulary project. *Nottingham Linguistic Circular* 11, 29–37.

Meara, P. (1990) A note on passive vocabulary. *Second Language Research* 6 (2), 150–154.

Meara, P. (1992) *EFL Vocabulary Tests*. University College Swansea: Centre for Applied Language Studies.

Meara, P. (1993) Tintin and the World Service. *IATEFL 1993 Annual Conference Report*, 32–37.

Meara, P. (1997) Towards a new approach to modelling vocabulary acquisition. In N. Schmitt and M. McCarthy (eds) *Vocabulary: Description, Acquisition and Pedagogy* (pp. 109–121). Cambridge: Cambridge University Press.

Meara, P. and Bell, H. (2001) P-Lex: A simple and effective way of describing the lexical characteristics of short L2 texts. *Prospect* 16 (3), 323–337.

Meara, P. and Buxton, B. (1987) An alternative to multiple choice vocabulary tests. *Language Testing* 4, 142–151.

Meara, P. and Fitzpatrick, T. (2000) Lex30: An improved method for assessing productive vocabulary in an L2. *System* 28, 19–30.

Meara, P. and Jones, G. (1990) *Eurocentre's Vocabulary Size Test: User's Guide*. Zurich: Eurocentres.

Meara, P. and Milton, J. (2003) *X_Lex, The Swansea Levels Test*. Newbury: Express.

Meara, P. and Wolter, B. (2004) V_Links, beyond vocabulary depth. *Angles on the English Speaking World* 4, 85–96.

Meara, P., Lightbown, P. and Halter, R.H. (1997) Classrooms as lexical environments. *Language Teaching Research* 1 (1), 28–47.

Meara, P., Milton, J. and Lorenzo-Dus, N. (2001) *Language Aptitude Tests*. Newbury: Express.

Melka Teichroew, F.J. (1982) Receptive vs productive vocabulary: A survey. *Interlanguage Studies Bulletin* (Utrecht) 6 (2), 5–33.

Milton, H. and Benn, T.V. (1933) Study of the vocabulary of thirty first-year French courses. *Modern Languages* 14 (1–3), 11–17, 43–47, 140–148.

Milton, J. (2004) Comparing the lexical difficulty of French reading comprehension exam texts. *Language Learning Journal* 30, 5–11.

Milton, J. (2006a) X-Lex: The Swansea Vocabulary Levels Test. In C. Coombe, P. Davidson and D. Lloyd (eds) *Proceedings of the 7th and 8th Current Trends in English Language testing (CTELT) Conference*, Vol. 4 (pp. 29–39). UAE: TESOL Arabia.

Milton, J. (2006b) Language lite: Learning French vocabulary in school. *Journal of French Language Studies* 16 (2), 187–205.

Milton, J. (2006c) French as a foreign language and the Common European Framework of Reference for Languages. In Proceedings from the *Crossing Frontiers: Languages and the International Dimension* conference, held at Cardiff University 6–7 July, and distributed by CILT, the National Centre for

Languages and the Subject Centre for Language, Linguistics and Area Studies. On WWW at www.llas.ac.uk/cardiff2006. Accessed 26.6.08.

Milton, J. (2007a) Lexical profiles, learning styles and construct validity of lexical size tests. In H. Daller, J. Milton and J. Treffers-Daller (eds) *Modelling and Assessing Vocabulary Knowledge* (pp. 45–58). Cambridge: Cambridge University Press.

Milton, J. (2007b) Vocabulary knowledge, language impairment and the language of education. Paper to BAAL 2007.

Milton, J. (2008a) Vocabulary uptake from informal learning tasks. *Language Learning Journal* 36 (2), 227–238.

Milton J. (2008b) French vocabulary breadth among learners in the British school and university system: Comparing knowledge over time. *Journal of French Language Studies* 18 (3), 333–348.

Milton, J. and Alexiou, T. (2009) Vocabulary size and the Common European Framework of Reference for Languages. In B. Richards, H.M. Daller, D. Malvern, P. Meara, J. Milton and J. Treffers-Daller (eds) *Vocabulary Studies in First and Second Language Acquisition: The Interface Between Theory and Application.* (pp. 194–211) Basingstoke: Palgrave.

Milton, J. and Daller, H.M. (2007) The interface between theory and learning in vocabulary acquisition. Paper presented to EUROSLA 2007, Newcastle, UK.

Milton, J. and Hales, T. (1997) Applying a lexical profiling system to technical English. In A. Ryan and A. Wray (eds) *Evolving Models of Language* (pp. 72–83). Clevedon: Multimedia Matters.

Milton, J. and Hopkins, N. (2005) *Aural Lex.* Swansea: Swansea University.

Milton, J. and Hopkins, N. (2006) Comparing phonological and orthographic vocabulary size: Do vocabulary tests underestimate the knowledge of some learners. *The Canadian Modern Language Review* 63 (1), 127–147.

Milton, J. and Meara, P. (1995) How periods abroad affect vocabulary growth in a foreign language. *ITL Review of Applied Linguistics* 107–108, 17–34.

Milton, J. and Meara, P. (1998) Are the British really bad at learning foreign languages? *Language Learning Journal* 18, 68–76.

Milton, J. and Riordan, O. (2006) Level and script effects in the phonological and orthographic vocabulary size of Arabic and Farsi speakers. In P. Davidson, C. Coombe, D. Lloyd and D. Palfreyman (eds) *Teaching and Learning Vocabulary in Another Language* (pp. 122–133). UAE: TESOL Arabia.

Milton, J. and Vassiliu, P. (2000) Frequency and the lexis of low-level EFL texts. In K. Nicolaidis and M. Mattheoudakis (eds) *Proceedings of the 13th Symposium in Theoretical and Applied Linguistics* (pp. 444–455). Thessaloniki: Aristotle University of Thessaloniki.

Milton, J., Wade, J. and Hopkins, N. (forthcoming) Aural word recognition and oral competence in a foreign language. In R. Chacón-Beltrán, C. Abello-Contesse, M. Torreblanca-López and M. López-Jiménez (eds) *Further Insights into Non-native Vocabulary Teaching and Learning.* Clevedon: Multilingual Matters.

Ministère de l'éducation (1966) *Le Français Fondamental.* (3rd edn) Paris: Insitut Pédagogique National.

Mitchell, R. and Myles, F. (2004) *Second Language Learning Theories.* London: Hodder Arnold.

Mochizuki, M. (1998) Understanding English affixes by Japanese learners. *Reitaku Review* 4, 100–120.

Mochizuki, M. and Aizawa, K. (2000) An affix order of acquisition for EFL learners: An exploratory study. *System* 28, 291–304.

Mondria, J-A. and Wit-de Boer, M. (1991) The effects of contextual richness on the guessability and the retention of words in a foreign language. *Applied Linguistics* 12, 249–267.

Nagy, W., Diakidoy, I.A.N. and Anderson, R.C. (1993) The acquisition of morphology: Learning the contribution of suffixes to the meanings of derivatives. *Journal of Reading Behavior* 25, 155–170.

Nagy, W. and Herman, P. (1987) Breadth and depth vocabulary knowledge: Implications for acquisition and instruction. In M. McKeown and M. Curtis (eds) *The Nature of Vocabulary Acquisition* (pp. 19–36). Hillsdale, NJ: Lawrence Erlbaum Associates.

Nation, I.S.P. (ed.) (1984) *Vocabulary Lists: Words, Affixes and Stems.* English University of Wellington, New Zealand: English Language Institute.

Nation, I.S.P. (1990) *Teaching and Learning Vocabulary.* Boston, MA: Heinle and Heinle.

Nation, I.S.P. (1993) Sixteen principles of language teaching. In L. Bauer and C. Franzen (eds) *Of Pavlova, Poetry and Paradigms: Essays in Honour of Harry Orsman* (pp. 209–224). Wellington: Victoria University Press.

Nation, I.S.P. (ed.) (1996) *Vocabulary Lists.* English Language Institute Occasional Papers No 17. Wellington: Victoria University of Wellington.

Nation, I.S.P. (2001) *Learning Vocabulary in Another Language.* Cambridge: Cambridge University Press.

Nation, I.S.P. (2004) A study of the most frequent word families in the British National Corpus. In P. Bogaards and B. Laufer (eds) *Vocabulary in a Second Language: Selection, Acquisition and Testing* (pp. 3–13). Amsterdam: John Benjamins.

Nation, I.S.P. (2006) How language a vocabulary is needed for reading and listening? *The Canadian Modern Language Review* 63 (1), 59–82.

Nation, I.S.P. (2007) Fundamental issues in modelling and assessing vocabulary knowledge. In H. Daller, J. Milton and J. Treffers-Daller (eds) *Modelling and Assessing Vocabulary Knowledge* (pp. 33–43). Cambridge: Cambridge University Press.

O'Dell, F. (1997) Incorporating vocabulary into the syllabus. In N. Schmitt and M. McCarthy (eds) *Vocabulary: Description, Acquisition and Pedagogy* (pp. 258–278). Cambridge: Cambridge University Press.

Ogden, C.K. (1930) *Basic English: A General Introduction with Rules and Grammar.* London: Paul Treber.

O'Neill, R., Kingsbury, R. and Yeadon, A. (1971) *Kernel Intermediate.* London: Longman.

Orosz, A. (2007) Gondolatok az angol nyelvoktatásról a 9–14 éves korú tanulók angol nyelvi szókincs mérése alapján. *Apáczai Napok 2006 Tanulmánykötet I* (pp. 262–266). Győr: Nyugat Magyarországi Egyetem Apáczai Csere János Kar.

Orosz, A. (2009) The growth of Young learners' English vocabulary size. In Nikolov, M. (ed.) *Early learning of Modern Foreign Languages.* Bristol: Multi-lingual Matters, 181–194.

Palmberg, R. (1987) Patterns of vocabulary development in Foreign Language Learners. *Studies in Second Language Acquisition* 9, 201–220.

Palmer, H.E. (1917) *The Scientific Study and Teaching of Languages.* London: Harrap.

Palmer, H.E. (1921) *The Principles of Language Study.* London: Harrap.

Paribakht, T.M. and Wesche, M. (1993a) The relationship between reading comprehension and second language development in a comprehension-based ESL program. *TESL Canada Journal* 11, 9–29.

Paribakht, T.M. and Wesche, M. (1993b) Vocabulary enhancement activities and reading for meaning in second language vocabulary acquisition. In J. Coady and T. Huckin (eds) *Second Language Vocabulary Acquisition: A Rationale for Pedagogy* (pp. 174–200). Cambridge: Cambridge University Press.

Parkinson, D. (ed.) (2005) *Oxford Business English Dictionary for Learners of English.* Oxford: Oxford University Press.

Pienemann, M. (1998) *Language Processing and Second Language Development: Processability Theory.* Amsterdam: John Benjamins.

Pienemann, M. and Håkansson, G. (1999) A unified approach towards the development of Swedish as L2: A processability account. *Studies in Second Language Acquisition* 21, 383–420.

Pitts, M., White, H. and Krashen, S. (1989) Acquiring second language vocabulary through reading: A replication of the Clockwork Orange study using second language acquirers. *Reading in a Foreign Language* 5, 271–275.

QCA (2002a) *Five Yearly Subject Reviews: Conclusions – French.* On WWW at http://www.qca.org.uk/nq/subjects/conclusions_french.asp. Accessed 6.7.03.

QCA (2002b) *Public Examinations: Views on Maintaining Standards over time: A Summary of the MORI/CDELL Project in Spring 2002.* On WWW at http://www.qca.org.uk/rs/maintaining_standards.asp. Accessed 6.7.03.

Quinn, G. (1968) *The English Vocabulary of some Indonesian University Entrants.* Department monograph IKIP Kristen Satya Watjana, Salatiga Indonesia.

Read, J. (1993) The development of a new measure of L2 vocabulary knowledge. *Language Testing* 10 (3), 355–371.

Read, J. (1995a) Refining the word associates format as a measure of depth of vocabulary knowledge. *New Zealand Studies in Applied Linguistics* 1, 1–17.

Read, J. (1995b) Validating the word associates format as a measure of depth of vocabulary knowledge. Unpublished manuscript.

Read, J. (2000) *Assessing Vocabulary.* Cambridge: Cambridge University Press.

Richards, B.J. and Malvern, D.D. (2007) Validity and threats to the validity of vocabulary measurement. In H. Daller, J. Milton and J. Treffers-Daller (eds) *Modelling and Assessing Vocabulary Knowledge* (pp. 79–92). Cambridge: Cambridge University Press.

Richards, B.J., Malvern, D.D. and Graham, S. (2008) Word frequency and trends in the development of French vocabulary in lower intermediate students during Year 12 in English schools. *Language Learning Journal* 36 (2), 199–214.

Rieder, A. (2003) Implicit and explicit learning in incidental vocabulary acquisition. *VIEWS* 12 (2), 24–39.

Rietveld, R. and van Hout, R. (1993) *Statistical Techniques for the Study of Language And Language Behaviour.* Berlin/New York: Mouton de Gruyter.

Rixon, S. (1990) *Tip Top Teacher's Book 1.* London: MacMillan.

Robson, W.F. (1934) The vocabulary burden in the first year of French. *British Journal of Educational Psychology* 4, 264–293.

Rodgers, T.S. (1969) Measuring vocabulary difficulty: An analysis of item variables in learning Russian-English vocabulary pairs. *International Review of Applied Linguistics* 7, 327–343.

Ryan, A.M.G. (1997) Learning the orthographical form of L2 vocabulary – a receptive and productive process. In N. Schmitt and M. McCarthy (eds) *Vocabulary: Description, Acquisition and Pedagogy* (pp. 181–198). Cambridge: Cambridge University Press.

Saragi, T., Nation, I.S.P. and Meister, G.F. (1978) Vocabulary learning and reading. _System_ 3/2, 72–78.

Schmitt, N. (2000) _Vocabulary in Language Teaching._ Cambridge: Cambridge University Press.

Schmitt, N. and Meara, P. (1997) Research vocabulary through a word knowledge framework – word associations and verbal suffixes. _Studies in Second Language Acquisition_ 19, 17–36.

Schmitt, N. and McCarthy, M. (1997) _Vocabulary: Description, Acquisition and Pedagogy._ Cambridge: Cambridge University Press.

Schmitt, N., Schmitt, D. and Clapham, C. (2001) Developing and exploring the behaviour of two new versions of the Vocabulary Levels Test. _Language Testing_ 18, 55–88.

Scholfield, P. (1991) Vocabulary rate in course books – living with an unstable lexical economy. _Proceedings of the 5th Symposium on the Description and/or Comparison of English and Greek_ (pp. 12–32). Thessaloniki: Aristotle University.

Schonell, F.J., Middleton, I.G. and Shaw, B.A. (1956) _A Study of the Oral Vocabulary of Adults._ Brisbane: University of Queensland Press.

Schur, E. (2007) Insights into the structure of L1 and L2 vocabulary networks: Intimations of small worlds. In H. Daller, J. Milton and J. Treffers-Daller (eds) _Modelling and Assessing Vocabulary Knowledge_ (pp. 182–203). Cambridge: Cambridge University Press.

Seashore, R.H. and Eckerson, L.D. (1940) The measurement of individual differences in general English vocabulary. _Journal of Educational Psychology_ 31, 14–38.

Seaton, J. (2004) Lexical levels needed for communicability. Unpublished MA Dissertation, University of Wales Swansea.

Segalowitz, N. (2003) Automaticity and second languages. In C.J. Doughty and M.H. Long (eds) _The Handbook of Second Language Acquisition_ (pp. 382–408). London: Blackwell.

Segalowitz, N. and Freed, B. (2004) Context, contact, and cognition in oral fluency acquisition: Studying Spanish in at home and study abroad contexts. _Studies in Second Language Acquisition_ 26, 173–199.

Segalowitz, N., Freed, B., Collentine, J., Lafford, B., Lazar, N. and Diaz-Campos, M. (2004) A comparison of Spanish second language acquisition in two different learning contexts: Study abroad and the domestic classroom. _Frontiers_ 10 (4), 1–18.

Shillaw, J. (1999) The application of the Rasch model to Yes/No vocabulary tests. Unpublished PhD thesis, University of Wales Swansea.

Shtrikman, S. (1994) Some comments on Zipf's law for the Chinese language. _Journal of Information Science_ 20 (2), 142–143.

Sinclair, J. and Renouf, A. (1988) A lexical syllabus for language learning. In R. Carter and M. McCarthy (eds) _Vocabulary and Language Teaching_ (pp. 140–160). London: Longman.

Smith, M.K. (1941) Measurement of the size of general English vocabulary through the elementary grades and high school. _Genetic Psychological Monographs_ 24, 311–345.

Soars, L. and Soars, J. (1993) _Headway Elementary._ Oxford: Oxford University Press.

Stæhr, L.S. (2008) Vocabulary size and the skills of listening, reading and writing. _Language Learning Journal_ 36 (2), 139–152.

Stevick, E. (1989) *Success with Foreign Languages: Seven Who Achieved it and What Worked for Them.* New York: Prentice Hall.

Stoddard, G.D. (1929) An experiment in verbal learning. *Journal of Educational Psychology* 20, 452–457.

Swan, M. and Walter, C. (1984) *The Cambridge English Course Book 1.* Cambridge: Cambridge University Press.

Tang, E. and Nesi, H. (2003) Teaching vocabulary in two Chinese classrooms: Schoolchildren's exposure to English words in Hong Kong and Guangzhou. *Language Teaching Research* 7 (1), 65–97.

Tharp, J.B. (1934) The basic French vocabulary and its use. *The Modern Language Journal* 19 (2), 123–131.

Tidball, F. and Treffers-Daller, J. (2007) Exploring measures of vocabulary richness in semi-spontaneous French speech. In H. Daller, J. Milton and J. Treffers-Daller (eds) *Modelling and Assessing Vocabulary Knowledge* (pp. 133–149). Cambridge: Cambridge University Press.

Tinkham T. (1997) The effects of semantic and thematic clustering on the learning of second language vocabulary. *Second Language Research* 13 (2), 138–163.

Tschichold, C. (2007) On the usefulness of word frequency information. Paper to BAAL, September 2007.

Tschichold, C. (2008) Vocabulary in tricolour: Do learners have a chance? Paper to BAAL September 2008.

Turner, I.P., Godwin, V.P. and Wilks, L.E. (2004) A measure of success: Changes in vocabulary usage on intensive EFL courses. In L.E. Sheldon (ed.) *Directions for the Future: Issues in English for Academic Purposes* (pp. 177–190). Oxford: Peter Lang.

Tyler, A. and Nagy, W. (1989) The acquisition of English derivational morphology. *Journal of Memory and Language* 28, 649–667.

University of Cambridge Local Examinations Syndicate (2001) *Cambridge Examinations, Certificates & Diploma: Regulations 2001.* Cambridge: University of Cambridge Local Examinations Syndicate.

Van Ek, J.A. (1990) *Waystage English.* London: Pergamon Press.

Van Ek, J.A. and Trim, J.L.M. (1990) *Threshold 1990.* Strasbourg: Council of Europe Publishing.

Vassiliu, P. (1994) Vocabulary profiles: A necessary prerequisite for course book selection. Unpublished MA dissertation, University of Wales Cardiff.

Vassiliu, P. (2001) Lexical input and uptake in the low level EFL classroom. Unpublished PhD dissertation, University of Wales Swansea.

Vermeer, A. (2000) Coming to grips with lexical richness in spontaneous speech data. *Language Testing* 17 (1), 65–83.

Vermeer, A. (2001) Breadth and depth of vocabulary in relation to L1/L2 acquisition and frequency of input. *Applied Psycholinguistics* 22, 217–234.

Vermeer, A. (2004) The relation between lexical richness and vocabulary size in Dutch L1 and L2 children. In P. Bogaards and B. Laufer (eds) *Vocabulary in a Second Language* (pp. 173–189). Amsterdam: John Benjamins.

Ward, J. (1999) How large a vocabulary do EAP engineering students need? *Reading in a Foreign Language* 12 (2), 309–323.

Waring, R. (1997) Comparison of the receptive and productive vocabulary knowledge of some second language learners. *Immaculata; The Occasional Papers of Notre Dame Seishin University*, 94–114.

Wesche, M. and Paribakht, T.A. (1996) Assessing second language vocabulary knowledge: Depth versus breadth. *The Canadian Modern Language Review* 53, 13–40.

West, M. (1953) *A General Service List of English Words.* London: Longman.

White, R. (1988) *The ELT Curriculum.* Oxford: Blackwell.

Wilkins, D.A. (1972) *Linguistics in Language Teaching.* London: Arnold.

Wilks, C. and Meara, P. (2007) Graph theory and words association networks. In H. Daller, J. Milton and J. Treffers-Daller (eds) *Modelling and Assessing Vocabulary Knowledge* (pp. 167–181). Cambridge: Cambridge University Press.

Wolter, B. (2001) Comparing the L1 and L2 mental lexicon; as depth of individual word knowledge model. *Studies in Second Language Acquisition* 23, 41–69.

Wolter, B. (2005) V_Links: A new approach to assessing depth of word knowledge. Unpublished PhD Dissertation, University of Wales Swansea.

Index